Values and Moral
Development

DEDICATION BY THE EDITOR

TO THE FIRST DELIBERATE MORAL EDUCATORS IN MY LIFE,

INCLUDING:

MY MOTHER AND FATHER,

THE SISTERS OF CHARITY AND LAYTEACHERS

AT ST. MONICA, JAMAICA, N.Y. and

THE BROTHERS OF THE CHRISTIAN SCHOOLS AND

LAYTEACHERS AT ST. AUGUSTINE'S HIGH SCHOOL,

BROOKLYN, N.Y.

Values and Moral Development

edited by

Thomas C. Hennessy, S.J.

Papers by:

Clive Beck

James W. Fowler

Harry B. Kavanagh

James R. Rest

Robert L. Selman

Norman A. Sprinthall

Edmund V. Sullivan

Reactions by

James R. Barclay	Ronald Hine
Wayne Bohannon	Robert Hogan
Barbara Geoghegan	Maureen Joy
Robert J. Havighurst	Alfred McBride
James E. Hennessy	John S. Nelson
Andrew Varga	

Paulist Press
New York/Ramsey/Toronto

Library of Congress
Catalog Card Number: 76-18053

ISBN: 0-8091-1972-2 (Paper)

Published by Paulist Press
Editorial Office: 1865 Broadway, N.Y., N.Y. 10023
Business Office: 545 Island Road, Ramsey, N.J. 07446

Printed and bound in the
United States of America

Acknowledgments

The article "A Developmental Approach to Interpersonal and Moral
Awareness in Young Children: Some Educational Implications of Levels
of Social Perspective Taking," by Robert L. Selman was first presented at a
Values Education conference held at Oakville, Ontario, 30 January - 1
February 1975. The article appeared as part of a volume entitled *Values
Education*, eds. John Meyer, Brian Burnham and John Chalvat, published
by Wilfrid Laurier University Press, Waterloo, Ontario, Canada, and is
used with permission of the publisher.

Contents

Introduction... 1
Thomas C. Hennessy, S.J.

1. A Philosophical View of Values and Value Education 13
Clive Beck

Reaction to Beck: Can Moral Values be Excluded? 23
Andrew Varga, S.J.
Reaction to Beck: The Importance of Exemplary Models
in Value Education 28
James R. Barclay
Reaction to Beck: A Hope: Research in Religious
Development.. 32
John S. Nelson

2. Moral and Psychological Development: A Curriculum
for Secondary Schools.. 37
Norman A. Sprinthall

Reaction to Sprinthall: But Is It Values Education?.................. 68
Barbara Geoghegan

3. Values and Issues in Counseling and School Psychology 74
Edmund V. Sullivan

Reaction to Sullivan: Helpful Relation of Theory and
Practice.. 96
Ronald J. Hine

4. The Research Base of the Cognitive Developmental
Approach to Moral Education 102
James R. Rest

Reaction to Rest: Ambiguities in the Research Base of the
Cognitive Developmental Approach to Moral Education........ 119
Robert Hogan and Wayne Bohannon

5. Moral Development in a High School Program....................... 124
Harry B. Kavanagh

Reaction to Kavanagh: Observations on Methodology,
Males and Religious Schooling 138
Maureen Joy

6. A Developmental Approach to Interpersonal and Moral
Awareness in Young Children: Some Educational
Implications of Levels of Social Perspective-Taking 142
Robert L. Selman

Reaction to Selman: Social Perspectives and the Development
of Moral Judgment 167
Robert J. Havighurst

7. Stages in Faith: The Structural-Developmental Approach 173
James W. Fowler

Reaction to Fowler: Fears about Procedure 211
Alfred McBride, O. Praem.

Reaction to Fowler: Stages in Faith or Stages in
Commitment 218
James E. Hennessy, S.J.

Bibliography 224

Contributors 233

Introduction

The Introduction is divided into two main sections. Section I contains in almost capsule form an overview of the Piaget and Kohlberg formulations. This overview is offered here in an effort (not wholly successful) to avoid repetition of this material on the part of many of the contributors to this book.

Section II contains brief summaries of the content of the papers and of the responses to them, together with the presentation of the rationales for the general and specific papers in this collection.

SECTION I

At the time when the work of Hartshorne and May was being widely circulated and provided the quietus to further research in regard to research on certain ethical questions, Jean Piaget in Switzerland was laying the foundation to a solid psychological foundation in moral development. His research methodology was brilliantly of the "grass-roots" variety. He closely observed the boys in his native town while they were playing marbles and made numerous inquiries of them about the rules of the game. Piaget observed that the youths went through a cycle of four stages regarding the rules of marbles, including a highly individualistic beginning stage and concluding with the codification of the rules of the game. A growth takes place from an original position (beyond the personalistic one) that the rules somehow have a kind of absolute divine origin, to an appreciation of the possibility of cooperation among players about the rules, and finally to the conviction that there are rules that are followed by everyone who plays this particular game. Thus the development has been from the egocentric view to a kind of absolutism and ended up with an agreed-upon set of rules that reflects a social perspective that influences the young adolescent.

After the publication of his *Moral Judgment of the Child*, Piaget changed the area of his research to the vast and difficult area of cognitive development. He reached the conclusion that young people go through a cycle that effects an intellectual transformation. Up to age two, the child experiences the sensorimotor stage which amounts to the interaction of the senses and the immediate environment. From about age two to seven, there is the intuitive or preoperational stage in which there is a dramatic growth in vocabulary, considerable learning based upon imitation, and much imaginative activity. From age seven to eleven there is the stage of concrete operations in which the child advances to an understanding of specific functional relationships and a kind of fundamentalistic adherence to logic and rules. From age eleven to sixteen the stage of "formal operations" flourishes. In this stage the adolescent can achieve the operations that are formally considered cognitive thinking in a logical rational manner and using abstract and generalized reasoning.

Some of the learnings that have been discerned from Piaget's cognitive research include the following: 1. Cognitive development takes place by stages, such that one goes through each stage in turn and one does not skip stages; 2. The environment (including the person-environment) is important as a stimulus to development from one stage to the next.

Lawrence Kohlberg is the next major figure in this picture. He did his collegiate and doctoral work at the University of Chicago after a period of internment for illegal refugee shipment to Israel. The internment was marked by deep reflection on ethics and morality. His doctoral dissertation on modes of moral thinking and choice incorporated some of Piaget's earlier work on moral development with his later cognitive developmental map. Kohlberg not only absorbed and integrated Piaget's work but provided his own additions and refinement, particularly in his now well-known Stages of Moral Growth (Table 1).

The main basis for Kohlberg's stages and his position regarding moral development is his interviewing of 50 Chicago-area males, middle- and working-class. They were first interviewed at age 10-26 and have been reinterviewed at three-year intervals from the mid-fifties to the mid-seventies.

Table 1. Definition of Moral Stages

I. Preconventional level

At this level, the child is responsive to cultural rules and labels of good and bad, right or wrong, but interprets these labels either in terms of the physical or the hedonistic consequences of action (punishment, reward, exchange of favors) or in terms of the physical power of those who enunciate the rules and labels. The level is divided into the following two stages:

Stage 1: *The punishment-and-obedience orientation.* The physical consequences of action determine its goodness or badness, regardless of the human meaning or value of these consequences. Avoidance of punishment and unquestioning deference to power are valued in their own right, not in terms of respect for an underlying moral order supported by punishment and authority (the latter being Stage 4).

Stage 2: *The instrumental-relativist orientation.* Right action consists of that which instrumentally satisfies one's own needs and occasionally the needs of others. Human relations are viewed in terms like those of the marketplace. Elements of fairness, of reciprocity, and of equal sharing are present, but they are always interpreted in a physical or pragmatic way. Reciprocity is a matter of "you scratch my back and I'll scratch yours," not of loyalty, gratitude, or justice.

II. Conventional level

At this level, maintaining the expectations of the individual's family, group, or nation is perceived as valuable in its own right, regardless of immediate and obvious consequences. The attitude is not only one of *conformity* to personal expectations and social order, but of loyalty to it, of actively *maintaining,* supporting, and justifying the order, and of identifying with the persons or group involved in it. At this level, there are the following two stages:

Stage 3: *The interpersonal concordance or "good boy—nice girl" orientation.* Good behavior is that which pleases or helps others and is approved by them. There is much conformity to stereotypical images of what is majority or "natural" behavior. Behavior is frequently judged by intention—"he means well" becomes important for the first time. One earns approval by being "nice."

Stage 4: *The "law and order" orientation.* There is orientation toward authority, fixed rules, and the maintenance of the social order. Right behavior consists of doing one's duty, showing respect for authority, and maintaining the given social order for its own sake.

III. Postconventional, autonomous, or principled level

At this level, there is a clear effort to define moral values and principles that have validity and application apart from the authority of the groups or persons holding these principles and apart from the individual's own identification with these groups. This level also has two stages:

Stage 5: *The social-contract, legalistic orientation,* generally with utilitarian overtones. Right action tends to be defined in terms of general individual rights and standards which have been critically examined and agreed upon by the whole society. There is a clear awareness of the relativism of personal values and opinions and a corresponding emphasis upon procedural rules for reaching consensus. Aside from what is constitutionally and democratically agreed upon, the right is a matter of personal "values" and "opinion." The result is an emphasis upon the "legal point of view," but with an emphasis upon the possibility of changing law in terms of rational considerations of social utility (rather than freezing it in terms of Stage 4 "law and order"). Outside the legal realm, free agreement and contract is the binding element of obligation. This is the "official" morality of the American government and constitution.

Stage 6: *The universal-ethical-principle orientation.* Right is defined by the decision of conscience in accord with self-chosen *ethical principles* appealing to logical comprehensiveness, universality, and consistency. These principles are abstract and ethical (the Golden Rule, the categorical imperative); they are not concrete moral rules like the Ten Commandments. At heart, these are universal principles of *justice,* of the *reciprocity* and *equality* of human *rights,* and of respect for the dignity of human beings as *individual persons.*

Kohlberg developed a series of moral dilemmas that were presented to individuals and groups to determine their moral stage and to stimulate discussion and thinking. The most well-known of these dilemmas is that of Heinz and the wonder drug. This story-dilemma is summarized here as there will be references to it in the course of the book. The story has as its background the fact that a druggist had discovered a radium-based wonder drug, and he was determined to make a great deal of money from the drug. So when a certain man named Heinz appeared to purchase the drug for his very ill wife, he was surprised to learn that the price for a small dose was $2,000. Heinz went to everybody he knew to borrow the money, but he could raise only about half the price. So Heinz went to the druggist and begged for a cheaper price or a chance to pay in full later on. But the druggist was adamant saying, "No, I discovered the drug and I'm going to make money from it." Three unusual events followed. That night Heinz became desperate and broke into the man's store to steal the drug for his wife. (At this point in interviews, the listener is asked: Should the husband have done that? Why?)

The second event took place between the doctor and Heinz's wife. When the stolen drugs were used, it was learned that they did not work and no other treatment was found. The patient was in terrible pain and was often delirious. She was so weak that a more than ordinary dose of painkiller would make her die sooner. In her calm moments she would ask the doctor to give her extra doses of ether, enough to kill her. She said that she couldn't stand the pain and would die in a few months anyway. (At this point in interviews, the listener is asked: Should the doctor do what she asks and make her die to put her out of her terrible pain? Why?)

The third event involved a third person. Heinz was given a 10-year sentence for stealing the drug but escaped from prison after a couple of years. He settled in another part of the country under an assumed name. He prospered and set up a factory where he gave his workers the highest wages and used most of his profits to build a hospital for work in curing cancer, which had taken his wife's life. But twenty years after the original robbery a tailor recognized the factory owner as being Heinz the escaped convict whom the police were still looking for. (At this point in interviews, the listener is asked: Should the tailor report Heinz to the police? Why?)

In the scoring and evaluation of the reports of the interviews, Kohlberg was not concerned with the actual solution offered to the moral issue but with the "why" response. The emphasis on the reasoning rather than the preferred kind of action is characteristic of Kohlberg's approach and is a basis for its acceptability to various elements of a pluralistic society. No religious or humanistic group feels that preferential treatment is afforded another group in the fundamental thrust of the moral growth paradigm (the details such as just what type of person ends up in the sixth stage is another matter).

Analysis of the responses to the dilemmas provided the data for the position that moral development, like physical and cognitive development, follows a definite pattern. In particular the following principles of moral growth have been evolved:

1. *Moral development takes place invariantly by stages*, i.e., one cannot get to a later stage without going through the earlier stage.

2. *In moral development, one cannot comprehend reasoning at a stage that is more than one stage beyond one's present stage*. This is a particular application of #1, and emphasizes the uselessness of inappropriate expectations such as appealing to a three-year-old's sense of principled justice.

3. *In moral development, one is cognitively attracted to reasoning that is one stage beyond one's present stage*. This principle is more than a positive statement of #2, in that it provides a reasonable basis for expectation for gradual moral growth.

4. *In moral development, movement is effected when cognitive disequilibrium is introduced*. This principle provides the basic orientation for the use of group discussion where different viewpoints are expressed and the participants are afforded the opportunity to see the perspective of others. If the others are trusted and there is a mutually empathic relationship in the group, the cognitive disequilibrium that brings out a clash of reasoning and of values is likely to be growth-productive for some of the participants. Kohlberg has also noted that at least up to stage four each stage represents an ability to think more abstractly and to identify with a more adequate perception of the social system.

Kohlberg has suggested that productive moral discussion is fostered when there is: 1. Exposure to the next higher stage of moral reasoning; 2. Exposure to situations posing problems and contradictions for the person's current moral position, leading to dissatisfaction with his current level; 3. An atmosphere of interchange and dialogue, combining the first two conditions, in which conflicting moral views are compared in an open manner.

There have been numerous criticisms of Kohlberg's work. Some such criticism is included in this book (such as Hogan and Bohannon's reaction to Rest's article) and only a brief summary of some criticism seems to be needful here.

Perhaps the most consistent criticism of Kohlberg's work centers around the distinction between moral reasoning and moral behavior: one can be rated high in moral reasoning but poorly regarded for one's actual level of behavior. This criticism has been summarized by Kurtines and Grief as follows: "There seems to be no evidence that each of the six stages by itself has discriminant validity or predictive utility." Kohlberg replied to this problem with the following points: 1. Moral judgment, while only one factor in moral behavior, is the single most important or influential factor . . . in moral behavior. 2. While other factors influence moral behavior, moral judgment is the only distinctively *moral* factor in moral behavior. 3. Moral judgment change is long-range or irreversible; a higher stage is never lost.

A second type of criticism has been proposed by Peters. He points out that Kohlberg has adopted the Kantian type of morality, currently represented by Hare and Rawls. Thus their emphasis on utilitarianism and the central principle of justice is challenged. Are there not other central themes that could be acceptable as the pinnacle of principled behavior? Peters mentions other possibilities: courage, a "romantic type of morality," and others. Certainly, the religiously oriented critic will see autonomous, principled behavior as presuming justice but centering on other foci such as love of God and man or a deep sense of obedience to God's will which has characterized saints from Moses to Mother Teresa.

A final difficulty that deserves mention pertains to inadequacies in research and particularly in certain aspects of the Moral Judgment Scale and of the Stages, particularly Stage Five and Six. It is not maintained by the critics that sufficient evidence has been compiled to discredit the Kohlberg model but rather that there are problems connected with the administration and scoring of the Scale and that there has not accrued enough positive empirical evidence to back up the theory after its being available for over 20 years.

Whatever the difficulties with Kohlberg's approach, many scholars who are interested in both morals and psychology agree that through his efforts a new stimulus, psychologically acceptable, has been made available to teachers and to researchers for attempting to foster the moral and psychological growth of future citizens. The approach has not been academically sterile. Instead it has been responsible directly or indirectly for numerous dissertations and research projects in psychology and related fields. It has already made its mark in many social-science curricula. It has influenced the field of religious education. Even if future analyses should completely replace Kohlberg's work, he has already provided a helpful model and a steady stream of data for one to feel a real sense of appreciation for him and his work. This appreciation goes so far as to disagree with a comment he wrote at the end of a recent article: "There is very little new in this—or in anything else we are doing." Without him, the tribute he gives to Dewey and to Piaget would be very general and vague. He gave a basic structure to moral development. We may end up by disagreeing with much of what he says, but the net result of the new conclusions will be based upon the initiatives and creativeness of Lawrence Kohlberg.

Before concluding this section it seems appropriate to offer some definitions that may be helpful to those who read this book. The words that seem to need defining are: cognitive psychology, moral education, and values. Each of these words deserves lengthy exposition but limitations of space require that only a short treatment be given to each.

Cognitive psychology (as differing from *affective* which deals with feeling and emotions, and *conative* which deals with acting, doing and striving) is the type of psychology that is preferred by most writers in the moral education movement. It focuses on cognition which is a general term designating all the various aspects and modes of knowing, including perceiving, recognizing, conceptualizing, judging and reasoning. Typically the developmental nature of human intellectual activity is emphasized such that the child's cognitive processes are regarded as distinctively different and so must be understood in their own right not simply as those of an undeveloped adult. Cognitive psychologists believe that basic mental operations are organized and have general characteristics that can be discovered through systematic theory and research. The behaviorist, psychoanalytic and humanist schools represent different traditions from that of cognitive psychology.

Moral education is the deliberate process in which the young members of society are assisted to develop from a naive self-orientation concerning their rights and obligations to a broader view of self-in-society and to a deeper view of self and all other reality (which for the religious person preeminently includes God).

Values as used in this book could be defined along the lines offered by Raths, Harmin and Simon (1966) as beliefs, attitudes, activities or feelings that are freely chosen after due reflection from among alternatives; they are prized and cherished, publicly affirmed, incorporated into actual behavior and are repeated in one's life. The emphasis is upon the free choice of values rather than the unreflective acceptance of values common to one's group.

SECTION II

As indicated above this section contains brief summaries of the papers and the responses. A rationale for the presentation and for the order of presentation is also offered.

There are three parts in the book. Part I is meant to introduce the philosophical groundwork for the analysis of moral and ethical growth. The philosophical contribution is illustrative of the inter-disciplinary efforts that are required for progress in this field. Additional papers might have been sought in this part from a sociologist, a theologian, or an expert in social studies to supplement the primarily psychological writings that are contained in the rest of the book.

Clive Beck has written extensively and exercised leadership in the area of moral and value education, particularly at the Ontario Institute for the Study of Education (OISE). The first part of his paper is devoted to terminology; he strongly prefers use of the word "value" to "moral." He then analyzes concepts implied in the word "value" and defends his reflective utilitarian approach. He then offers an overview of several approaches to value education and this provides a good background for the papers that follow. He concludes with a controversial note on the relation between values and religion.

Because of the central importance of philosophy to this volume three reactors were asked to write a response to Beck's paper. Andrew Varga, a philosopher, challenges Beck's rejection of the distinctly moral element in his analysis. James Barclay, who has written extensively of the relationship between philosophy and aspects of psychology, would add to the analysis of growth in value the importance of value models, including parent, peers and the media and others. John S. Nelson, a religious educator, develops and clarifies some statements and implications in Beck's paper regarding Christianity and religion, especially religion-as-function. Nelson, anticipating some of Fowler's work, sees a likely stage development in religious commitment to parallel Kohlberg's stages of moral development.

Part II is devoted primarily to papers that emphasize programs that are directed to fostering growth in moral-related areas among students.

Norman Sprinthall, who with other associates while he was at

Harvard, pioneered programs in deliberate psychological education, presents a well-reasoned background (from psychology and educational inadequacies) for the need for active programs that sponsor moral and general ego development. The definite program he reports is called the class in the psychology of counseling. This class is concerned with empathy, listening skills and a related practicum. Responsibility and social development are cited as goals of the program. Sister Barbara Geoghegan, an educational psychologist, finds Sprinthall's program "exciting and fascinating" but doubts that there are enough Sprinthalls for the schools' needs and fears an outbreak of amateur psychologists in the schools if many of them adopted the proposed type of program. Furthermore, she feels that admirable though Sprinthall's program is in many aspects, it does not aim directly enough at moral and ethical education.

The second paper in the programs part of the book is written by Edmund Sullivan, who has worked with Piaget and specialized in moral education. He analyzes certain activities of counselors such as testing and dialoguing with counselees and from a moral-value orientation urges heightened self-awareness and understanding of the real-life setting. He also encourages the counselor to become involved in school policy decisions so as to protect children's rights and foster value-moral education. In addition, in disputes in schools, the counselor should be viewed as a kind of combined negotiator and student advocate, a difficult combination. To remove certain pressures on his work, perhaps his main work-site and the administration over him should be located away from the school building. Sullivan views the counselor's work as tending toward the counter-culture, and so it will probably develop into a new, as yet unspecified role that will attract a new type of person to fulfill that role. Ronald Hine, a religious educator, continues the analysis of Sullivan's concern about the domination of counselors by scientific psychology and calls for a more complete knowledge of the disciplines of philosophy and psychology and for a better integration of the knowledge obtained from them. He calls for a self-awareness of one's philosophical and psychological stance. Hine reacts eloquently to the phrase "blaming the victim" and urges better understanding of clients, of the environment and of dialogue.

Part III is devoted to four papers that describe and report research in moral education and related areas.

James Rest, a cognitive developmental psychologist and researcher, reviews the differing psychological approaches and offers a special summary of the contentions of cognitive developmental psychology. Rest also offers the rationale and details of his efforts to standardize a moral development scale, his DIT. Hogan and Bohannon challenge several of Rest's interpretations of research and testing materials. One such interesting challenge is to the value system that places the social contract thinking at Stage 5 while the Kantian ideal is placed at Stage 6. They point out and welcome Rest's independence of Kohlberg in various factors of his DIT, and wonder how he can still identify with the cognitive developmentalist tradition.

Harry Kavanagh, an educational psychologist, reports on his moral education research at the high-school level. Using filmed presentations of moral dilemmas, students reacted under varying conditions: some in peer-led groups, others in counselor-led groups, and others reacted only in writing. Readers may be surprised to learn which group showed the highest gain. Maureen Joy takes a critical look at Kavanagh's work, including research methodology. She urges that research in this area be more extensive in its time dimension. She also puts her finger on the problem of emphasis on the male as decision-maker in Kohlberg's work and points out the importance and opportunity for research in moral education in religious (e.g. Catholic) schools.

Robert Selman, a cognitive psychologist-researcher, reports on his work in the area of perspective-taking which is regarded as an important element in the social growth of those who go beyond the first egocentric level in the Kohlberg scale. Selman explains how his perspective-taking fits into the structural-developmental approach and then offers the educational implications and methodology that accompany his findings. Finally he describes a pilot research project that is important to his studies. Robert Havighurst, the University of Chicago social psychologist, in reacting to Selman, offers a brief overview of his own work on character development, and indicates that he can readily integrate Selman's and Kohlberg's models into his own. He raises the problem of cognition versus behavior in these studies.

The final major paper is offered by James Fowler, a theologian and developmental psychologist. Using a special definition of faith (more broad than religious faith), he proposes and describes six stages and the variants within each stage of faith development. He describes the research procedure and some results of his semi-clinical interviews in faith development. Finally, he shows how his approach agrees with and differs from concepts of mystical stages and from Kohlberg's approach. There are two reactors to Fowler's paper. Alfred McBride, a religious educator, is rather negative regarding the developmental psychological part of the paper but positive from the viewpoint of insight and perspective. James E. Hennessy, a theologian, takes a positive stance towards Fowler's paper and urges him to continue his research along more specifically religious faith lines.

I should feel remiss if I do not add a word concerning the importance of the moral education movement in my judgment. First let me say that I do not agree with the historians who point out with glee that the ancient Greeks and Egyptians voiced their concern about the youth of their day, who it turned out developed pretty well. Our moral, ethical, value, social and faith (in Fowler's generalized sense) conditions among larger and larger segments of the population have plummeted. A cursory glance at the newspapers regarding politicians, big and little business, and crime statistics, especially for youth, illustrates that trend. The fears that people express about being out after dark or using public transportation show how widespread the conviction of diminished morality has become. While the other side of the coin indicates a contrary trend on the part of a moral elite group to become more developed (a trend toward Teilhard de Chardin's point Omega) than ever before, the net picture of the total world population reveals a true crisis in morals.

It seems to me very fortunate that at this time the moral education movement has caught the attention of many concerned individuals, including educators. It is my conviction that the group has brought a new sophisticated respectability to the analysis of moral growth among psychologists and educators. There is a grave need, however, among the latter group to make a deep study of the current contentions of moral educators before they embark upon a program among their students. It's easy to poke fun at a misunderstood vocabulary or to say "I tried it and nothing happened" when you haven't really studied it deeply. One of the major elements of the moral education movement that should prove attractive to educators is its primary concern about the "disequilibrium" that sponsors growth on the part of those who are ready for it. I suggest that this growth element should make its goal link up very well with the general purposes of education.

A final word regarding religious educators and the moral education movement. There is the same need among religious educators to develop a deep understanding of this approach before "trying it

out" as obtains among all other educators. Furthermore, upon
learning well what Kohlberg and others are teaching, the religious
educator has the additional chore of attempting to translate its literature and even its scales to the needs of those in the religious tradition. It is my belief that when this kind of work is done well, a
great harvest (even a hundredfold) will be the result for those who
seek the growth of others in religious education. It will represent a
marriage of developmental psychology and religious education, and
I for one would like to be around to bless the wedding and to
express my optimism for a fruitful progeny.

All but one of the papers presented here have been written
especially for this book. They are revisions of lectures given at the
institute in Moral and Ethical Issues in Education, held on Satur-
days in the spring of 1975 at the School of Education, Fordham
University at Lincoln Center, New York City.

The one paper that has been published elsewhere is that by
Robert Selman. One part of the paper was contained in an article
by Robert Selman and Marcus Lieberman in the *Journal of Educational Psychology,* 1975, 67, 712-716, under the title "Moral Education in the Primary Grades: An Evaluation of a Developmental
Curriculum." *(Copyright 1975 by the American Psychological Association. Reprinted by permission.)* In addition, most of the article
"appeared as part of a volume entitled *Values Education,* Meyer, J.,
Burnham, B. & Cholvat, J. (Eds.) published by Wilfred Laurier University Press, Waterloo, Ontario, Canada, and is used with the permission of the publisher."

1.
A Philosophical View of
Values and Value Education*

Clive Beck

In this paper I have chosen to write of "values" and "value education" rather than "morals" and "moral education." Such a choice of terminology deserves some explanation.

The term "values" in this context is preferable to the term "morals," in my view, because it suggests greater breadth of concern, and because it discourages preoccupation with the notion of a narrow and separate moral domain. There are many value dimensions with which humans concern themselves—aesthetic, cultural, educational, political, economic, and so on. Furthermore, the word "moral" in recent times has tended to be used in such a way as to imply that the right approach to human conduct lies in the unreflective adherence to a set of rather specific rules. The word has absolutist and conventionalist connotations. Of course, one could retain the word "moral" and broaden its meaning, stressing the need to take account of an interconnected set of fundamental life-concerns when dealing with moral problems. But the danger of constant misunderstanding is so great that it would seem advisable to use the word "value" instead.

The other alternative is to see moral value as just one type of value among many, with certain distinctive characteristics. However, after many years of attempting to identify a distinctive moral domain, I have been forced to conclude that there is no such domain. There *appears* to be, if one views human conduct from a conventionalist, absolutist perspective. But if one weighs human conduct in terms of more fundamental life goals or life concerns one sees that all decisions are life decisions and there are no distinctively moral decisions. In what follows, however, I will occasionally use

*This paper arose in part out of the OISE Moral Education Project, funded by the Ministry of Education, Ontario.

the term "moral" in deference to those writers who continue to find a use for it.

An Approach toward Reflecting on Values

It is necessary to distinguish between values in the sense of *valuings* and values in the sense of *valuables* (things that really *are* valuable). A person may value something that is not in fact valuable: it is possible to be mistaken in one's value beliefs, to have unsound or inappropriate valuings. In this paper we are concerned chiefly with "values" in the sense of things that really are valuable. Our interest is in the origin of *sound* valuings in human beings.

It should be noted, however, that soundness in valuing is almost always a matter of degree: objects are more or less good or bad, valuings are more or less sound or unsound. Probably there is a grain of soundness in almost every human valuing (even when, on balance, the valuing is grossly unsound). And probably there is an element of unsoundness in even the most appropriate of valuings. Just as there is no such thing as the perfect way of life, so there is room for improvement in any one sub-area of a person's value system.

There is no end to the debate over what makes a value (or valuing) sound, just as epistemologists have been unable to resolve the problem of what makes a belief true. However, for practical purposes, a value may be declared sound if it passes certain tests, the tests varying somewhat from context to context and from person to person. I would like to refer to the process of testing and hence arriving at sound valuings as "reflection," and discuss several types of reflection on values.

(i) First, reflection on valuings is obviously important in order to ensure that one is not making a straightforward mistake about "the facts of the case." For example, one may value a business associate for his honesty and resourcefulness but find on reflection (including appropriate inquiry) that he is neither honest nor resourceful. The need for this kind of reflection on values is unproblematic and widely acknowledged. However, there are three other fundamental kinds of reflection on values that are not so commonly recognized.

(ii) Second, one must through reflection bring the values one is not sure about into line with the values one is sure about. For example, one may, upon reflection, be somewhat unsure about the value of competitive sport. By reflection upon a complex of values one is sure about—health, happiness, friendship, and so on, in certain forms—one may arrive at either a rejection of competitive sport as valuable or a conception of competitive sport such that one can legitimately value it. Adjustment of one's values to one another in this manner may appear so obviously sensible as not to merit mention here. However, it is amazing the extent to which people compartmentalize their valuings, not noticing that certain values for which they have no sound basis can be rejected, modified or justified in the light of other values that they are sure about for good reason.

(iii) Third, one must through reflection bring means-values into line with end-values (insofar as one is sure that the end-values in question really are valuable). One may believe, for example, that promotion in one's profession is a good means to happiness and security but recognize on reflection that one would be happier and more secure at the promotional level one has at present. Here again, it is common for people not to engage in reflection of this kind and to value things that in fact militate against the achievement of their fundamental life goals.

(iv) Fourth, it is necessary through reflection to arrive at a set of fundamental or ultimate life goals—things that one values for their own sake—in the light of which one can assess specific and intermediate values. It would appear that for the great majority of people, the following are ultimate life goals: survival, health, happiness (enjoyment, pleasure, etc.), friendship (love, fellowship, etc.), helping others (to some extent), wisdom, fulfillment (of our capacities), freedom, self-respect, respect from others, a sense of meaning in life, and so on. These are ultimates in the sense that to a large extent (though in varying degrees) they provide a final resting place for questioning about value and purpose. If asked "Why do you want to be happy, fulfilled, wise, free?" one may legitimately reply "I just do, that's all." By contrast, if asked "Why do you want to go to a university?" or "Why do you want to get a new job?" it is not legitimate to reply "I just do, that's all"; achieving such goals as these is only worthwhile if it enables one to achieve a certain quality of life, characterized by the fulfillment of ultimate life goals. The "Why?" questions must be asked and answered.

Of course, different people vary in the emphasis they give to ultimate values such as survival, happiness, and fulfillment, and part of the reflection process for a particular person involves determining the emphasis one is going to give to each value. Even at this ultimate level, there are degrees of ultimacy and an interdependence between ultimates. Further, one has to refine the *type* of survival, health, happiness, etc., one is after (for oneself and others) and under what circumstances. This is in part one with determining what specific and intermediate values one is to have; but it is also a matter of determining what, *ultimately*, one seeks in life. This self-knowledge is an essential basis for the other kinds of reflection on values.

In stressing the importance of reflection on values of the kinds described above I am proposing a type of utilitarian approach (Smart, 1967) to the origin of values and also giving a major place (though by no means an exclusive place) to the cognitive dimension. This requires some defense, since there are many people who have misgivings about means/ends distinctions, utilitarian outlooks, and placing emphasis upon the cognitive in value matters (Peters, 1963; MacIntyre, 1964; Ellul, 1964). My defense takes the following form.

It appears to be a fundamental characteristic of humans that they have rather strong and definite wants and desires. A human being who had no wants or desires would probably be dead, or at least in a state very similar to death in most respects. Further, it is characteristic of humans that they value very highly a general sense of assurance that their wants will be satisfied in some degree. This sense of assurance, which has reference both to physical wants and psychological/spiritual wants, might be described as a sense of security. Now, it is widely acknowledged that human beings have a right to security and a sense of security. Security is often defined in physical terms, with reference to assured provision of food, shelter, clothing and the like. But equally humans must have security and a sense of security with respect to their psychological/spiritual wants. A person wants to know as he lives his life that he is not constantly making mistakes, "barking up the wrong tree," heading toward disappointment and disillusionment. Often the desire for security is disparaged by moralists and ideologues; but clearly, in an important sense of the term, a measure of security is fundamental to human well being. If, then, one is to have the degree of security that humans commonly desire, one must reflect on one's way of life in the light of one's ultimate life goals, and develop through reflection and appropriate action a well-grounded assurance that one's way of life is indeed such that one will achieve at least some of one's ultimate life goals in some degree. One must determine what, *ultimately*, one is after in life and establish a pattern of life appropriate to these ultimate concerns. Thus, reflection on one's values, in the manner I have outlined, is fundamental to a satisfactory human existence.

While stressing the importance of reflection, however, we must avoid certain stereotypes concerning the manner in which reflection on values is conducted. To begin with, it should be noted that the reflection that gives rise to sound values need not be carried on in a highly skeptical, critical spirit. One can be thoughtful about values without adopting a negative stance toward existing values. One may reflect on the value of promise keeping, for example, without being predisposed to reject promise keeping as a principle of living. The result of reflection on commonly accepted values will in many cases—perhaps the great majority of them—be simply that one will refine the values in certain ways, come to understand their point more fully, learn how to implement them more effectively, and be more solidly committed to them than one was before.

Further, reflection on values may take place with full respect being given to the weight of tradition and authority relevant to the values in question. For example, the values proposed by a particular religion may be taken very seriously. A value that has stood the test of time or that is strongly advocated by a reliable authority is for that reason to be given careful attention. Tradition and authority provide much of the essential raw material for the development of values. Traditions and authorities must be assessed in terms of the likelihood that the values they support are sound. But very often one will not be in a position to develop a value for oneself and will have to accept it from a tradition or an authority that one has good reason to believe can be relied upon with respect to the value issue in question.

Again, while one reflects on values as an individual, one very often does so in a context of dialogue and social participation in which it may be very difficult to distinguish one's own judgment from that of others. A whole group or set of interconnected groups engage in joint inquiry into values and we are inevitably influenced by the values of our community even when we have been unable to make an independent assessment of these values.

Yet again, reflection on values does not exclude the influence of feelings, intuition and conscience in guiding us toward sound values (Beck, 1972). In many cases we are aware that we do not have the time or the capacity to question the directions suggested by semi-automatic mechanisms of these kinds. We may plan at some future date to assess our intuitions or educate our conscience, but we recognize that we cannot do better than rely on them at this moment on this particular issue. Reflection is still operative here, but it moves to the higher (or lower) level of acknowledging that an assessment "from scratch" is not appropriate under the circumstances.

Finally, reflection on values, in the broad sense in which I am using the term, includes drawing on information and ideas derived from published material, films, lectures and the like and from life experiences, planned or unplanned. Reflection includes engaging in inquiry or utilizing the inquiry of others relevant to the value issues on which one is reflecting. Thus, reflection on values in school settings, for example, will involve study of a wide range of topics and use of multi-media sources and personal-involvement techniques such as classroom simulations and community activities.

In summary of this section, we say that the meaning of values can be grasped through a process of reflection (including inquiry) with four major aspects: reflection on relevant facts of the case; reflection which brings values one is not sure about into line with values one is (more) sure about; reflection which brings means-values into line with end-values; and reflection on one's fundamental or ultimate life goals, for oneself and others. The justification of this whole process is the basic human need for a sense of security, the assurance that one is achieving and will achieve those things in life that one values for their own sake. However, while emphasizing the role of reflection in giving rise to sound values, we must recognize that this reflection takes place in a positive spirit, and with due regard for tradition, authority, dialogue, social participation, feelings, intuition and conscience.

Value Education

A major concern in value education is with helping people come to live in accordance with their values. A lot has been said about this subject by Peter McPhail (1970), John Wilson (1973), Lawrence Kohlberg (Beck et al., 1971), and Sidney Simon (1972), among others. Simon, for example, has described a large number of specific techniques by means of which people may become more aware of their values and more committed to them cognitively, emotionally and behaviorally.

Our concern in this paper is rather with another major aspect of value education, namely, that of helping people arrive at sound values in accordance with which to live. The discussion will follow from the points made in the preceding section about reflecting on values. The process of reflection on values described in that section is central to the value-inquiry aspect of value education.

Despite differences among various schools of thought—

McPhail, Wilson, Values Clarification, Kohlberg, the OISE Project—
one message comes through loud and clear from the modern movement in moral/values education: students should not have values
imposed on them, but rather should (a) be introduced to certain
general procedures for arriving at values and (b) be exposed to
various ideas and arguments in the area of values as a stimulus to
thought.

Now, it seems to me that the theory of value reflection presented in the preceding section can be used to spell out this basic
message, and within the reflection procedure a synthesis of the
various contemporary schools of thought on value education can be
achieved. We will look in turn at each of the schools of thought
mentioned.

Peter McPhail has argued convincingly that school students
need a context in which they may simulate real life situations without many of the insecurities and immediate pressures of real life, a
context in which they may engage in social experimentation leading
to the discovery of more satisfactory human relationships (McPhail,
1975). He accepts the fact that students have fundamental human
values such as happiness, fellowship, and fulfillment, but maintains
that in everyday life they do not have sufficient opportunities to try
out new ways of achieving these values. He claims that the basic
motivation is there, but the means chosen are defective. Clearly,
this position can be related to the theory of value reflection proposed earlier. Through discussions and personal-involvement techniques students are helped to bring their specific modes of social
coping—their means-values—into line with their fundamental
human values or ultimate life goals—their end-values.

John Wilson has shown that being moral involves a much
more complex set of attitudes, knowledges, skills and tendencies
than we have commonly supposed (Wilson, 1973). It is not sufficient for a child to "know" that it is right to be considerate to
others. He must have a basic concern for others, he must understand what "others" are like, he must be able to see things from the
point of view of others, he must know how to help others, he must
have the necessary social skills to help others, and so on. Thus, in
accordance with the theory of reflection outlined earlier, a child
must acquire relevant knowledge of "the facts of the case," he must
recognize within himself a fundamental concern for others along
with other basic values, and he must develop specific and intermediate values that enable him to achieve his fundamental values,
within the context of the facts of the case. Of course, Wilson goes

beyond the theory of reflection into additional aspects of moral motivation, but the approach to moral education inherent in his theory of moral components may be integrated with the theory of reflection.

Sidney Simon, the chief exponent of the values-clarification approach, has stressed the importance of being aware of all of one's values—specific, intermediate and ultimate—and being conscious of the consequences of committing oneself to these values. Simon has sometimes been criticized for suggesting that what a child's values are does not matter, so long as he is aware of them and is committed to them. However, statements by members of the values-clarification school in recent years have suggested that there is a concern for the modification of values as a result of reflection; and whatever the emphasis within the approach may be, the various techniques for facing up to one's values, becoming clear about them, and becoming aware of their consequences can certainly be utilized in a total process of reflective reconstruction of one's values such as was discussed in the first section.

Lawrence Kohlberg's proposal for arriving at sound values is tied to a theory of moral development that sets what some would see as rather pessimistic limits on the moral insights one can attain in a given problem area at a given stage. However, the general form of the reflective process is much the same as the one I have proposed: values are not imposed, but rather students are exposed to relevant facts, arguments and value ideas and engage in an active process of achieving equilibrium between the various elements of their value outlook. Thus, even if one were to disagree with Kohlberg's empirical psychological claims about the patterns of moral thought at different ages and stages, one could heartily endorse his nonauthoritarian, interactive, reflective approach to arriving at values.

The project of the Ontario Institute for the Study of Education (OISE) of which I am a representative, has tended to stress discussion techniques in which attention moves constantly back and forth between value principles and specific examples. It has been felt that while the detailed study of a particular case study or moral dilemma is useful from time to time, it is necessary to review a great many examples, most of them rather close to home, in the course of reflecting on a value concept or principle. Further, it has been felt that while simulation activities and values-clarification techniques are undoubtedly useful, progress toward the development of a sound value outlook will be very slow unless individual insights are drawn together in a somewhat explicit manner. Nevertheless, the OISE Project is very concerned (as this paper illustrates) to stress (a) that there are many very useful techniques and approaches in value education in addition to the principled discussion approach, and (b) that there is more to value education than arriving at a sound value outlook: one must also learn how to apply one's value outlook in practice (which will in turn lead to a further refinement of one's value outlook). Thus, while the OISE Project also has stressed certain aspects of the total reflective process more than others, its position can be integrated into that process as it has been described in the present paper.

It would seem, then, that despite differences of emphasis and differences in technique, some agreement is emerging with respect to the value-inquiry aspect of value education. It must be an open, reflective, nonindoctrinative process, with exposure to relevant information and various arguments and points of view. The precise list of fundamental human values provided in the first section above may not be accepted by all, but the notion that students should be trying to arrive at sound values—specific, intermediate and ultimate—by an open, informed, reflective process is gaining very wide acceptance.

A Concluding Note on the Relation Between Values and Religion

In a paper on values the absence of extensive reference to religion may to some seem rather surprising. It might be argued, for example, that the "ultimate life goals" I have mentioned are not ultimate enough: that such life goals require in turn a further justification of a religious or metaphysical nature. By way of illustration, let us look at this issue in terms of a theistic religious position, namely, Christianity.

It has sometimes been said that the principles of Christian ethics are to be followed not because they are self-justifying but because they are found in God's revealed Word or, more simply, because God wills that we follow them. This, it is said, is the ultimate justification for being moral. Now there is perhaps a grain of truth in this view for some people, for it would seem that a sense of meaning in life is a fundamental human value, an ultimate life goal, and if one's sense of meaning in life is bound up with a Christian perspective, reference to the will of God may have some place at the ultimate level. But it can have only a limited place at the ultimate level. For the question any reflective, mature Christian must be able to answer is: "*Why* does God want me to follow the principles of

Christian ethics?" And the same is true of any other religion.

The inadequacy of a purely authoritarian, unreflective approach to Christian ethics is brought out by the question: Is an action good because God wills it or does God will it because it is good? The latter alternative is rather obviously the correct one. And if God wills good actions because they are good, we can presumably find out the criteria of good actions and hence be in a position to arrive at value conclusion by a nonauthoritarian, reflective process. Further, we—and our students—*must* find out the criteria of good actions; for unless a person understands at least in part why a principle of action is sound he will not be able to follow it satisfactorily. To some extent the argument over inculcation *versus* education in values is a nonargument, for values cannot be inculcated. Unless a person is allowed to explore and reflect upon the nature and purpose of a value principle, he will not know when the principle applies, when to make an exception, when to modify the principle, and so on. He will simply not have the principle. Thus, even within a religious context, attempts at the unreflective inculcation of values are self-defeating.

How, then, does the reflective, "ultimate life goals" approach to values and value education that I have advocated relate to a religion such as Christianity? In the first place, Christianity, along with all other major religions, endorses ultimate life goals of the kind listed earlier. God is represented as wanting people, by and large, to survive, be happy, be fulfilled, have friendships, and so on. Accordingly, general theory of reflective valuing can be applied and developed in a religious context.

Second, because of this common ground between religious and "nonreligious" approaches to life, people of religious and "nonreligious" persuasions can help each other in value matters. (I put the term "nonreligious" in quotation marks because I am not sure what it would mean to be nonreligious; but that raises issues too large to be discussed here.) Despite metaphysical differences, then, a "nonreligious" teacher can help a religious child to a considerable extent in value matters, whether in a counseling situation or in general value inquiry; and equally a religious teacher can help a "nonreligious" child.

Third, while not everyone needs religion (in a traditional sense of the term), it is very likely that some do, in order to have optimally sound values. One does not have values in a cultural and metaphysical vacuum; and a person's most satisfactory cultural and metaphysical context may include a traditional religion, depending upon his background, upbringing, temperament and general outlook. The main issue is whether religion is functional in a person's life, and one cannot prejudge this question for a particular individual.

Reaction to Beck: CAN MORAL VALUES BE EXCLUDED? *by* Andrew Varga, S.J.

The term "value" is a relatively new acquisition of the philosophical vocabulary and, unfortunately, it is frequently used in a confusing way. As there is no universally accepted theory of value, one turns to the reading of an essay on this topic with the hope that at least some aspects of the question will be somewhat clarified and some light will be shed on the issue. Reading Professor Beck's study, however, one cannot escape the feeling of disappointment as he injects a rather disturbing factor into the discussion by excluding moral values from his consideration at the very beginning and states that such values do not exist at all. Furthermore, he affirms that the word "moral" in recent times has tended to indicate an "unreflective adherence to a set of rather specific rules." This would mean an "absolutist and conventionalist" approach to morality in our times or, according to accepted terminology, a positivist interpretation of morality.

The task of philosophy is to analyze and understand reality, and consequently it must not exclude from its investigation that which at least appears to belong to the realm of reality. It is the common experience of the man in the street and of the philosopher that we frequently refer to moral values as they are distinguished from economic, aesthetic, cultural, scientific, or in one word, nonmoral values. We are convinced that there is a difference between a cultured person and a morally good person. A great scientist is not necessarily a good person, because he may deliberately and freely use his scientific knowledge to strengthen the rule of a tyrant in exchange for monetary reward. (For a brief analysis of the moral and nonmoral senses of value, see Frankena, 1973, p. 62.) The common experience of men concerning moral value must not be left out of our investigation of the origin of values. If Professor Beck, after a thorough analysis of this experience, arrives at the conclusion that there are no moral values and morality only means "an unreflective adherence to a set of rather specific rules," we would like to know the reasons for this judgment. Furthermore, the statement that the word "moral" has an abolutist and conventionalist connotation does not seem to express the experience of our era, especially of the decades after the Second World War. If anything is striking in the moral consciousness of the "masses" and individuals, it is a turning against conventionalism in morality, a revolt against moral laws imposed either by civil or religious authority. All the restlessness, activism and revolutionary tendencies of the past decades indicate that people do not identify moral value with obedience to conventional rules, but they rather base their judgment of morality on some value found within the act and not in the power of authority external to the act. Moral positivism attributes the origin of moral value to positive laws whether they are the result of positive enactment or of the forces of tradition and convention. It is not only the younger generation today that emphatically rejects this interpretation of morality; it seems rather characteristic of our times to scrutinize positive laws and conventions to determine whether they are just or unjust, whether they express or contradict true intrinsic values. The absolutist and conventionalist approach to morality is in disfavor today and it is difficult to find many representatives of this school. It appears to be a false reading of contemporary thinking to state that the prevalent theories of morality today are some forms of unreflective moral positivism. Fashionable and prevalent thinking, however, cannot furnish decisive reasons for the validity of a theory, and an incorrect appraisal of the present situation does not invalidate Professor Beck's opinion either. His main reason for rejecting moral values is found in his statement that, after many years of research, he cannot identify a distinctive moral domain among the different types of values and hence he concludes that there is no such domain. In his opinion, one could retain the word "moral" and broaden its meaning to include an "interconnected set of fundamental life concerns," but this would create a constant misunderstanding. Any further analysis of the problem of moral values is dismissed because, weighing human conduct, one finds no distinctive moral decisions.

In response to Professor Beck's opinion, let us attempt to trace the origin of moral values in a brief analysis. Man is not born good but becomes good by performing good acts, i.e., by good conduct. Among the varied activities of man we find some actions and values that make man good purely and simply as man without adding a qualification as, for instance, a good composer, good sportsman, good scientist, etc. Is this judgment based on some subjective and arbitrary evaluation or is there any objective basis for judging a person a good man and thus stating that there is a specific domain of values which makes man specifically or, in generally accepted terminology, morally good? Can this domain be identified in some way to distinguish it from other types of values?

Goodness has to be found in some way in the acts that we can freely perform and which are directed to goals we can realize. If a man lacks musical talent and does not become a great musician, he does not become a morally bad person because of the lack of this value. The study of medicine does not make a person a morally good man, but the neglect of acquiring the necessary knowledge to perform a surgery successfully makes a practicing surgeon morally deficient because his neglect has moral connotation and produces a moral disvalue. The objects of free human acts must lie within our control to acquire moral qualifications. This, however, is not enough to affirm that a certain act is morally good. We also have to find the basis for certain acts being morally valued while others are not. Analyzing the different classes of human actions, one finds that there are certain types of actions which particularly add to the building of the genuinely human in us, actions which contribute to the realization of what we hold really human. Man is not a finished, completed being at birth but builds his humanity throughout his life; while he is conscious, he performs acts some of which contribute to his becoming more of a human being and others that degrade his humanity as they go against his rational and social nature. To act in an inhuman way is to act immorally, and to act in a human way is to become a morally good person.

Professor Beck may object to this understanding of morality because it is too broad and it contains the unknown element of true humanity. One could answer that any other understanding of morality unduly restricts its domain and perhaps identifies it with religion or the practice of a few virtues. Many of our actions that in themselves have no moral significance may have moral references because they contribute to the building or weakening of the human in us on account of some circumstances. Playing golf in itself can be considered as a nonmoral act but it may gain moral significance if a person spends too much time on the golf course and neglects his duty as a cabinet minister. The neglect of one's duty weakens the truly human in a person because it disturbs a rational and social cooperation that should be a constitutive part of our true humanity. Moral problems surround us everywhere in our daily lives whether the question is of disconnecting the respirator for a terminally ill patient or going on strike as a teacher, fireman or police officer, or refusing to serve in the military. Our everyday decisions are usually less dramatic than the examples mentioned. They are nevertheless just as much moral because they build the truly human in us or on the contrary they make our conduct less human.

According to these considerations, morality is derived from the quality of free acts that contribute to the building of the real human. The understanding of this relationship, however, presupposes a sufficient knowledge of what it means to be really human because the idea of man is the end that specifies the morality, the rightness or wrongness, of actions. One may wonder whether we can really know what the truly human is. We could answer that some understanding of the truly human is part of our consciousness and can be attained by self-reflection. We can analyze our own tendencies and drives, and apprehend the requirements of a truly human living. Human nature, our true humanity, should not be taken, then, in a static but in a dynamic sense as the goal that organizes and coordinates our actions and directs them toward an ever more perfect realization of our humanity. We comprehend the essential characteristics of our humanity in the experience of our existential drives and relationships with our fellow human beings. This initial and implicit knowledge, to be certain, needs refinement and explicitation. A more precise knowledge of our humanity, however, is not impossible to achieve with the help of the human sciences. Thus the discernment of the truly human is an ongoing process regarding both the individual and the human race as we scrutinize and penetrate our nature more and more in the light of the new discoveries of the sciences.

In spite of their great differences, most ethical systems appear to have a common concern of "humanizing" life, that is, bringing human conduct in conformity with the human ideal as much as possible. Even the philosophically uneducated man speaks about conduct that dehumanizes or humanizes us, condemns actions that are "inhuman" and commends actions that conform to "human dignity." The agreement of an action with one of the human existential drives does not make a person necessarily morally good because it may not substantially confer to the general humanization of man. Great knowledge does not turn a man into a morally good person because such a person can use his knowledge to make his own life or the life of many persons "inhuman." Using knowledge, however, to enhance our own humanity and that of our fellowmen, becomes a morally good act. It is obvious from these considerations that the understanding of what man essentially is, constitutes

the key element of our discovering what man should be by his conduct, or in other words, what actions are morally valuable. Thus a
philosophy of man or a philosophical anthropology is necessary for
the study of morality.

After having dismissed moral values as a special distinctive
domain in the realm of values, Professor Beck proceeds to examine
the "origin of *sound* valuings in human beings." A value is sound,
in his judgment, if it passes certain tests and he calls the process of
testing "reflection." He discusses four main types of reflection on
values. He follows a utilitarian approach and his reflections and observations are clear and well presented. The fourth type of reflection deals with "fundamental or ultimate life goals—things that one
values for their own sake." He mentions a set of fundamental or ultimate life goals. It seems that his justification of why these are ultimate values is an intuitive knowledge. In his opinion, one cannot
give an explicit reason why one wants to be happy, fulfilled, etc.
This is, of course, the usual answer of the utilitarian theory. Utili-
tarians, however, must have some idea of what man is, otherwise
they could not propose actions of social reform to improve the
quality of life. It is some idea of man that governs their judgment
when they propose a conduct that is good for man. As Professor
Beck proceeds to justify his utilitarian approach, he arrives at some
description of his idea of what man is. "It appears to be a fundamental characteristic of humans that they have rather strong and
definite wants and desires." Thus he implicitly admits a final cause,
i.e., man's nature to be realized by human conduct. That is the
foundation that explains why certain actions are valuable. This ad-
mission, however, remains implicit as in his concluding summary,
he reverts to placing the origin of values in the process of reflection. I could agree with his analysis if he had just said that reflection *reveals* the connection of certain actions and facts with fundamental life goals, and the quality of the free actions that
promotes and achieves the fundamental life goals is the reason why
théy are valuable.

To sum up my observations, I want to state *first* that I do not
accept Professor Beck's rejection of moral values. I tried to show in
a brief analysis that there is a special domain of moral values and
that the morality of an act consists in its contributing to the building up the genuinely human in us. Human nature, to be realized
more and more perfectly, is the final cause of our moral development and it provides the reason why certain actions constitute
moral value and others moral disvalue. Human nature has to be un-

derstood as the dynamic source of all our activities and not as the biological functions of man.

Second, I find Professor Beck's *description* of the valuing process clear and logical but I wish he had gone beyond description and had explicitly indicated the genuine (ontological) basis of values which, in my view, is more important in assessing the meaning of values than the account of the valuing process.

Reaction to Beck: THE IMPORTANCE OF EXEMPLARY MODELS IN VALUE EDUCATION *by* James R. Barclay

Recently, my wife and I were seated in a restaurant specializing in seafood. There was an elaborate menu in which a lobster played an important role with a large drawing indicating the specialty of the house. A young family came in and sat next to us. They had three children. One was about five, another about seven, and the youngest about three. The waitress presented all but the youngest with a menu. Shortly thereafter the seven-year-old pointed to the lobster and said: "Daddy I want that!" The father looked at the child and said, "Ah—that's spider chicken." The child examined the menu closely and then turned to his mother and said, "Is that right Momma?" She laughed and said, "If your father says it's spider chicken, it is."

We laughed at this internally, but on second thought the situation really represents a profound fact in value determination. The father (and others) often serves as an interpreter of reality. Though obviously the father wished to order something like chicken for his son, perhaps to save money, he was acting as an interpreter of what is real and what is valid. The son checked out the epistemological verity by consulting his mother, who agreed with the father's interpretation.

Rightly or wrongly, a considerable amount of value determination is not simply a question of experiencing various alternatives either in simulation exercise or real life, but a question of who believes what for what reasons. Thus, the exemplary model provides a key to the question of value determination.

I have little to disagree with in Beck's discussion of value education as he presents it. Who can really disagree with the idea that students should be presented with cases, simulations and the like? But there is an important element missing in this discussion of value education. Values are not decided upon simply by some problem-solving method in which alternate solutions are posed and rational judgment used to decide the best alternative. Values are related to modeling. Children as well as adults tend to place a value on the valuer. They tend to look at the model and his or her particular personality as it is subjectively judged and it plays a significant role in their own value determination.

Perhaps what is implicitly involved in the personal identification of values is the credibility of the model's preference. If a child believes his father is nearly omnipotent, then he may be inclined to accept his valuings or interpretation of reality. Naturally, there comes a time when the father (or mother) may be seen as less than omnipotent. This event arrives sooner or later in the lives of all individuals. But there are then other significant persons who by reason of either reinforcement, or modeled behavior, or status in a situation assume important person roles. Thus the judgment about people is, I think, an important determinant to the possible acceptance of values.

In our society the peer group has often taken on an important role as the interpreter of values. I tend to think that this has occurred because the family nucleus has failed to present an authoritative model. I mean specifically authoritative in the sense that father and mother indicate the source and basis of their values—advocating a specific form of values because they believe in them, but not imposing them in an authoritarian manner. Thus, I feel that a distinction must be made in values that are promoted between the authoritarian "Accept what I say, regardless, because it is right," the authoritative, "We believe these values to be right and we hope you will agree," and the laissez-faire, "We don't know and/or we don't care." Naturally, at times it may be difficult to distinguish between authoritarian and authoritative but the distinction is a real one. The authoritarian position simply advocates acceptance of a value position on the basis of authority. But the authoritative position indicates a thought-out position that is positively held, but not foisted on others. Baumrind (1971), in an extensive study of family styles of nurturance that lead to socially responsive and responsible behavior in elementary children, found that children from families where an authoritative stance was taken on value determination were much more socially responsive and responsible than children from families where either an authoritarian or laissez-faire attitude was manifested.

Initially and maximally parents serve as models for their children in value determination. But children quickly distinguish whether parents truly exemplify what they advocate. It is not appropriate to command children to attend church services when the parents exclude themselves. Nor is lip service to racial equality acceptable when parents give vent to racist expressions. On the other hand, children can also make distinctions between the actions of parents when angry and disturbed vis-à-vis their normal behavior.

The emergence of the peer group or members in the peer group as a criterion of modeling may be in part related to the failure of adequate parental models. But not always. The existence of a formidable mechanism of cultural control and values in our society must be accepted for what it is—a major determinant to value judgment. I refer to mass media and specifically to television where the criterion of value appears uniformly to be what is new, what is more efficient, what will bring about more "peak" experiences.

The effect of television and a variety of popular as well as professional magazines and journals is cumulatively unrest. There is always a lingering suspicion that somehow one is not getting the "most" out of life. The incessant flow of books and articles that suggest new ways to enjoy sex more, the feverish pitch to continually buy more unneeded consumer goods, the equation of love at Christmas with a volume of gifts, represent a value system that is pegged squarely to the notions that: (1) what is new is better and cheaper, (2) what is old is outdated, and (3) "if it feels good, do it."

The school as an organized interpreter of values comes off a very poor third or fourth in the ranking of value experiences. However, if the school itself could call into question the spurious pseudo-criteria of the media, then it might be in a better position to provide adequate criteria for value determination. Much of the media message argues implicitly that what is good for one's self is right, and what is not good is not right. Thus the criterion of goodness appears to be related to what is self-fulfilling. Personal self-enrichment of experience thus becomes the criterion of good-evil and right-wrong. The continual modeling of violence, self-aggrandizing behavior, and the consequent passive-viewer status role prepares hosts of children for the acceptance of group values. The school's role in value determination thus becomes a very poor alternative.

There is one bright light in this discussion. The role of the model is still most important. The teacher is an exemplary model.

Parents continue to function as exemplary models. Both teachers and parents function as interpreters of values and their importance in such interpretation is directly related to the impact of their personality. Bandura (1969) tells us that status is an important factor in modeling. Reinforcement from a person of high status is more important than reinforcement from a person of low status. Thus respect and status appear to be related. Where parents value education and teachers and where positive models of decision-making exist in an authoritative, but not authoritarian method, children have something to model their behavior after.

Though it may sound traditional to echo these views, I do not believe that values can be discovered by some simulation game process. Nor do I think it possible to consider value alternatives with the dispassionate decision-making one makes in selecting alternate brands of light bulbs. Value evolution is related to both epistemological certitude and the nature of reality. Perhaps in many subtle ways, children, like adults, continually seek exemplary models. And I believe that the crucial disposition is the appeal to reason, the behavioral consistency, and the genuineness of these models. Making the valuing process conscious is one thing. This can be done by education. But I suspect strongly that effective models cannot approach the process with a dispassionate method and be effective.

To make the argument more concrete, as a university professor, I guess I can accept quite well the rational and positivistic arguments of my son's astronomy professor. Even though I personally think his view of the universe is myopic, I can respect his judgments lectured with a conviction that influenced my son. Most of all, as I discussed this with my son I recognized that he has viewed his professor's opinions as indicative of his values toward the universe. I did pose some opposing arguments to his position which I think were recognized by my son. I suspect that eventually my son will make some resolution of his own values that may include both his astronomy professor's views and my own. But the point I am suggesting is that effective models do take positions.

In summary, I suggest that value determination is a conscious process in which models play an important role. Simulation, I submit, is a valuable procedure for making the process conscious and explicit, but personal integration of values is strongly aligned to the perception of the validity, authority—and yes—the wisdom of the model.

Reaction to Beck: A HOPE: RESEARCH IN RELIGIOUS DEVEL-
OPMENT *by* John S. Nelson

Theory has run ahead of research with regard to how values
and religion relate to one another. Since we do not have at hand
much hard data, it becomes us in modesty to be open and un-
finished on this topic. In this spirit may I register some personal
agreement and disagreement with Dr. Beck's concluding note on
the relation between values and religion, then express briefly the direction of my own thought.

I concur most with Beck when he observes that persons involved in value education and persons concerned with religious development share a common ground: ultimate life goals. In the light
of this, he infers:

> Second, because of this common ground between religious
> and "non-religious" approaches to life, people of religious
> and "non-religious" persuasions can help each other in
> value matters. (I put the term "non-religious" in quotation
> marks because I am not sure what it would mean to be
> non-religious; but that raises issues too large to be dis-
> cussed here.)

This parallels what has been called "a common-ground morality" as a basis for ethical consensus among persons of different
faiths and different cultures. Given the pluralistic world and nation
in which we live, we have no other alternative for communication
and harmony with most of our neighbors. In a similar way, persons
who respond to the question of God in markedly different ways can
work together in value education because they share ultimate life
goals, because they respect the differences in one another, and because they try to explore and reflect upon value principles in a
nonproselytizing way.

Here I have one reservation. We should take into account all
the dynamics that contribute to growth toward moral maturity.
This includes the support of a tradition-bearing community as well
as freedom of choice amid positive alternatives. It seems to me that
inducing cognitive disequilibrium in the manner of Lawrence Kohlberg or clarifying values with exercises from Sidney Simon, while
valid and worthwhile, both neglect the impact of a relatively homogeneous community upon how our values become specified as we
grow.

My disagreement with Beck revolves around how he uses two words: Christianity and religion. Perhaps the brief space he allotted to his concluding note did not allow him to develop and nuance his thought, as he did much more carefully when treating the origin of values and value education. Perhaps I am reacting to what he does not say but what I hear him implying in some of his generalizations. To be fair, let me cite what I find inadequate and explain why I react negatively.

We read:

> It has sometimes been said that the principles of Christian
> ethics are to be followed not because they are self-justify-
> ing but because they are found in God's revealed Word,
> or, more simply, because God wills that we follow them.
> This, it is said, is the ultimate justification for being moral.

Beck then shows the inadequacy of such a position by asking the critical question: Is an action good because God wills it or does God will it because it is good? He chooses the latter alternative. Well and good—I for one agree with him. So would Thomas Aquinas. My problem is that Beck leaves the reader with the impression that Christians by and large favor the first alternative. This simply is not so. In the roomy tradition of Christian ethics some have emphasized the will of God, some the mind of God, and some a combination of the two as the ultimate justification for the rightness or wrongness of human behavior. For those in the Catholic tradition, there is a long and still living history of a "natural law" which in some way mirrors an "eternal law" in God's mind. For those in the Protestant tradition, there is a dialectic between the uniqueness of the divine imperative and the more general orders of creation. In brief, so wide and varied is the Christian approach to ethics that the·impression should not be given that it favors an approach which is voluntaristic or authoritarian or unreflective. I would contend, though I cannot prove, that this is true not only among its theorists but also among ordinary Christian believers.

Similarly, my second disagreement concerns what Beck connotes to me by "religion." The final paragraph of his paper reads:

> Third, while not everyone needs religion (in a traditional
> sense of the term), it is very likely that some do, in order
> to have optimally sound values. One does not have values
> in a cultural and metaphysical vacuum; and a person's

most satisfactory cultural and metaphysical context may include a traditional religion, depending upon his background, upbringing, temperament and general outlook. The main issue is whether religion is functional in a person's life, and one cannot prejudge this question for a particular individual.

What is religion "in a traditional sense of the term"? A check through books on my shelf that deal with religion from theological, psychological, and sociological points of view makes clear to me that responses are so varied and nuanced as to make the term relatively useless unless defined by the person employing it. Its implications in the paragraph cited above leave me uneasy; I feel that "traditional religion" is expressing a stereotype or a caricature of a much deeper and more meaningful reality. It implies a heteronomy, a law from the outside replacing one's own independent autonomous decisions. Yet religious development, as moral growth, can move from preconventional to conventional to postconventional levels.

Two phrases in particular sound to me wide of the mark: "while not everyone needs religion" and "the main issue is whether religion is functional in a person's life." For the believer, religion expresses a relationship that is analogous to such experiences as love or patriotism. The main issue is not whether the loved one or native land is needed or functional. Friend and country do serve a purpose, but the purpose is not the reason for the relationship. To my way of thinking, to instrumentalize religion is to misunderstand the real meaning that it has in the life of the believer and of the believing community. It is legitimate to ask what function religion has in the believer's ethical thinking and moral behavior. It is a distortion to reduce religion to this function.

Finally, may I express the direction of my own thought. In his remarks on the relation between values and religion, I would have wished that Beck had developed his personal insight stated in his introductory remarks:

But if one weighs human conduct in terms of more fundamental life goals or life concerns one sees that all decisions are life decisions and there are no distinctively moral decisions.

This makes much sense to me. On the empirical level, we can

distinguish between what people recognize as moral behavior from what is called religious practice. We can then establish verifiable criteria for both areas so as to ascertain the correlation between the two. To my knowledge, empirical studies on this topic have come to the conclusion that moral behavior and religious practice vary independently of each other.

Beck's insight, however, suggests to me that the correlation between values and religion should be pursued at a deeper level, because on the empirical level religious practice can be an ambiguous and unreliable indicator of religious belief. Merton Strommen, for example, in his studies of church youth was perplexed by the degree of prejudice and stereotyping that he found among them. In probing the question, he found a high correlation between biased persons and "consensual" Christians, that is, Christians whose religion was more external observance than internal conviction and commitment. In terms of what mature Christian faith should be, poor attitudes on social questions went together with faulty religious belief, despite a high degree of such observable religious practice as church attendance.

What I have in mind requires a vocabulary that expresses the roots within us of both our moral and our religious life. My own preference lies with those who say that the human person is open to self-transcendence in a way that no other earthly creature is. This self-transcendence takes many forms: over the particularity of sense experience through abstraction and reflection, over the determinism of instinct and passion through choice and freedom, over external law or heteronomy through principled autonomy, over inward isolation through relationship with others in various degrees of self-giving, over all the limitations of this present life through belief in a transcendent God. The list could go on. My point is this: the ultimate reason why men and women are morally responsible for their actions, while cows and pigeons are not, is the same as the ultimate reason why men and women worship God, whereas sharks and tigers do not. If this is so, then we may reasonably infer that to the stages of moral development, such as described by Lawrence Kohlberg, there correspond stages of religious development. We would expect that the structure of a person's believing in some way resembles the structure of his or her decision-making. I am not looking for an identity here; even within one area of development, that of moral decision, the same person can be in different but neighboring stages when making judgments on various case histories. I am anticipating some kind of parallelism and interrelationship, since it is one and the same human person who is developing through stages toward ethical and religious maturity.

In conclusion, I wish to observe that I detect in Beck's approach an openness to change, to modify and to deepen his thinking in this important area. I concur with these attitudes and I believe that we share the hope that we both will develop new approaches in the light of the hard data still to come.

2.
Moral and Psychological Development: A Curriculum for Secondary Schools

Norman A. Sprinthall

Schools and Adolescents: The Problem of Development
Studies of the current impact of schooling upon teen-agers provide evidence toward the urgency of needed educational solutions: new forms, new programs, and new experiences designed to enhance rather than impede human development. Paulo Freire has correctly pointed out that there is no such thing as a neutral educational process. By definition education is not a value-free concept. Richard Shaull in his Foreword to Freire's work notes, "Education either functions as an instrument which is used to facilitate the integration of the younger generation into the logic of the present system and bring about *conformity to it,* or it becomes the 'practice of freedom,' the means by which men and women deal critically and creatively with reality and discover how to participate in the transformation of their world" (Shaull, 1972, p. 15).

A series of recent extensive studies has researched the psychological impact of schooling upon the adolescent pupils. Such studies provide a searching illustration of the extent to which schooling in general becomes the "practice of freedom" or something quite different. A rash of recent books and articles depict graphically what is really "learned" in school (Coleman, 1961; Friedenberg, 1959; Jackson, 1968; Kohl, 1967; Kozol, 1967; Leacock, 1969; Goodlad & Klien, 1970; Silberman 1970). Research on teaching (Hoetker & Ahlbrand, 1969) indicates that teaching is still predominantly telling and that pupils typically are intellectually passive and dependent on teachers.

All of these studies raise profound questions about the basic objectives of schooling. Multiple failures of the institution of schooling are implied. The "common" school as the goal of public education, as Peter Schrag (1965) and others point out, is simply a convenient myth. Schools tend to perpetuate, rather than reduce, social and educational differences among children. Seeley et al. (1956) indicated the extent to which the values of secondary-age pupils are a reflection of the family backgrounds, a result more recently cross-validated through the massive Coleman (1966) study on the equality of educational opportunity. The explosive situation in slum schools heightens our awareness of the problems created by schooling that systematically avoids the person, personal development or human growth as major and direct educational objectives. It is now obvious that poor black and white children have learned, and indelibly so, to regard themselves with self-contempt as a result of schooling (Kohl, 1967; Kozol, 1967; Coleman, 1961). What else they may have learned (reading, spelling, writing) may be "academic" and esoteric in the most literal sense. It is also obvious if we listen to the voices from the ghetto that what the adults want for their children is the opportunity to develop a strong and stable self-concept, a sense of personal identity.

Without overstating the case or romanticizing the problems, it also seems that the frustrations with schooling (particularly its dehumanizing side) that are finally exploding in the cities are paralleled by serious questioning of the suburban or "model" schools. Fantini and Weinstein (1967) argue that the urban child, especially the black urban child, has become the spokesman for the middleclass child as well. Major school reform is by definition an immense, complicated and yet essential job. In any case, the concern over education in the suburbs is now growing, largely because of the dislocative effects in the personal lives of secondary-school adolescents noted at the outset. The pressure to achieve academically, the importance of grades (as rewards and, more importantly, as sanctions), the increasing necessity to postpone responsibility and "adult" status (yesterday high school, today college, tomorrow graduate school—all "necessary" steps)—such elements have created the conditions of student revolt. Bitterness, alienation or a cynical "going along" are implicit atmospheres in many suburban schools. "School is dead" theology or pessimism for the sake of pessimism has nothing to do with our belief that public schools are in trouble, deeply so in the city, subtly so in the suburb. Both institutions run on a thin edge of credibility (Sprinthall & Mosher, 1971).

In general then, schools—city, suburban or rural—have tended to define their role as the transmitters of academic ideas and skills. Recent efforts at reform have been directed at revitalizing the existing academic curriculum and its teaching. Very little intellectual

energy or funding has been directed toward reformulating education—that is, the development of essentially new curriculums and
new educational interventions that will promote healthy psychological growth.

The School's Role in Psychological and Ethical Education

Until recently, schools have generally assumed that their mission was to focus on the intellectual and/or skill development of
their pupils. The ethical and psychological growth of the pupils
was ruled off-limits for the regular classroom experiences. Of
course, it was hoped that through studies in the standard curriculum the personal development of pupils would be positively influenced, at least as a by-product. Healthy personal growth, a secondary objective, was supposed to occur while the intellectual and
skill-training objectives were being implemented. Ironically, the recent research on the impact of schooling (including Coleman, 1961;
Jackson, 1968; Minuchin et al., 1969; Ojemann, 1958; Silberman,
1970; Sprinthall & Mosher, 1971) indicates that just the reverse actually happens. The schools are providing an ethical and psychological education for the pupils, yet the effect is negative. The so-
called hidden agenda or implicit curriculum of most schools teaches
for negative outcomes. Intrinsic interest in learning *declines* the
longer a pupil remains in school. Negative self-concepts *increase*
with time spent in school. Stereotyped "surface" and judgmental
thinking *increases*. Self-confidence in problem-solving *decreases*.
Personal autonomy in learning tasks *decreases*. Personal alienation,
inhibition and isolation *increase*. The litany mounts, yet the conclusion is inescapable. The schools are psychological educators. For example, in the various subject-matter disciplines, the adults may also
teach that teachers have power, that children are impotent, irresponsible and should be intellectually and personally dependent.
The emphasis on achievement, competitiveness (or cheating) and a
belief that self-worth is tied to academic achievement are further
examples. This is a harsh critique of the school, but evidence suggests that this hidden curriculum is typically more inimical and
psychologically crippling than it is positive and developmental.
That these effects of schooling are largely unrecognized (and presumably unintended) is hardly an extenuating factor.

We should recall that the original question was from Freire—
"Do schools seek to induce conformity or can they stimulate the
practice of freedom?" The evidence strongly suggests that the
general impact is negative. This does not mean all schools fail, nor

that all teaching is narrow, pedantic and passive. There are always exceptions, yet it is clear that for most pupils, in most schools, the mainstream experience is still largely listening to teachers transmitting information.

William James many years ago pointed out the fallacy of learning as the exclusive transmission of knowledge in the classroom. The teacher was to "Work your pupil into such a state of interest in what you are going to teach him that every other object of attention is banished from his mind; then reveal it to him with devouring curiosity to know the next steps." (James, re-issued 1968, p. 25). The difficulty with this model of stimulation was in part that the teacher actually did almost all the work of culling and sorting through the "Library of Congress" for the most vivid illustrations and categories for information presentation. Also, as James tellingly comments, that process leaves the pupils free to their own devices in a manner similar to an enemy commander in wartime. The pupil "Is working away from you as keenly and eagerly as is the mind of the commander on the other side."

It is both interesting and disheartening to note that recent studies of actual classroom interaction in most schools is still predominately a "teacher-talk-pupil-listen" mode. Studies from as far back as 1912 found that over 80 percent of all classroom talk consisted of teacher talk in the form of brief direct factual questions at the rate of about four per minute. In studies conducted in the 1960's, fully 50 years later, the results were astonishingly similar. Teacher talk accounted for 70 percent of all classroom talk, again mostly in the form of brief direct factual questions at the rate of two to three per minute.*

James Coleman has recently suggested that the school must shift its function from such limited and classical objectives. We need to reduce the school's dependence on such goals so that it can take on new ones. "The new goal must be to integrate the young into functional community roles . . . since the school's function will no longer be to protect the child from society but rather to move him into it. The school must be integrated with service organizations, such as those providing medical services so that the young can help in them" (Coleman, 1972).

In Coleman's view the critical general education goals are to make responsible, productive human beings, "Who can *lead* in a

*These studies are more fully summarized in Sprinthall, R. C. and Sprinthall, N. A. *Educational Psychology: A Developmental Approach*, Reading, Mass. Addison-Wesley, 1974, Chapter 2.

task or follow, and who are able to live with the consequences of their actions."

It is clear throughout this entire rationale that adolescents need and deserve responsible roles to play and schools need and deserve new programs to meet such reciprocal needs. Dr. Harvey Scribner, the former head of the largest school system in the country, accurately perceived the problem as arising from the false dichotomy of intellectual vs. personal learning. As a result he has called for a redefinition to eliminate the distinctions between acquisition of skills vs. psychological development. The effective school, he suggests, is the one "which defines its curriculum as opportunities to grow simultaneously both in skills and psychologically" (Scribner, 1972).

Ralph Tyler, an eminent educational psychologist, has called for similar changes in curriculum experiences for adolescents. "Schools have failed to provide opportunities for young people to mature through assuming responsible social roles. The schools tend to serve children, to plan *for* them when the need is for the teenagers to serve and plan for others" (Tyler, 1974).

If the school is to enhance the "practice of freedom" on the part of the growing citizens in its charge and if we are concerned about the quality of human beings who enter adulthood, we will have to look further than new ways to teach history or physics, for example, or tinkering adjustments in administrative arrangements such as modular scheduling.

Schooling is not a benign psychological, moral, and ethical experience. Schooling, however, can become, in the view of this writer, a positive growth-inducing experience. As a step toward that goal, we will review the question of educational objectives vis à vis a cognitive-moral and ethical developmental framework. From this suggested framework, we will next present procedures that may be actually employed to reformulate classroom learning atmospheres as well as some current evaluations. Finally we will conclude with a discussion on value development as both a sufficient and necessary objective of the educational enterprise of a democratic society.

Psychological and Ethical Development: Issues

Throughout the first section of this paper, we have indicated the need to create a series of learning experiences designed to promote psychological maturity. In this section we will outline some of the theoretical considerations connected with the assumptions as to the nature of such development. There is the need to build a framework to understand the nature of such growth. We obviously cannot simply refer to the process of change in such broad and general terms. Personal growth, psychological maturation, and moral education are by themselves too imprecise as educational objectives. So too, with the general term "development." Thus the objective of this section is to provide a framework and a variety of perspectives on the nature of psychological development during adolescence. Admittedly such a framework will be loose, given the nature of the state of theory at the moment. Hopefully the framework can be viewed as a series of important proximate constructs to clarify the nature of adolescent development and its relationship to actual proposals for curriculum reform.

Developmental Stages: The Egg, Caterpillar, Butterfly

The concept of a stage of development is central to the theorists mentioned below. It was, of course, John Dewey who originally formed the idea that children and teen-agers move through stages of development. A child is not, in this view, a midget-sized adult who simply grows from small to large in a quantitative sense. Instead children and teen-agers grow and develop in a series of qualitatively distinct stages. Each stage is unique, a special way of organizing the thought process as to how a person makes meaning and understands the world. Qualitative growth can be compared to the transformations of the egg to caterpillar to butterfly sequence. Each stage of development is unique and separate; yet the succeeding stage builds upon and is dependent upon the prior stage.

As a pupil develops, then, there is a major shift at specific age-related points in terms of general cognitive process. Whether or not growth and development occurs from stage to stage, however, depends upon the kind and quality of interaction with the environment. This is a crucial point, if not the most important aspect of developmental theory and practice, namely, that growth does not take place automatically nor unfold unilaterally. Instead, a person needs a series of significant experiences—interactions with the environment at particular times to promote the shift from a lower to a higher stage of development. Without significant experiences at critical times a person will cease psychological growth and prematurely stabilize at stages below his or her potential.

From a developmental standpoint adolescence is a stage in which almost all persons can learn to function at relatively high levels of intellectual, moral, ego, and personal development.

Whether such learning takes place depends upon the general educational experience which occurs. We shall now detail four aspects of psychological development during adolescence and underline the relationship between such growth and educational programs such as the ones currently under development in deliberate psychological and ethical education.

Cognitive Growth

Piaget (1952) has been a most important source of psychological knowledge concerning adolescence. He has suggested that *only* during adolescence, and *not before*, is an individual capable of certain modes of thought. What Piaget calls "formal operations" in thought provide an opportunity for an individual to think in modes qualitatively different from those possible during childhood. An adolescent can conceive of possibilities and probabilities: he can think abstractly about himself, his sense-of-time perspective changes, and he can perceive himself in a variety of ways both now and in the future. Such a new mode of perceiving and understanding is tremendously significant if we are concerned about personal development/personal knowledge. The Piaget framework suggests that during adolescence it is not only possible but most appropriate to focus on such personal questions. If a pupil is capable of thinking about himself in a *nonabsolutist* way (e.g., children tend to categorize along such dimensions as good-bad, white hats-black hats) and *conceive of self and future* in probability trends and possibilities (e.g., children tend to see their futures as already determined) and *change hypotheses* as new information is brought to light (e.g., children tend to "hang on" to hypotheses in spite of new and contradictory evidence), then an educator has an opportunity for deliberate education. Piaget theoretically created a rationale for intervention that would become relevant to an adolescent pupil.

All the programs described in the next section are heavily oriented toward understanding the nature and complexity of human behavior, conceptions demanding the potential for formal operational thought. Learning to counsel has an obvious relation as a technique to the process of thinking about human behavior, both in self and others in nonabsolutist ways. Abstract thought about a variety of personal and subjective possibilities also is central to effective counseling procedures when the topic is "self." Finally the ability to genuinely see and understand someone else's problem or plight connotes the abstract ability to place yourself in someone else's shoes in order to genuinely resonate with that person's subjective experience. Genuine empathy, then, connotes the ability of entering someone else's subjective world to understand and experience from that point of view.

One of the major shortcomings of schooling, particularly the so-called standard curriculum, has been the failure to promote the use of formal operations. Estimates indicate that only 50 percent of the secondary-school pupils actually develop the ability to use formal operations. While almost all are potentially able to learn abstract thinking, a substantial number do not achieve it (Kohlberg and Gilligan, 1971). A major reason for this outcome derives from the fact that much of the regular secondary-school curriculum assumes rather than promotes cognitive development. Similarly, regarding skill in empathy, there is the assumption that pupils can vicariously place themselves in the position of Achilles, Macbeth, Evangeline, Willie Loman, or Scarlet O'Hara et al. Without significant experience, however, many students never really understand the point of it all. Likewise, an analysis of other subject-matter areas, such as social studies and natural sciences, indicates parallel difficulties, namely that much of the teaching assumes that students already can think in formal abstract operations. Although pupils may learn to emit the "proper" response in these areas, careful inquiry will usually reveal a lack of genuine understanding as to the meaning of such concepts.

Moral Development

In this area the recent work of Lawrence Kohlberg (1970) is particularly significant. Based on a long series of field interviews designed to find out how humans actually think about problems of social justice, Kohlberg discovered that the process of making judgments actually formed a developmental sequence of six stages. After investigating people in different ages, different social and economic classes and different cultures, Kohlberg like Piaget found a parallel sequence of stage growth. He also found that the majority of teen-agers stabilize in moral-judgment thinking between Stage Three and Stage Four. This means that most high-school pupils employ a system of thought which assumes that justice means going along with the crowd. (other-directed) as Stage Three, or to rigidly apply a standard of law and order regardless of circumstances as Stage Four. Without significant new interactions with the environment most teen-agers enter adulthood with rather stereotyped systems of thinking about major questions as to legal and moral justice. Most unfortunately the system of thinking undergoes few changes after adolescence as society and current educational practice is organized. As we noted in the previous section on Piaget, cognitive growth to the use of formal and abstract thinking demands a stimulating curriculum—the need to promote not assume development. The same holds true for the development of moral and social-justice thinking and judgment. Teen-agers need opportunities to be directly confronted with major problems of the human condition. Such real interaction can provide an experience-base upon which to build a more adequate system of thinking and acting upon moral questions.

Research has shown from a developmental standpoint that a person's level of moral-judgment thinking tends to lag slightly behind his or her general stage of intellectual development. Thus while almost 50 percent of adolescents in this country do reach formal, abstract thought, about 30 percent reach Stage Five in moral judgment. This is understandable when we realize that problems of social justice are more complex, more subjective, and more personally involving than general abstract thinking. Also, as is perhaps obvious in these days of the so-called post-Watergate morality, in general, educational experience is usually quite limited in responding to major moral questions. Schooling has tended to avoid direct interaction with questions of social justice and value problems. Society, writ-large, has also eschewed such questions, usually under the guise of either a narrow-minded literal moralism or more likely an atheoretical pragmatism.

In Kohlberg's view, based on his findings, all humans do think about questions of social justice, and these systems of thought represent a series of distinct and qualitatively different stages. Thus we are all "moral philosophers" yet use different systems of thought. Both Kohlberg and Piaget use the phrase, "the child and the adolescent as moral philosophers." This means that humans at those stages do ponder questions such as the meaning of human experience, what is right from wrong, under what conditions do I help another human, etc. The form or structure of our thinking, however, is distinctively different depending upon our stage of development.

Ego Development

Jane Loevinger (1970), based on extensive field interviews, has created a framework to comprehend stages of ego development. She sees "ego" as a master trait of personal growth in a manner similar to other theorists such as Gordon Allport and Robert White. Ego is a construct for that part of human personality that acts as an executive—co-ordinating, choosing, selecting and directing a person's activities. Loevinger's work suggests that there are special qualities of ego functioning, how adequately or inadequately a person chooses, makes decisions, etc. At different stages of development the ego functions in distinctly different patterns. At higher stages the ego functions more adequately, takes in more aspects of a given situation, views problems with greater complexity, sees more broadly, selects from a greater variety of possible actions. As the accompanying chart shows, there are qualitative differences to the various stages, each one building on the previous at higher levels of differentiation and integration.

Research has indicated that most teen-agers are classed in Loevinger's Stages Three and Three/Four. This means the system employed by teen-agers to understand and make meaning from their own experience involves the characteristics of these stages. The similarity to the stages of moral development is obvious. Kohlberg's Stage Three is similar to Loevinger's Stage Three and Three/Four. This means the major preoccupations of the teen-age "ego" are with concepts like conformity for its own sake, superficial niceness, the importance of appearance, social acceptability and the use of stereotypical thinking. These findings also cross-validate the earlier mentioned classic research on adolescence by James Coleman. Loevinger, however, provides a broader framework since she charts the nature and structure of higher stages. The educational objectives, then, become apparent: to stimulate ego development during adolescence to go beyond Stages Three and Three/Four. In other words, we can specifically define ego developmental objectives as promoting self-evaluation, mutuality, intensive responsible concern for others, communication, differentiated feelings, understanding complex human motives—all aspects of Stage Four *and* the groundwork to Stage Five.

Personal Development: Erikson & Elkind

In his classic work, Erikson has viewed adolescence as involving the stage task of identity formation versus identity diffusion. We will not repeat his position here except to underscore the importance that Erikson places upon the need for broad experience as a mechanism for growth. His famous concept moratorium, however, does not mean a period of time in which a teen-ager merely floats around in a magical process of finding his or her "self." Instead Erikson sees the need for broad and significant experience, not episodes, upon which the adolescent can reflect and examine in order to gain self-knowledge.

SOME MILESTONES OF EGO DEVELOPMENT
Jane Loevinger and Ruth Wessler

STAGE	IMPULSE CONTROL, CHARACTER DEVELOPMENT	INTERPERSONAL STYLE
Presocial		Autistic
Symbiotic		Symbiotic
Impulsive	Impulsive, fear of retaliation	Receiving, dependent, exploitive
Self-pro-tective	Fear of being caught, externalizing blame, opportunistic	Wary, manipulative, exploitive
Conformist	Conformity to external rules, shame, guilt for breaking rules	Belonging, helping, superficial niceness
Consci-entious	Self-evaluated standards, self-criticism, guilt for consequences, long-term goals	Intensive, responsible, mutual, concern for communication
Autonomous	Add: Coping with conflicting inner needs, toleration	Add: Respect for autonomy
Integrated	Add: Reconciling inner conflicts, renunciation of unattainable	Add: Cherish-individuality

Note: "Add" means in addition to the description applying to the previous level.

Source: Loevinger, J. and Wessler, R. *Measuring Ego Development*, Vol 1, Jossey-Bass, Inc., 1970. (Editor's note: three columns of the original source have been omitted here.)

David Elkind has tellingly commented upon the nature of personal growth during adolescence. If we accept the idea that developmentally adolescence is the appropriate time to consider personal questions such as one's own values, then we must also accept one other aspect of adolescence as a developmental stage which if not acknowledged will, in our view, raise havoc with any educational curriculum designed to elicit the personal domains. Piaget indicated that when a person advances from one developmental stage to the next, a special transition point occurs before the person fully comprehends the new stage. Piaget called the transitional phase a tendency to egocentric thinking—a shift in modes of thought to focus on the self. Piaget's scheme indicates that a person moves up developmentally one level and then shifts within the new stage to egocentric concerns. Thus a child at the sensorimotor level starts in that stage egocentrically. Elkind (1967) showed that even in the first year of life a baby progresses through the sensorimotor from an egocentric position to a more differentiated view of self and the world (called decentering). Similarly during the elementary years a child leaves the sensorimotor stage and enters a period called "concrete" operations. He can classify objects, combine properties and like-minded tasks. However, as Elkind (1967) noted, "This system of concrete operations . . . which lifts the school-age child to new heights of thought, nonetheless lowers him to new depths of egocentrism" (p. 1028). This was demonstrated rather indelibly when elementary-age pupils took positions on certain issues and then were so wedded personally to their views that they refused to change them in the face of overwhelming contradictory evidence. The egocentric mode tends to encourage early perceptual closure on problems and only gradually subsides as the child enters the new stage more fully and confronts enough new experiences to give up egocentric thought.

The same sequence probably occurs during adolescence. A pupil leaves concrete operations and enters the stage of formal operations during adolescence, a step up the developmental scale. Then he may shift "sideways" to egocentric modes once again.

Cognitive Stage	*Mode*

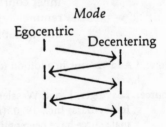

Sensori-motor/Intuitive (0-6 yrs.)

Concrete Operations (7-11 yrs.)

Formal Operations (12-18 yrs.)

Egocentric — Decentering

From the standpoint of a curriculum designed to promote personal/psychological growth during adolescence, this creates special difficulties. The shifts upward from concrete to formal operations provides the opening to help adolescents learn who they are. Not only does the stage provide that opportunity, but there is some evidence at least indirectly from Kohlberg's work on moral development that if growth experiences do not take place during that stage the individual ceases any further development. At this point then it seems more than appropriate to consider a curriculum in psychological education. The pupil emerges from concrete thought to formal operations, a growth change that almost beckons for a responsive curriculum designed to deal with the new sets of issues at the new stage.

The second aspect of development during adolescence, the shift sideways to egocentric thought, however, may "lower him to new depths" (Elkind, 1967, p. 1028). When designing curricula, we must be concerned with this issue as well. In particular we would need to create conditions that do not foster or necessarily encourage further movement to egocentric thinking, especially about self. The problem is, in fact, the opposite: how to develop procedures and experiences that will help an adolescent to move from the limits of egocentric thinking to a more differentiated and integrative mode.* Again Elkind noted that egocentric thinking in adolescence causes the adolescent to become preoccupied with himself, the uniqueness of his appearance, feelings and ideas. The adolescent's self-consciousness derives in part from the belief that others are as totally concerned about him as he is, and that he is the only one who has ever felt such feelings. "This complex of beliefs in the uniqueness of his feelings . . . might be called a personal fable, a story which he tells himself and which is not true" (Elkind, 1967, p. 1031).

The educational problem is thus particularly clear. It might seem appropriate to develop programs that would allow an adolescent as he enters the period of formal operations to focus on himself, his new abilities to think abstractly about himself, his ability to differentiate his own mental constructions from others, and his concern somehow to put all these new parts of himself "all together." This would make sense because of the shift upward from the previous stage. However, the paradox becomes evident if the

---

*The emergence of relativistic thinking during adolescence can promote egocentrism. Anyone who has worked with teen-agers, especially those from so-called sophisticated middle-class communities, is forcefully struck by the amount of self-centered relativism. To "Do your own thing" can be in practice a justification for a hands-off, laissez-faire view that encourages privatism under the guise of individuality.

programs used to accomplish this would lock the adolescent into the egocentric mode rather than deliberately aim to lead him out of that mode. A program for ethical/psychological education thus must take into account both aspects of development if it is to promote psychological growth.

Summary of Objectives

From a variety of perspectives we can now see how general educational objectives can be viewed in developmental terms. One attempt to list such objectives follows:

A CURRICULUM IN INDIVIDUAL AND HUMAN DEVELOPMENT: PSYCHOLOGICAL OR AFFECTIVE OBJECTIVES

To enable the individual to listen to people—to their ideas and to their feelings.

To enable the individual to attend to and identify feelings—to subjective reactions in general.

To enable the individual to accurately perceive people—to judge people correctly and efficiently.

To enable the individual to understand himself—who he is at a given time.

To enable the individual to express feelings of his own.

To enable the individual to be spontaneous and creative.

To enable the individual to respond to other people's feelings.

To enable the individual to relate to others—to have more complex, more profound interpersonal relations.

To enable the individual to act in behalf of a personal value.

To assist the individual to perceive—articulate—who he wants to become.

To enable the individual to begin to change in the directions he chooses:

    teach him ways to see and formulate personal problems;

    teach him ways to make personal decisions;

    teach him ways to achieve.

To enable the individual to formulate a set of personal meanings—a personal philosophy.

To enable the individual to make personal meaning with regard to issues that concern him (e.g., how to communicate with others, college or job choice, drugs). Individual begins to form judgments concerning the type of life he wants to lead: Who am I? What do I stand for?

Each of these objectives relates to the concepts of intellectual growth stages from Piaget, moral judgment from Kohlberg, ego development from Loevinger, and personal growth from Erikson and Elkind. In a more common sense, the strands of intellectual, ethical, and personal growth can be seen as separate yet related facets of development as an aim of educational experience.

Gisela Konopka (1972) has perhaps summarized it best when she stressed that the critical psychological task during adolescence was the development of human interdependence. She sees the classic battle during adolescence between excessive dependence and independence as the expression of the entrance toward mutual interdependence. To build a strong sense of personal identity based upon the ability of reciprocal helping, sharing together with genuine communication and understanding, becomes a major overall goal of psychological maturity for adolescence. In this sense we are directly suggesting that schooling accept the educational responsibility implied by a developmental framework. In Dewey's view this means that ethical, psychological, and personal development as well as the more traditional domain of intellectual growth all become the aim of deliberate education intervention.

Ethical and Cognitive Development: A Curriculum Example

In order to illustrate how classroom learning atmospheres can be altered to achieve important developmental objectives we will present in some detail one high-school course currently in process. This will be followed by brief reference to a number of analogous high-school classes as well as the current evaluations.

From a developmental standpoint, how we learn involves two basic domains: (1) significant experience, in interaction with (2) careful reflection. Growth does not occur in a vacuum, nor do we merely think our way to higher stages. To provide pupils with lectures and/or exhortations on the need for ethical and psychological growth will accomplish little. We are reminded that Jeb Stuart McGruder of Watergate fame enrolled in a course in Ethics taught by William Sloan Coffin as an undergraduate at Amherst College. More systematic studies by Flanagan (1973) on the impact of traditional methods of curricula have revealed similar outcomes. Less than two-thirds of a huge sample of secondary pupils in English (N=250,000) could understand one-half of Robert Louis Stevenson (and that's *Treasure Island*). Less than one-third understood Rudyard Kipling and only 8 percent Jane Austin. In social studies the picture was no more optimistic. Scrivan reported that less than one-quarter of the teen-agers in this country can present a two-page outline with arguments for and against democracy as a form of governance and that approximately two-thirds of the general public in this country resolutely opposes every practical instance of free speech (Scrivan, 1972).

William James perhaps best summarized the inadequacy of the rote memorization approach (thinking without experience) with the following example: "A friend of mine, visiting a school, was asked to examine a young class in geography. Glancing at the book she said, 'Suppose you should dig a hole in the ground, hundreds of feet deep, how should you find it at the bottom—warmer or colder than on top?' None of the class replying, the teacher said: 'I'm sure they know, but I think you don't ask the question quite rightly. Let me try.' So, taking the book, she said: 'In what condition is the interior of the globe?' and received the immediate answer from half the class at once: 'The interior of the globe is in a condition of igneous fusion' " (James, 1958, p. 106).

On the other hand, learning through experience alone is clearly not a credible alternative. Experience for its own sake will not necessarily stimulate growth to more complex stages. Supposedly when a teacher candidate presented himself to John Dewey with the claim, "I've been teaching for ten years," Dewey's question was, "Ten years? Or one year ten times?" Romantic educational critics have wrongly assumed that Dewey's dictum of learning by doing did not include the parallel component, namely hard thinking and disciplined inquiry. Experience by itself can be educative or miseducative depending upon what analysis the learner accomplishes. Obviously not all experience is similar. There are qualitative differences in what and how much learning can be drawn from a variety of experiences. The old philosophical chestnut that asserts that "push-pin [an English child's game] is not the same as poetry" is to the point.

In our view, a developmental approach to learning involves both significant (not simply trival) experience and careful inquiry. Since we are directly concerned with the process of psychological and ethical development, it is appropriate to select particular types of human experience and guided examination as a means of promoting growth to higher, more complex and comprehensive stages of human development. Thus the parameters of our approach to curriculum involve a deliberate blending of real experience and thought, of process and content, of action and reflection, and of doing *and* thinking. We seek to combine a seminar approach with a practicum experience. The specific experience involves significant social role-taking. We place teen-agers in "learning roles" that require participation in learning how to help and be responsive to other human beings. Personal ethical responsibility becomes an objective. We do not assume that teen-agers, nor indeed humans in general, are already engaged in such activity. Rather we seek to promote instead of assuming development. The course outline follows.

The Psychology of Counseling Class

This course is designed as a practicum and seminar experience to promote the learning of listening skills and the development of empathic responses through actual peer-counseling experience. The practicum sessions consist of sequential training in role-play exercises, examinations of counseling tapes, and counseling of high-school peers. The seminar sessions include readings on communication, discussions of counseling films and tapes and an integration of this with the practicum units to encourage reflection and cognitive restructuring of the total learning experience. This class, like others in the overall program, was offered on a pass-fail basis and was an elective. In this particular school almost one-half of all the academic classes are offered as electives. The instructional approach represents an attempt to balance and integrate the process and content of counseling psychology. Thus actual process-experiences in learning counseling techniques, active listening skills and learning to rate appropriate versus inappropriate responses are balanced by content experiences through readings, writing assignments and discussions of counseling films.

Introductions

The first phase of the class begins with personal introductions by each participant. In previous classes we tried out a series of procedures for these introductions including structured exercises, games and simulations. We found that the development of listening skills, building the class as a group, and the creation of a collegial atmosphere between the pupils and the instructional staff could best occur without the use of such so-called simulation techniques. Instead we asked each person to take about 5 to 10 minutes to introduce him/herself, say something that would help us get acquainted and mention some significant learning experience in the past week or so. The class co-teachers would then respond to the introduction in a manner designed to indicate that they heard and understood both the content and some of the feelings that the person introducing him/herself was experiencing. There are some moments of awkwardness and self-con-

sciousness in this procedure which the co-teachers acknowledge as well as a
sense of relief when a person gets through his/her turn. To speak about
"self" in front of 25 to 35 classmates and staff is a significant and difficult
experience; yet the procedure is designed to provide a common experience-
base for the initial stages of the class as well as a demonstration of difficulties of both sending and receiving communication messages. At the conclusion of this phase we ask everyone to fill out a two-page question guide on
the introductions:

> Please describe your *thoughts* and *feelings* as you introduced
> yourself.
> How uncomfortable were you just prior to your turn?
> Did you prepare something to say in your mind?
> What were your feelings while you were talking?
> Can you describe how you felt afterward?
> Did you have a sense that the class was listening to you? Were
> any specific individuals helpful with their questions?
> Did you have difficulty at times listening to others?
> Did you learn new ideas, more about your classmates, teachers,
> during the introductions? Any new thoughts and ideas about
> yourself?

We then summarize the comments for the pupils as a means of
helping them understand that everyone in the class including the
staff is somewhat uncomfortable, would like to say more about
themselves, felt they were slightly incoherent, had difficulty in really listening to others, etc. Such information gleaned from their
reflections upon the experience helps to promote an equalization
and democraticizing of the classroom process. Also it is noteworthy
how many times pupils comment that it's the first time they knew
anything about many of their colleagues more than a name. The
procedure also helps to begin to break down some of the previously
formed teen-age cliques.

Teaching Active Listening Scales

Immediately following the introductions we start direct teaching of the Active Listening Scale. We found that by modifying the
original Rogerian Empathy Scale into two components, response to
content and response to feeling, we could teach the skills more effectively. We could more easily focus on the particular domain that
the pupils were having difficulty mastering by separating the dimensions. We described the scales briefly and handed out one-page
copies to each pupil.

ACTIVE LISTENING SCALE

Response to Feelings—Emotions

5. Goes well beyond the person's expressed feelings. Provides the person with a major new view of the emotions he/she is experiencing.

4. Goes to a slightly deeper feeling than expressed. Helps person understand his/her own feelings in more depth. Goes just beyond the emotions expressed.

3. An accurate understanding of feelings and/or emotions, expressed in your own words. An accurate reading of feelings.

2. A slight distortion of the feelings expressed—a near miss.

1. No awareness of feelings expressed, the wrong feelings—or a genuine put-down.

Response to Content—Ideas

5. Goes well beyond the stated meaning. Provides new insight.

4. Goes slightly beyond the meaning stated. Provides some new insight. More concise. Helps the person understand his/her own ideas better.

3. An accurate understanding of the content—a restatement in your own words of what the person said.

2. A slight distortion of meaning—just misses what the person said.

1. Dead wrong—the opposite of what was said. A complete miss as to meaning or an active disinterest.

Practicing Listening Skills

Through practice such as writing down single responses to stated "role play" or actual concerns, the pupils gradually develop skill and comfort with the scales. It is a slow process to move from the artificial and somewhat "plastic" experience of writing single responses to the point of maintaining verbal dialogue with a role-play counselee and requires patience and support. The students' initial resistance to practicing the scales tends to be somewhat high. We have found, however, that this structured approach seems to

yield positive outcomes in skill learning. Also, we usually play audio-tapes from some actual initial counseling interviews made by graduate students. By showing some of these first awkward interviews between real clients and graduate counselors-in-training, the high-school pupils see firsthand the difficulty in accurately identifying and responding to content and feelings. We emphasize the two-stage nature of these learnings, (a) to accurately pick-up, hear, and identify content and feelings, and (b) to frame a response, "Using your own words which communicate to the role-play client that you do accurately understand the message." The pupils then learn to score responses both on the audio-tapes and on the single response in-class practice sessions. By teaching the pupils to "judge" their own as well as others' responses, learning the scale is hastened. The pupils become conscious of the dual process of identifying on one hand and responding on the other to understand and experience the process itself.

We have also used practice role-play responses to videotaped excerpts as one further aspect of this skill-training phase. We play an excerpt on video to the class, stop the tape, and ask them to write a response that captures both content and feeling. These excerpts can be "home-made" simply by asking pupils in a drama class to make up a problem that teen-agers often experience and then tape a series of statements describing the problem. After showing the taped excerpts we then go over the responses in class, usually listing on the blackboard all the content responses and then all the feeling responses to each excerpt. This particularly teaches a language for identifying emotions when we as a group pick out from the list on the board the responses that seem most accurate. The pupils then rate their own responses on the two five-point scales. Thus the process teaches judging or rating skills and a language system for identifying emotions simultaneously.

Adding Nonverbal Skills

After the first three or four weeks on the active listening scales we introduce a third aspect of counseling and communication training—the nonverbal components. The summary below represents a framework around which we focus the questions of body-language. In the same way as the content-feeling dimensions are presented, we have the students learn to *identify* nonverbal messages and then after some practice sessions in class, we routinely assign a pupil the task of process observation of role-play counseling sessions. Thus with the one-page handout as a guide a pupil will jot down examples of body-language "talk" while observing the class practicing active listening responses. At the end of each exercise the process-observer will make a short presentation of his/her findings. This helps to illustrate the three major aspects of communication: content, feelings and the nonverbal aspects.

1. *Nonverbal Cues:* *Body-Language Signs*
                                                Quality

Voice	Harsh/Overly Sweet	Genuine
Facial Expression	Stone-face or disinterested	Interested
Posture	Leans away. Tense, rigid or too casual	Leans toward-relaxed
Eye Contact	Avoidance of eye contact or excessive staring	Maintains reasonable eye contact
Touching	Avoids all contact or smothers (back-slapper)	Contact appropriate to situation
Gestures	Closed: guarded or overly jovial	Open, Flexible
Spatial Distance	Too far or too close	About "right" Comfortable

2. *General Congruence*

Similarity of verbal and nonverbal cues—how "together" is the talk and the body-language.

Examples: "Oh, I'm not embarrassed." (Face reddens)
"I really enjoy lecturing to students." (Knuckles white)
"It's so nice to see you." (Voice tight)
"The test you gave us was a useful learning experience." (Eyes like black darts)

3. *Three Areas of Communication: A Summary*

Verbal Content (5 pt. scale)	Feelings (5 pt. scale)	Nonverbal Cues Congruent/Dissonant

These three dimensions provide us with information on the *content* of what is being said, the *feelings* behind the content, and the *body*-language. Sometimes the feelings and the nonverbal language are referred to as the "hidden agenda"—the messages just below the surface. If we learn to "see" and respond to these dimensions, we will tend to increase our own understanding of the complexities of "where the other person is coming from" or that we will become more accurate in "reading" of another person. Often when we say the "Medium is the message," we mean, *how* a message is communicated (the feelings and the body language) is more important than the content itself. Actions speak louder than words, feelings are more significant than rhetoric, are other ways of saying this same concept.

Writing Assignments

Following these process learnings, we then handed out short reading assignments such as *Barriers and Gateways to Communication* by Carl Rogers (1952), and *Parent-Child Communication Skills* by the National Education Association (1971). We also showed the Gloria films *(Three Approaches to Psychotherapy)* with counseling segments by Rogers, Ellis and Perls. We asked the students to prepare papers examining the communication issues. The format for one such writing assignment was as follows:

1. Read the Rogers' article, "Barriers and Gateways to Communication."

2. Write a reaction paper, 2-3 pages, due next week. Hand in to your small-group leader.

3. Almost any format will do since the purpose is for us to see how understandable and significant his comments are for you. If you wish, you can (1) *Describe his basic idea:* How clearly does he state his position? Is his language too "academic"? Does he explain his view adequately or is it too vague, too trivial, too Utopian? (2) Put his ideas in your own words, e.g., this is like a level 3 response. How would you say what he says if you were talking with him? (3) Without being too judgmental, *how do you evaluate the significance* of his view for everyday life? (4) *Other comments:* Did he seem much different on "paper" than

in the film? Does he make more sense in action with Gloria than in the paragraphs? Are his nonverbals and body-language congruent (all together) with his words?

After completing the film of Perls and Ellis including Gloria's addendum, we hand out another writing assignment seeking to synthesize or integrate the three approaches to our overall goal of effective communication in all three modes. The writing format follows:

Writing Assignment

Write a reaction paper (2-3 pages) comparing Rogers, Perls and Ellis. Again, your paper may take almost any format that best fits your method of description and examination of the issues.

1. Gloria summed it up that Rogers responded to her emotions, Ellis to her mind, and Perls to her as a person. You might start by explaining in your own words what she meant by this.

2. Also, you could comment on your own reactions to her choice at the end—surprise, disbelief, dismay—that she chose Perls!

3. You also might comment on how complete are any of the single communication systems depicted in the films. For example, is it complete just to focus on content (Ellis), feelings (Rogers), or body-language (Perls)?

Is it possible to consider a "super-gestalt" of communicating in all three basic modes? Can a person learn to accurately identify content, feelings, and body-language simultaneously (or is it like a three-ring circus!)? And further, can a person learn not only to *identify* in the three areas but also to respond accurately?

The Shift from Role Plays

As we proceed through the term we follow the same overall format employing part of the class time on process skills and part on intellectual discussion and writing assignments. As the class proceeds the skill training aspect of the process work declines. Instead the pupils begin to bring in their own "real-life" concerns. The role-play counseling shifts to actual problems, and the pupils start using their newly learned active listening skills on these genuine issues. The range of issues is substantial from one student expressing anger over being falsely accused by a teacher of stealing a book, another concerned over the loss of her dog, to yet another who has an overprotective mother and feels suffocated. Students have the opportunity to both counsel their peers and be counseled in turn by these same peers.

Reciprocal Helping

At an experiential level, we were stressing the reciprocal nature of counseling and communication. We were not interested in creating a professional cadre of teen-ager counselors as one class of helpers with the balance of the school population as helpees. Instead we wanted the concepts of helping, caring, active listening to remain an essentially democratic responsibility. Pupils were asked to note the difference between this approach to counseling and communication and the regular professional approach with its univocal focus.

Transfer-of-Training Issues

As the class neared the end of the term, we then stressed the transfer-of-training problem. We examined the issues involved in moving from the context of the particular class into the "outside" world. We asked the pupils to make brief communication audiotapes with friends as a means of trying out their skills with non-classmates. This provided for a significant discussion when the pupils realized both how much they had learned as well as how difficult it was to transfer such learning to different situations. As a final test of transfer we administered Counseling Skill tests to the class as a whole and reported those results at the final class.

Continuing issues that we stressed throughout this transfer-of-training phase concerned the questions of choice and the meaning of behavior in general. In the first instance we would focus on the responsibility that accompanies the use of active listening and helping others. As pupils learned to use these skills in the real world they often found themselves confronted with difficult choice questions such as "Should I respond to my friend now that I can hear the pain?" or, "I'm not really sure that I like this at all. I was happier not listening to others" or, "I was really surprised to find out how complicated the problem was, but now what?" We try to help the pupils understand that they can become effective helpers to one another, are genuine resources and can themselves be helped by their peers.

Also we point out that the process of active listening as helping provides all of us with an understanding of how complicated and multifaceted are problems of human behavior. In a sense the communication training becomes a means of teaching pupils that behavior is not the result of a single cause-and-effect sequence (we call that view the billiard-ball theory of human behavior). Instead the process becomes the road to multiple causation and what it means to say is that human behavior is overdetermined. Learning to explore and examine for meaning and the series of factors that are involved in almost any aspect human behavior becomes our way of teaching for nonstereotyped thinking about human behavior and its causes. The process of developing psychological and personal maturity on the part of teen-agers is aided, in our view, by these learnings. To understand the complexities of behavior in ourselves and others is certainly a step toward the development of genuine empathy.

Counseling Skills, Social Role-Taking and Moral Development

From a theoretical standpoint we were hypothesizing that counselor-skill training would represent a new and more comprehensive social role for teen-agers. Moral-development theory and research suggests that cognitive restructuring, growth to higher stages and/or horizontal decalage, occurs as a result of significant experience and reflective examination in new and more responsible social roles. Social role-taking under conditions which require a more comprehensive set of responses to other humans and higher levels of empathy seemingly represents the instructional process. Kohlberg has noted somewhat wryly that the process involves an iron discipline of listening, of systematically setting your "self" aside and attempting to genuinely resonate to another's emotional and intellectual agenda. He has suggested that although professional psychotherapists in this country may not be successful in helping others, their skill training improves their own level of functioning (Kohlberg, 1971). To be sure we were not seeking to train pupils as psychotherapists. Rather we were seeking to expand the pupil's humane role (an awkward phrase, to be sure), to increase their levels of empathy and responsiveness to others. Also, we wanted to increase their abilities to become reciprocal helpers to one another. As the training sessions progressed the pupils experienced both roles of counselor and client. They could offer helping conditions to one another in turn as the counseling practice moved toward genuine personal problems.

The class, then, represented a deliberate attempt to promote the human and humane development of the pupils. We have been critical of schooling in general and curriculum materials specifically for assuming rather than promoting development. In a Kohlbergian sense the majority of high-school pupils can be classified at Stage Three, a stage in which other-directedness predominates. The evaluation of the counseling class indicated that the pupils learned the counseling skills and could apply those communication procedures effectively. Their empathy "scores" improved from 1.17 (on a 5-point scale) to 2.76 in one study. Other replication studies indicated the same significant improvement in counseling skills. At the same time measures of general psychological growth, namely the Kohlberg Scales of Moral Development and the Loevinger Scales of Ego Development also indicated significant shifts to higher cognitive-structural stages. These results are presented in the following table along with the results from other courses currently under development. All of the classes that have been successful in stimulating moral and personal growth have two similar components: (1) learning through real experience and (2) a careful and rigorous examination of the meaning of the experience. Thus each has a cycle of action (or "doing") followed by reflection. Also important is the quality of the experiential component. As we noted, "push-pin" is not the same as poetry and working at the "Rub a Dub-Dub" Car Wash is not the same as learning principles of child-care in a nursery school for visually impaired children.

In one sense all of the successful classes involve learning under real conditions, as opposed to vicarious experiences, with genuine social responsibility, and a rigorous examination of meaning. Teenagers learning to perform significant adult roles is another way of stating the same idea.

Other Classes

In addition to the detailed class in the Psychology of Counseling, we have developed a sequence of courses designed to promote development growth. Under the direction of Professor Ralph Mosher at Boston University, a series of classes in teaching high-school pupils to teach and lead moral-dilemma discussions has proved highly successful. At Minnesota a continuing series of courses has emerged with equally positive results. Erickson has developed a course designed to stimulate moral and personal development by secondary-school female pupils (Erickson, 1975). Rustad and Rogers (1975) have replicated and created a more systematic curriculum in the Psychology of Counseling course originated by the highly innovative work of Dowell (1971). Hurt and Sprinthall (1975) have tried out a counseling curriculum with college students. The table (page 64) presents the evaluations of these classes.

Development through Social Role Taking

As the data table illustrates, all of the classes that involve active learning stimulate similar shifts in moral/ethical and psychological/personal development. The scores of the Kohlberg test show a consistent shift from Stage Three to Stage Four. The Loevinger results also indicate a shift from Stage Three to Stages Three/Four and Four. The shift was from wary, self-protective to more trust and open communication and higher self-respect and complexity. Essentially, this is a shift from other-directedness to the beginnings of a more integrated inner-reliant and less egocentric stage. The Kohlberg results, while not as dramatic, statistically confirmed the trend shift. The pupils moved from Stage Three toward Stage Four. The content of those stages is analogous to the Loevinger, except that it is much more difficult to move through an entire stage in the Kohlberg system. It usually takes teen-agers two or three years to move from Stage Three to Four and even then a substantial minority never make it past Stage Three. Thus the smaller quantitative shift in the Kohlberg results may well be more significant theoretically. Certainly the changes are internally consistent across all these studies. The one class that did not stimulate change was Schaeffer's (1973). In that course, the pupils actually studied the theory (both Kohlberg and Loevinger) and attempted to apply the theory to their own classroom discussion of moral dilemmas. The class, however, had no "outside" component in the sense of a practicum. The pupils did not have to apply their classroom learning to real situations. Thus the only difference pedagogically in this instance was the lack of significant social role-taking. In the other courses, the pupils all participated in social roles such as teacher, counselor, interviewer, and child-care helpers. Such participation would thus seem requisite for growth. In the discussion class the pupils essentially remained just that, pupils. The learning was more traditional and passive even though the content of the class was directly related to the theory of Kohlberg. It would seem that active social role-taking on the part of adolescents represents a promising method of stimulating cognitive structural growth in the learner.

As we noted earlier, one of the basic assumptions from Dewey is the concept of qualitatively different stages, or systems of think-

ESTIMATES OF PSYCHOLOGICAL DEVELOPMENT*
Kohlberg Moral Dilemmas and Loevinger Ego Level
Rest—Defining Issues Test
DATA RESULTS

The Psychology of Counseling		KOHLBERG SCORES					LOEVINGER SCORES (10 point scale)				
		PRE	POST	t Value	p Value (one-tailed)	Follow-Up (1 yr. later)	PRE	POST	t Value	p Value (one-tailed)	Follow-Up (1 yr. later)
Dowell (1971) (Jrs. & Srs.—H.S.)	E(N=18)	322	356	1.84	.08	—	5.21	6.42	8.54	.001	—
	C(N=20)	295	285	—	N.S.	—	5.70	5.30	-1.49	—	—
Rustad-Rogers (1975) (Jrs. & Srs.—H.S.)	E(N=13)	370	401	1.35	.10	402	4.70	6.04	8.12	.001	6.64 (N=11)

REST, DEFINING ISSUES TEST

Hurt & Sprinthall (1975)		KOHLBERG SCORES					LOEVINGER SCORES		
		PRE	POST	t Value	p Value (one-tailed)	Follow-Up (1 yr. later)	Pretest-Post	Experimental	Control
	E(N=28)	28.6%	32.1%	1.94	.05		Shift to a Higher Level	10	2
(Jrs. & Srs.—Coll.)	C(N=23)	31.3%	32.9%	1.05	N.S.		No change or lower level	18	21
									$X_2 = 5.13$ .02

Cross-age Teaching

Sullivan & Mosher (1975)		Kohlberg Scores					Loevinger Scores				
		Pre	Post	F Value	p Value	Follow-Up	Pre	Post	F Value	p Value	Follow-Up
(Jrs. & Srs. H.S.)	E=14	301	344	9.64	.001	383 (N=21)	5.43	7.21	47.3	.001	—
	C₁=14	263	272				5.78	5.57			
	C₂=14	234	239				5.07	4.57			

Womens Development

Erickson (1973) (Sophs.—H.S.)		Kohlberg Scores					Loevinger Scores				
		Pre	Post	t Value	p Value	Follow-Up (1yr)	Pre	Post	t Value	p Value	Follow-Up (1yr)
	E(N=23)	298	330	1.55	.07	383 (N=21)	6.04	6.39	1.78	.05	7.38 (N=21)
Moral Dilemma Discussion Class Schaeffer (1974) (Jrs. & Srs.—H.S.)	(N+30)	372	380	.742	N.S.	357 (N+11)	4.51	4.46	—	N.S.	5.40 (N=10)

*All courses except the Mosher/Sullivan were 1 term (12 to 16 weeks) that course was over a two-semester period.

ing. Growth and development then represent a series of milestones, or qualitatively distinct schemas, each more comprehensive and complex than the previous one. The structural changes toward Stage Four thinking on questions of social justice by the teen-agers represent an important step to higher order-complexity, especially vis-à-vis questions of empathy. The pupils were no longer as concerned over what the "leading crowd" might think or do, but rather gained an increasing ability to understand genuinely another person's perspective—to feel at an experiential level what a human different from one's self may be confronting in his or her own life. Similarly the shifts in ego development represent a higher-order structural change implying greater differentiation (seeing and understanding at a more complex level).

Recently an eminent theorist on the nature of adolescence, Gisela Konopka, has challenged our adult society to develop effective educational programs for the teen-agers of the country. She notes that the degree or the extent to which adolescents experience responsible participation in society will determine and maximize their human development. This does not suggest that adolescence is simply a transitory stage that humans merely pass through. If such were the case we could all survive the process through forbearance. Instead Dr. Konopka notes the special opportunity that adolescence as a stage presents to all adults concerned about maximizing effective human growth. "We believe adolescents are persons with specific qualities and characteristics who have a participatory and responsible role to play, tasks to perform, skills to develop" (Konopka, 1973, p. 292). Adolescents should not be viewed as preadults, preparents, or preworkers but as growing, developing persons. The kind and quality of their development does not unfold automatically, romantically, or idealistically. Their development is seen as a function of their interaction with society writ-large. Erik Erikson has commented that society rebaptizes its youth during adolescence. The rebaptism can sponsor youths as active, psychologically healthy, mature, significant humans with a strong sense of personal identity or the obverse, namely, passive, dependent inferior and other-directed humans with a confused and diffused identity. If we exploit, demean, order and direct the growing adolescent we can inflict permanent scars, prematurely inhibiting healthy development. Such damage may not be as visible as a physical handicap but the scars remain, only inside.

Instead the results indicate that there are alternate educational paths to follow.

General Implications: A Plea for Value Development

We have tried to make a strong case for schools to take development seriously as an educational objective. From a framework that encompasses a series of complementary yet multiple perspectives on development, namely intellectual, ethical/moral, and personal/ego, we have attempted to demonstrate the legitimacy and importance of a deliberate educational focus toward these domains. Healthy development does not unfold magically, in fact just the reverse. For too long, in our view, educators have attempted to beg the question of values. Somehow epistemology was to remain separate from axiology. Knowing was to occur in a "sanforized" atmosphere in classrooms without entertaining questions of valuing. The distinction, of course, was artificial and as we have shown the schools were most assuredly engaged in value education. The hidden agenda or implicit curriculum of each school was instructing and inculcating particular sets of values—namely, stereotyped thinking, conformity to group norms of the leading crowd, extrinsic motivation for learning, privatism and self-centeredness.

Perhaps the best way to put the case for value development is to examine briefly the present social costs of our failure as a society to promote development. As we have noted, research on moral development indicates that only one-third of our adult population reach the stage of principled moral thinking. Thus the great silent majority of adults and adolescents view moral questions and social justice in highly conventional terms. In this light it is understandable that a random group of 38 citizens would look away during the two hours that Kitty Genovese lay dying. It is also understandable that all but one soldier of Lieutenant Calley's 200-member platoon would follow orders obediently and shoot everything in sight at My Lai. Finally, it is also understandable that in the results of the famous social-psychological experiment, the Milgram study, fully two-thirds of the subjects from all walks of life were willing to follow orders and inflict a series of apparently painful electric shocks on an innocent, pleasant, middle-aged man (Milgram, 1963). If we compare these results with concepts of free and interdependent citizens in a free society we may have concern for these larger issues. The roots of a democratic society reside in the soil of the educational experience of its citizens. The quality of that experience is critical if we are to promote maximal development for all. We believe that failure to develop is at base a failure to educate. The human costs of such failure is tragic. Educators need a deeper vision. Our task is central and compelling—how can we help the pupils of today, the leaders of tomorrow, to think and act sensitively and humanely on the basic moral and social-justice questions that represent the burdens of a democratic society?

How will they understand the agony of a J. Robert Oppenheimer as he confronted the question of obedience to governmental authority and the "angel of death"—the Hydrogen Bomb?

How will they understand during this country's recent Vietnam period that the Nuremberg principle cannot apply only to the Germans?

Or how will the future female leaders of this country understand that Barbara Jordan's speech during the House impeachment hearing was more than rhetoric, was more than merely opposition to the status quo, but rather a call for justice for all?

How will today's pupils understand Martin Luther King's call from a Birmingham jail in 1963? In answering the question, "What justifies breaking laws?" he answered: "How does one determine when a law is just or unjust? A just law is a man-made code that squares with the moral law or the law of God. An unjust law is a code that is out of harmony with the moral law. To put it in the terms of Saint Thomas Aquinas, an unjust law is a human law that is not rooted in eternal and natural law. *Any law that uplifts human personality is just. Any law that degrades human personality is unjust.*"

And who will teach them to understand why Martin Luther King would willingly sacrifice his own life to upgrade the lives of 1,300 black garbage men in Memphis?

These and other great issues of tomorrow will be solved or not by our pupils. The quality of our civilization depends ultimately upon how values are taught. F. Scott Fitzgerald said of the youth of the 1920's that they found all wars fought, all gods dead and all faith shaken.

Such a view is equally possible today. On the other hand, perhaps more optimism is in order. Perhaps our young, given the opportunity to grow and develop, can and will understand and act upon the great issues of tomorrow. Perhaps it can be said of them as men and women as was noted at the time of Robert F. Kennedy's death: "He was a good and decent man who saw wrong and tried to right it, saw suffering and tried to heal it, saw war and tried to stop it."

Reaction to Sprinthall: BUT IS IT VALUES EDUCATION? *by*
Barbara Geoghegan

In reacting to Dr. Sprinthall's interesting and exciting paper,
this individual finds herself riding off in at least three directions:
one, pointing toward agreement and admiration; another, toward
crossroads pointing both to agreement and honest differences of
opinion; the last, toward strong disagreement.

Dr. Sprinthall's cogent and succinct presentation of the problems of today's adolescent, of youth's confusion and instability in a
world marked by vast and rapid technological, social, and economic
upheaval, should contribute greatly to the reader's understanding
of adolescent behaviors and attitudes. Those concerned with and
about our young people—parents, teachers, social workers, all helping adults—can be grateful for these insights and interpretations.

Sprinthall faults the high schools for failing to meet the needs
of the adolescent of the 1970's, for tardiness in "developing essentially new curriculum and educational interventions" conducive to
healthier psychological growth. Those who are familiar with the
perennial three-track and other traditional approaches to high-
school offerings in many school districts must wholeheartedly concur. However, there *are* more than a few giant steps being made
toward loosening of the rigidity of the old-type high-school curriculums. Indeed, such strides have already brought more than a few
isolated school systems to an assortment of "alternative" programs
(Miles, 1964). With varying emphases, these programs stress individual choice and responsibility on the part of the student, make
wide use of community resources, and show surprising decrease in
lock step organization—all aimed at enhancing the young person's
development during these identity-searching years (Clark, 1970;
Sand, 1970; Jennings, 1970). Indirectly, and in various ways, such
programs can contribute to the moral development of adolescents as
they require young people to be more active in the decision-making
process and to be accountable for their own progress often outside
the classroom walls and without direct adult supervision (Graubard,
1972; Hapgood, 1971). Such plans help the youth toward a more
positive self-concept as he sees himself as competent in dealing
with his self-chosen and self-planned program effectively and pro-
ductively (Guskin and Guskin, 1970). In other words, I am suggesting that Dr. Sprinthall paints too dark a picture of educational efforts to meet the needs of our young people for whom the
"traditional" approaches to learning are sterile. Certainly, many of

these "traditional" programs are also changing, along less revolutionary lines, as schools adopt and adapt to technological aids to curriculum and methods of implementing them (Eurich, 1970). In fine, while his charges are undoubtedly justifiable for some schools in some places, his wholesale indictment of the secondary system seems to me to paint too pessimistic a picture of the total scene.

Developmental Stages: The Egg, Caterpillar, Butterfly

Those working with adolescents in the helping professions who are unfamiliar with the stage approaches of Piaget in cognitive development, Kohlberg in moral development, Loevinger on ego development, Erikson on sociopsychological growth, will find in this part of Sprinthall's paper a remarkably complete and succinct presentation of these theorists' concepts applied to the adolescent. The inclusion of Elkind's description of successive shifts in egocentrism through successive stages is helpful in completing the picture of the adolescent as a young person now more or less capable of abstract thinking, stabilized in moral thinking between Kohlbergian Stages Three and Four, in a state of identity confusion which will hopefully eventuate in attainment of a sense of selfhood, of "me." Readers of this paper are fortunate to find so much insight encompassed within so excellent a summary.

From the stage concepts, and the needs of the adolescent at the stage he has attained, Kohlberg has evolved a sequence of curricular objectives, objectives aimed at psychological (affective) growth that might well serve as the basis for a series of faculty seminars. Every high-school teacher might well apply these to his/her own subject-matter field, and look for answers to the question: What in my teaching-field content will contribute toward attaining these objectives by the young people with whom I am working?

It is at this point that Sprinthall leads us to his answer to the problem of moral and ethical development of the adolescent:

> The strands of intellectual, ethical, and personal growth can be seen as separate yet related facets of development as an aim of educational development.

and he suggests that

> to build a strong sense of personal identity based upon the ability of reciprocal helping, sharing together with genuine community and understanding becomes a major overall

goal of psychological maturity for adolescence.

He reminds us that Kohlberg has shown that moral development lags behind intellectual stages of development and states that teenagers need opportunities for direct confrontation with major problems of the human condition.

At this point, Sprinthall offers his contribution to moral and ethical development in the course he has designed in the psychology of counseling:

> . . . designed as a practicum and seminar experience to promote the learning of listening skills and the development of empathic responses through actual peer-counseling experience.

The description of this course is exciting and fascinating: one would wish that all might profit by such an experience under this sensitive and skilled psychologist.

One observation: The fortunate students who profited by this course under Dr. Sprinthall's leadership developed good insights and understanding into selves and others, and attained a degree of skill in communicating. But I wish to pose a question: How many schools have available to them the services of a capable and experienced psychologist to direct such a program? There are few Sprinthalls able and willing to give of time and experience to such a project. What threats lie in putting this sort of instrument in the hands of inexperienced and amateur psychologists? Therapists and counselors are learning from sad experiences of their clients the dangers following from poorly conducted, insensitively handled encounter groups for young people, from what Cottle has termed "the informal practice of clinical psychology in the classroom" (1975). There is little reason to believe that a program such as this one would be set up in terms of capable, proficient and adequately prepared leaders in our high schools. Here, then, is part of my disagreement.

But supposing for the sake of discussion that the above-stated objection could be met—that we could somehow supply the necessary personnel. There still exists a question—a doubt that the course in counseling for high-school students will attain moral as well as psychological growth in the adolescent. "Autonomous people," suggests Chazan, "may frequently choose immoral action" (p. 145).

The objectives of psychological development, stated as preface to Sprinthall's exposition of his counseling course, are summarized and critiqued as follows:

> (1) to enable the individual to listen to others; to attend and identify feelings; to perceive others accurately; to respond to others' feelings; to relate to others; to perceive and to articulate what the person wants to become; to understand himself.

My question is: Does self-improvement, better understanding of self, more honest view of self, improved relations with others, necessarily bring about higher levels of moral judgment and behavior? True, among those objectives are several with moral implications.

> (2) to enable the individual to act in behalf of a personal value; to begin to change in the directions he or she chooses; to formulate a set of personal meanings—a personal philosophy; to make personal meaning with regard to issues which concern him; to begin to form judgments concerning the type of life he wants to lead: Who am I? What do I stand for?

But all of this is very general and unspecified. Many high schools today are approaching the problem under the heading of "values clarification." The objectives just named refer to values— but values of themselves can be socially and/or morally positive or negative. A value is "a preference for something cherished or desired; it is linked to one's satisfaction of his needs, his realization of goals, and the maintenance and enhancement of his self-concept" (Perkins, 1974, p. 580), but it is entirely possible that the preference for things cherished or desired may be for behaviors that are antisocial and morally wrong. The assumption in (1) and (2) above is that the individual will aim toward goals considered by society to be desirable and good, will adopt a philosophy that contributes toward self-actualization and the good of others, in the sense of Maslow's self-actualizing person (1972). But so long as these objectives are implied with regard to their moral and ethical aims, and not specified, we must class them as incidental rather than as direct outcomes of the course in counseling. It is a truism long expressed in education courses that incidental learning may or may not occur; that it is wise not to take for granted that which may or may not occur; in other words, it is important to spell out objectives in clear and understandable statements (Block, 1974; Popham, 1974). Admirable as is the course in psychology of counseling for high-school students, it does not seem to meet the objectives of moral and ethical education adequately. We must meet this need head on or indirectly in other ways. Kohlberg's discussion approach has been shown to help people clarify their moral judgments, and to bring them to another level of judgment as outlined in his stages. Further, he has found that higher levels of moral judgment are correlated with higher levels of moral behavior (1969, 1971).

Some approach has been made to Kohlberg's dilemma using his stories of Heinz and others. Other efforts have introduced dilemma situations nearer to our young people's situations, either in collected stories in books, in filmstrip-tape materials, or in films. Using Kohlberg's scheme, such discussions can open ways to thinking about problems that will hopefully terminate in ways of behaving. Archambault says that the function of the school is to promote rather than to teach understanding (1973, p. 164), and direct presentation of moral or ethical situations does seem one means of so doing. The "value clarification" approach—which apparently is a device to steer clear of the threatening term "moral"—of Raths and his coauthors (1966) makes extremely good sense for those interested in a direct approach.

Where direct approach in the form of curricular offerings is not possible, the fact remains that courses in social studies, literature, and history are inexhaustible sources of "dilemma situations." The political and economic events of our own times constitute a rich vein for classes in history, civics, economics, and current events. The point to be kept in mind, as in the case of Sprinthall's course in counseling, is that we cannot expect such thinking to take place automatically or incidentally, it must be planned for, stated as a definite objective, and given considerable thought and consideration in preparing the background before the class meets (Stake, 1972; Block, 1973; Wenacel, 1973).

In short, moral and ethical education constitutes areas of learning that are too important to be left to chance, or to be included as incidental to other purposes (Chazen and Soltis, 1973).

In a recent review for the *Saturday Review*, Sara Sanborn had this to say concerning the writer of *Sins of a Generation:* "To differ with him is always an exercise in critical thinking. I disagree with his book, but recommend it" (page 27).

I should like to close this response to Dr. Sprinthall by paraphrasing Sanborn: To differ with Dr. Sprinthall is a demanding exercise in critical thinking. I agree with much of his paper, and recommend it, with the reservations I have above stated.

3.
Values and Issues in Counseling and School Psychology

Edmund V. Sullivan

INTRODUCTION

For the past five years the school has seen a resurgence of interest devoted to the general area called values education and more specifically moral education (Sullivan, 1975). During this period there has been an accent on the value implications of social studies, history, religion and moral education courses proper. For the most part, interest in values has been a concern to teachers and to some extent to school administrators. Interest in values has therefore generated a considerable amount of theory and research that can be seen in some of the other chapters of this book (e.g., Sprinthall). In contrast to the teaching personnel's interest in values and moral education there is the relatively minor interest that school psychologists and counselors devote to these areas. This is seen most clearly in the emphasis, or lack thereof, given to value and moral issues in their programs of training and certification. This paper attempts to break some ground in this area and will therefore focus on the more specific relationships and responsibilities of counselors and school psychologists rather than on curriculum interests and teacher participation.

EDUCATION AND VALUES FOR THE
COUNSELOR AND SCHOOL PSYCHOLOGIST

Approaching the topic of value issues in counseling and counseling education is a complex process, and the direction and posture that an author takes will indicate some of the underlying values that the author may have in this area. Ordinarily, one would expect some discussion of the ethical guidelines laid out by the counseling profession itself. Usually these are spelled out in terms of a set of principles which delineate rights and duties that the counselor has toward the counselee and the institution in which the counselor works and society in general. By and large, these principles are abstract, that is, they are not related to any particular concrete social contexts. Supposedly, abstract principles are guidelines for dealing with particular ethical issues, the application of these principles being arrived at through some complex system of casuistry. This will not be the approach taken in this chapter and the option for its exclusion is deliberate. The principles approach to ethical issues of a profession is *a-historical* with a penchant for separating *theory* from *practice*, *is* from *ought*, and *facts* from *values*. This type of ethics was developed out of liberal social theory and finds its appeal in what can be safely called the "liberal mentality." The approach taken here can best be identified as "radical" since radical social theorizing has programmatically been *historical* in its approach to value issues and has been habitually critical of systems of ethical theorizing that have rigidly separated the *is* from the *ought*; *theory* from *practice* and *facts* from *values*. Thus the approach taken here will be purposively sensitive to *historical* issues and also to concrete social contexts. Thus, in discussing ethical issues in counseling and counseling education, we will locate this professional in concrete historical contexts and will systematically look at his role as it has developed historically in a society where *expertise* is a commodity which serves many social purposes, not all of them, on closer scrutiny, being morally edifying to say the least.

SOURCES OF VALUE CONFUSION

Psychology's Domination by Scientific Psychology
     One of the first sources of value confusion that the counselor* will meet is the discipline of psychology proper. First of all, much of a counselor's training in the discipline of psychology will be outside of a school context. Although a practitioner by nature, the counselor will be systematically withdrawn from the practical setting of the school as he pursues the theories and research methods proliferated by psychologists in university settings. In other words, this part of his career will evidence, in whole or in part, a retreat from the societal context in which he will make his livelihood. Although not inevitable, he will be subject to the influence of the university's attitudes toward society in general. These attitudes are by no means *neutral* and in many ways downright *hostile*. Seymour

*Counselor and school psychologist will be used interchangeably throughout this paper.

Sarason (1974) has characterized these negative attitudes with the appellation "the myth of contamination by society." Sarason (1974) contends that the discipline of psychology, in its penchant for cleanliness from natural, real-life settings, has gone to extreme lengths not to be contaminated by them in its general methodology. The contamination myth has been part of an ideology propounded by academic psychology and has served as an obstacle not only to applied work but also to productive theorizing and research about man in natural settings, in our case the school setting. It strikes me, then, that one of the first value crises that a counselor will have to face when he embarks on training is his own self-alienation. This self-alienation ensues when a goodly portion of his certification program is hostile to the future settings in which he will be working. The counselor along with the school psychologist is a practitioner by profession; it is here that he will have to initially deal with the radical bifurcation between theory and practice that psychology as a theoretical discipline has systematically pursued as an historical option since the beginning of this century. If this were the only area (i.e., separation of theory from practice) producing self-alienation, his ethical problems would be contained. But there are many more subtle hazards embedded in his training for certification. The most prominent hazard, which contains a multitude of other *demons* that may have to be eventually exorcised, is that the discipline of scientific psychology can potentially alienate him from his own values by systematically masking them from his view. It is to this issue I would now like to turn, by briefly looking at some of the historical underpinnings of contemporary psychological science. Suffice to say this is a thumbnail sketch with many of the finer distinctions being ignored for purposes of the present argument.

Psychology's Divorce from Philosophy

The development of contemporary psychology is a series of historical options made in the context of the values of our contemporary society. Although these options reflect a pluralism as witnessed by the establishment and development of several schools and programs of research strategy, it may safely be said that all of these schools reflect a common core of contemporary societal values (i.e., an ethos).

One of these core options was an attempt to systematically separate the discipline of the psychology from its mother discipline, philosophy; and, with the exception of William James and Jean Piaget, the first half of the twentieth century saw the birth of a discipline that has purposely distanced itself, in a rather disdainful way, from philosophical inquiry. The rationale for this was that psychology was to be a science and philosophical inquiry was pre-scientific in its approach to human problems. The sum total of this effort was to mask the philosophical underpinnings of scientific understanding, leaving the discipline of scientific psychology unre-flective and therefore uncritical of its own philosophical preunder-standings. In actuality, psychology is embedded in a particular philosophical ethos called logical positivism that was rampant at the turn of the century. This school of philosophical thought was pri-marily interested in the developments of the natural sciences and its concomitant emphasis on *quantification* and *empiricism*. More im-portant, however, was the positivistic belief that *is* questions (i.e., ontological and epistemological questions) could and should be sep-arated from *ought* questions (i.e., ethical questions) and ensuing from this, that *facts* could be separated from *values*. Finally, using the metaphor of supposedly natural sciences (i.e., more specifically physics) positivistically oriented psychology would couch its ex-planatory apparatus in a language that saw man as a mechanism in the physical order of nature.

Some Necessary Elements in the Education of Counselors

(a) *Awareness of Real Life Settings.* From some of the pre-vious criticisms of psychology in its *modus operandi*, it is impor-tant that a counselor keep in touch with the real-life settings in which he will work and use this as the basis of any process of psy-chological reflection. This type of approach would appear logical but it has little support in contemporary psychology to date. The utility of moving from the practice setting to theory is outlined in Sarason's (1974) work on the role of community psychology. In the counselor's case, he will be using the school as the setting in which to reflect on complex social processes and their moral ramification. In the school setting he will have to develop a sensitivity to the val-ues and moral status of the individuals he will be working with over extended periods of time. Some of the areas of sensitivity would seem to me to be such things as social class, ethnicity and stage of development. It seems apparent that these contextual con-cerns will raise their own unique moral concerns that can be under-stood after some reflective process, but can hardly be predicted by some theory in advance. Obviously, the rich have different moral problems than the poor. Blacks have different value concerns than Chinese, and children have different moral concerns than adolescents and adults. Although this appears obvious, in many instances the counselor's training may direct him away from these important background conditions. Specifically, in relation to children he should become aware of the budding literature that is beginning to emerge on the "rights of children."

(b) *Awareness of Self.* When I allude to an awareness of self I am not speaking about some obscure profound philosophical experience. Specifically, this awareness involves a continuing sensitivity to one's own values in relation to others. It involves a recognition of, and responsibility for one's moral status as a psychological expert and the problems that this entails. More specifically this revolves around the fact that the public invests a certain credibility and trust in the role of a counselor regardless of the real competence that the person may have occupying that role. The glibness that some psychologists have in venturing interpretations in many instances is indicative of the disdain that they have for the public that invests its trust in them. Finally, awareness that one's values grow and change should precipitate a certain tolerance for the client's values that may be different from one's own. The reason why this type of awareness is stressed here is because much of one's psychological training may be systematically masking the values that are involved in the counselor-counselee relationship.

(c) *Focused Study in Moral Education.* It may seem novel and far-fetched but where possible it could be beneficial if a counselor could do some focused study in the area of moral education in general. First of all, it would systematically expose him to philosophical and psychological theories that deal with values and morality in an explicit fashion. Most counseling programs ignore this possibility completely in their certification sequence. A few counselors have taken some of my courses in moral education and I think they find it helpful in their work. For example, exposure even to Kohlberg's theory has some beneficial effects for them since it sensitizes them to the possibility of seeing a moral component in their psychological experiences. It also is a challenge to the unreflective value relativity which seems pervasive in psychological programs. Second, it exposes the counselor to those areas of the curriculum (e.g., social studies) that may deal with value conflict areas of a society and more specifically the value conflict areas of student life. The issue of the legitimacy of authority is a moral issue and conflicts in this area among students, school personnel and parents in many instances are fair game in a counselor-counselee relationship. The lack of interest in this type of issue in many instances makes counselors unreflective legitimatizers of unjust authority institutions in the school. More concretely, counselors may be simply unwitting sympathizers of the authority of school principals and teachers over students. More about this later. Finally, exposure to some aspects of moral education may counteract the present lacunae of a value-component in counselor- and school-psychology training. At present the idea of psychology as a "value-free enterprise" still prevails as an accepted idiom in psychological circles. The net effect of having these underlying assumptions are manifold and we will discuss only a few aspects here for our purposes. First of all, psychology would share with many of the other social sciences the belief that its endeavors are value neutral or value free. Second, there is the conviction that the gathering of factual evidence is *disinterested* in scientific inquiry and therefore interested value dimensions are eschewed. Third, in following the metaphors of natural sciences, the drift of psychology would reflect in the social sphere how the natural sciences have related to nature. Specifically, where the natural sciences have attempted domination and control of nature, the social sciences and specifically psychology have professed a desire to have *domination* and *control* over man, a moral issue if ever there was one.

The student of psychology, and in this case the counselor, is submerged in a discipline where he/she is not encouraged to reflect on value dimensions. He/she will assume that questions of *objectivity* and *rationality* are arrived at through *disinterested* inquiry. He/she is directed away from the possibility that social-scientific inquiry is quite *interested* and more specifically *class interested* from a more radical perspective (Habermas, 1972). And finally, the counselor is embedded in a discipline that takes prediction, control and domination of its *subjects* as one of its predominant motifs. This ultimately leads to a psychology that is nondialogical in nature and naively involved in the practice of oppression. I will return to the latter contention in the next section of this chapter.

SOME FUNCTIONS OF THE COUNSELOR
AND MORAL EDUCATION

The Technology of Testing

One of the most pervasive mandates that counselors and school psychologists have in terms of their vocational responsibilities is psychological testing. The administration of psychological tests in North American schools started with the institution of the intelligence test and has progressively accelerated into other numerous areas of human capacity. We now have tests for reading readiness, moral development, creativity, hyperactivity and you name it. The psychological test is believed to be the most *objective* test for the assessment of human capacities and there has developed a myth about this that has now reached epic proportions. The public projects capabilities on the psychological test situation that is totally out of proportion to its real or potential value. In all honesty, the profession of psychology is, by and large, much more reserved about what these tests could and should do. Nevertheless, the test has become one of the focal points for crucial policy issues in a variety of areas in the American educational setup. The famous Jensen controversy on black intelligence is just one illustration of the important ramifications of the type of important educational issues that the test raises for American educational policy. Daniel Moynihan is reputed to have said on the publication of Jensen's (1969) article in the *Harvard Educational Review*, "the winds of Jensenism are sweeping Washington."

Counselors or school psychologists are related to these controversies since they are usually charged with the testing of students in the school. It is clear that the ordinary school counselor does not see his role as one who is involved in large educational social-policy questions, but rather, as one who is involved in the ongoing policy questions of a particular school or school district.

At the school level, what are the reasons for administrating psychological tests? By and large tests are used for classifying students for a variety of purposes. They are used for the assessment of intellectual or emotional maturity or deficit. They are used for simple normative comparisons among schools. They are used to *serve as* the basis of tracking students into different programs that are reputed in line with the students' educational needs. The public rationale for any type of testing will always be couched in a language that will put the test in a positive light. I do not wish to say that there are no positive values in the use of tests, but in line with the theme of this paper I would like to bring out some of the unreflective negative consequences of testing since it bears on the crucial questions that are now looming on the important area of the rights of children (Magnusson, 1975).

Let me focus on the most commonly used test in the school setup, the intelligence test. The reason why I use I.Q. is that it raises so many moral issues and is therefore a good example for our purposes. In the sense that the construct of intelligence is derived from a particular set of measurement operations, it is obviously an abstraction that has no real existence apart from these operations (Ausubel and Sullivan, 1970). Nevertheless, insofar as the construct is logically tenable and derived from relevant and technically appropriate operations, it is by no means merely an arbitrary and fictitious invention of psychologists. It is definitely related to an existing state of affairs in the world and has much theoretical and practical value both in explaining cognitive and other aspects of behavioral development, and in predicting the cognitive level at which individuals function (Ausubel and Sullivan, 1970). The intelligence quotient (I.Q.) has historically been correlated with skill acquisition measured in the school's achievement tests. In this context, the I.Q. has been closely associated with ability grouping and tracking. The I.Q. was taken to be a good predictor of a person's success and speed in school achievement. The rationale for ability grouping was based on the assumption that school achievement could be enhanced if students could be tracked into classes that were commensurate with their intellectual capacities (i.e., high or low I.Q.). By and large, the low-ability student (slow learner) received the same material in his class, but at a slower pace than the high-ability student (fast learner). The ultimate effect of this type of innovation has had less than salutary effects for some of the students involved. The research findings indicate that I.Q. classification effectively separates students along racial and social class lines, raising the question of whether this type of tracking may well cause injury to minority-group children (Kirp, 1974). Mercier (1974) for instance, found that minority children were particularly burdened with school-specific stigmatizing labels. A host of studies reviewed in this area suggest that adverse classifications stigmatize students, reducing both their self-image and their worth in the eyes of others (Kirp, 1974).

The counselor or school psychologist in the testing role is not ordinarily involved in consciously sorting students on the basis of race. Student classification in large school systems is routinely handled by school officials who know nothing about a given student except his or her academic record (Kirp, 1974). When counselors discuss appropriate track placement with their students their recommendations are premised on estimates of student ability and school needs. Although not racially motivated, it ends up that minority children are tracked in less advanced programs (Kirp, 1974). Since counselors, not students, frequently make these decisions by matching school offerings to their own estimates of each student's

ability or potential, Kirp (1974) makes strong pleas for joint decision-making (i.e., dialogical) in an area that is of such crucial importance to the student's future educational life.

It goes without saying that victimization is not restricted to the
I.Q. test, but is rather potentially present in all forms of psychological testing and psychological attribution. Zuniga (1975) stresses the
point that social scientists select problem groups for study not un-
like the criteria by which the broader culture selects certain groups
as scapegoats. Not only the definition of the problem and the causal
interpretations, but also the recommendations for policy-making
gets centered on the "person's" problems and ignores the social
conditions. This process is cogently discussed in William Ryan's
book *Blaming the Victim* which I would like to quote at length
because of its evocative expository manner:

> Twenty years ago, Zero Mostel used to do a sketch in
> which he impersonated a Dixiecrat Senator conducting an
> investigation of the origins of World War II. At the climax
> of the sketch, the Senator boomed out, in an excruciating
> mixture of triumph and suspicion, 'What was Pearl Har-
> bor *doing* in the Pacific?' This is an extreme example of
> Blaming the Victim.

> Twenty years ago, we could laugh at Zero Mostel's carica-
> ture. In recent years, however, the same process has been
> going on every day in the arena of social problems, public
> health, anti-poverty programs, and social welfare. A phi-
> losopher might analyze this process and prove that, tech-
> nically, it is comic. But it is hardly ever funny. Consider
> some victims. One is the miseducated child in the slum
> school. He is blamed for his own miseducation. He is said
> to contain within himself the causes of his inability to read
> and write well. The shorthand phrase is "cultural depriva-
> tion," which, to those in the know, conveys what they
> allege to be inside information: that the poor child carries
> a scanty pack of cultural baggage as he enters school. He
> doesn't know about books and magazines and
> newspapers, they say. (No books in the home: the mother
> fails to subscribe to *Reader's Digest*.) They say that if he
> talks at all—an unlikely event since slum parents don't talk
> to their children—he certainly doesn't talk correctly.
> (Lower-class dialect spoken here, or even—God forbid!—

Southern Negro. *Ici on parle nigra.*) If you can manage to
get him to sit in a chair, they say, he squirms and looks
out the window. (Impulse-ridden, these kids, motoric
rather than verbal.) In a word he is "disadvantaged" and
"socially deprived," they say, and this, of course, accounts
for *his* failure, they say, to learn much in school.

Note the similarity to the logic of Zero Mostel's Dixiecrat
Senator. What is the culturally deprived child *doing* in the
school? What is wrong with the victim? In pursuing
this logic, no one remembers to ask questions about the
collapsing buildings and torn textbooks, the frightened,
insensitive teachers, the six additional desks in the room,
the blustering, frightened principals, the relentless segre-
gation, the callous administrator, the irrelevant curriculum, the bigoted or cowardly members of the school
board, the insulting history book, the stingy taxpayers, the
fairy-tale readers, or the self-serving faculty of the local
teachers' college. We are encouraged to confine our attention to the child and to dwell on all his alleged defects.
Cultural deprivation becomes an omnibus explanation for
the educational disaster area known as the inner-city
school. This is Blaming the Victim (Ryan, 1971, pp. 3 and
4).

Service professions such as counseling easily fall into *victim
blaming* because it is a subtle process. It is usually couched in a
humanistic outlook and occurs due to the lack of critical awareness
in professional training that I have pointed out at the outset of this
paper. Psychometricians do it, humanistic psychologists do it, behavior modifiers do it because our profession is singularly blind to
the impact that larger social-structure variables have on personality
development. Moreover, it is not done in the absence of generous
motives. It is usually carried out in the express interests of the
student involved. So it still holds true that the devil makes his way
best in this world when he is parading as the father of lights. The
subtle way in which psychological technology has tended toward
"victim blaming" should make the counselor or school psychologist
very wary about the labeling of his clients and to what purpose. I
can only touch on this problem here since this is a very complex
area. My intent is to point out that the labeling process is not simply a value-neutral technological innovation, but rather an in-

herently moral and political enterprise. Those involved in these
tasks should be sensitized to some of the value implications of their
work, especially some of the possible negative aspects. Let me conclude this section with a quote from Magnusson (1975), since he
deals with the issue of testing and labeling in relation to possible
abuses to student rights. In the context of student classification:

> What we see here is a serious threat to the rights of stu-
> dents—in some instances an outright denial of rights—aris-
> ing from various actual abuses of psychological test re-
> sults, learning theory, and normative psychological data.
> Durable and essentializing deviance labels have arisen re-
> peatedly from incomplete individual histories of learning,
> from a child's inability or refusal to adapt to the conven-
> tions of learning theory as practiced in his school and
> from intelligence and achievement testing. The misuse of
> psychological data has had serious moral and ethical re-
> percussions for "slow learners" or "poor readers" who are
> emotionally damaged by overt and covert sanctions that
> extend beyond the beneficial intentions of the labels.
> Where the misuse has camouflaged social and political
> challenges to the accepted order of the schools, the accep-
> tability of psychological data for educationally valid
> "diagnosis" and "treatment" has been abused since the
> generalization to this type of political issue is logically and
> ethically an unwarranted extension of scientific data
> (Magnusson, 1975, pp. 109-110).

The lucrative profession of testing raises many complex moral
issues and those involved in it cannot ignore some of its negative
possibilities if they wish to remain morally sensitive persons.

Dialogical Function
   (a) *The Expert.* The testing situation is an asymmetrical relationship but it is quite typical in terms of how psychologists relate
to their clients. In general the psychologist has become the *expert*,
he does the asking, his clients the answering. Dialogue would not
be the paradigm for this type of relationship since the parties involved are not on an equal plane. What I would now like to advance is the notion that the dialogue should be the paradigm for

human relationships and communication and that the psychologist-client relationship should reflect dialogue if it is to be a humanizing activity. The idea of the "*expert*," which has become commonplace in our culture, is contrary to the kind of dialogical activity that I am suggesting. Let me elaborate on this aspect.

(b) *The Counselor as Professional Expert.* With the development of modern technology we find the ascendence of advisors in all walks of life called *experts*. Within the school context, counselors are considered experts in their understanding of students. This expertise is accepted in the area of the interpretation of psychological test results, learning theories and other types of normative psychological data. The expert becomes, then, the focal point for decisions in the school structure. The idea that the expert "knows best" eventually can open the way to robbing people of their own moral judgment. Illich (1973) goes so far as to say that with the ascendence of the expert knowledge has become a cognitive disorder. He calls it a cognitive disorder because an illusion is created that makes people less critical in interpreting their own experiences. The *expert*, the *professional*, has the "objective" answers to problems whereas the individual citizen does not. This so-called "expert" knowledge is then expected to be the data base for a process called "decision-making."

The language of "decision-making" in the school system is couched in a framework which makes it appear "value neutral." As we have already indicated earlier, value neutrality in psychology is simply a veiled moral ideology. Within the school context the "supposed by neutral (scientific) and beneficial act of "educational" labeling educators and its consequences are distinctly moral and political, reflecting a covert institutional and social bias toward the labeled individuals (Magnusson, 1975).

Let me give just one example of how this *expert* mentality can distort the situation and ultimately become miseducation. Although I use "behavior modification" as an example, the process should not be construed as confined to this particular approach. The specific example is a "behavior-modification" sequence cited by Burger (1972) which intends, as an objective, the teaching of language to six-year-old Navajo children. Burger is attempting to show how the psychological *experts* in the school are, in many instances, insensitive to the social and cultural world of the people that they are trying to help. He observed with these Navajo children that the behavior modifier directed the teacher to seat the children a few inches apart from her and with their backs close to the wall. At this, the children became uneasy. Apparently the Navajo is accustomed to open spaces and an anthropologist who was aware of this suggested that the children would be more at ease if they were allowed to have more space between them. The anthropologist further observed that the teacher might exchange positions so that the pupils could back off into an open area. The "behavior modifier" ignored this suggestion and felt no need to accommodate this cultural information into his modification sequence. Here and in several other examples cited, Burger (1972) develops the thesis that the *expertise* of operant behaviorism neglects the complexities of the culture. The expert, in his hubris, assumes means, goals, and rewards of the majority culture, hence imperializing the human subjects who tend to be in minorities. Paulo Freire (1972) would label the above procedures *"cultural invasion"* and he sees the expert's role in a more negative light:

> Cultural invasion, which like divisive tactics and manipulation also serves the ends of conquest. In this phenomenon, the invaders penetrate the cultural context of another group, in disrespect of the latter's potentialities, they impose their own view of the world upon those they invade and inhibit the creativity of the invaded by curbing their expression. . . . (p. 150) To this end, the invaders are making increasing use of the social sciences and technology, and to some extent the physical sciences as well, to improve their action (note, p. 151).

The example given is just one instance of a more pervasive phenomenon which puts psychologists in relationships with their clients in such a way that the paradigm for these relations is one of a monologue. When a psychologist is trained in a methodology that encourages *manipulation* and *control* he tends toward a monological world view. In order to counteract this influence, it is imperative that counselors or school psychologists expose themselves to a psychological ethos that reflects the importance of dialogical communication. The problem here is to find programs that reflect a dialogical idiom and it is to this type of consideration I would now like to turn in distinguishing dialogical from nondialogical psychology.

Dialogical Psychology
Probably the most seminal work on the notion of dialogue and

dialogical relationship is Martin Buber's *I-Thou* (Buber, 1970). Buber contrasts two core relationships that man can have with his world, that is, the "I-Thou" and the "I-It." The notion of I-Thou connotes a relationship of mutuality and reciprocity between two persons. The notion of an I-It relationship signifies how a person relates to objects other than persons. The I-It is an impersonal relationship that allows the entrance of manipulation and control of a person (I) over some aspects of an objective (It) world. A relationship of mutuality and reciprocity between persons is a dialogical relationship, and Buber considers this the paradigm for human relationships. Because psychology has attempted to mimic the natural sciences, much of its methodology falls into the sphere of nondialogical relationships (I-It). Where manipulation, prediction and control stand as an ideal in methodology, there stand I-It relationships. Freire's work *The Pedagogy of the Oppressed* extends the dialogical paradigm of Buber in analyzing macro-social relationships that have predominent "I-It" components and portrays them as unjust oppressive relationships. Following from the above contentions, I would venture to say that much of contemporary psychological methodology fosters unjust oppressive social relationships since the predominant motif is that of the "I-It." Nondialogical (I-It) psychology directs one to treat its subjects or clients as objects to be manipulated. Our own contention is that a psychological perspective which, in the process of studying its subject matter, turns *subjects* into *objects* is a depersonalizing, dehumanizing, anti-dialogical and oppressive psychology. A psychological perspective, be it behavioral or humanistic, which in word or in deed gives primacy to the use of *technique* will probably be weighted toward a theory of oppressive action. A psychological perspective that does not reflect on the possible negative effects of *expertise* or *professionalism* (i.e., elites) will tend toward an anti-dialogical and oppressive psychology. When all or some of the above conditions are present one can expect the proliferation of *unjust* and *oppressive* institutions parading under the name of human liberation. From a perspective of revolutionary action, emancipation from these types of institutions and social relationships are in order.

The distinction of I-Thou versus I-It extends throughout the whole process of psychological inquiry. In a sense the distinction requires different types of knowledge. The first is our knowledge of persons as persons (I-Thou); the other our knowledge of persons versus objects (I-It). David Hunt and I have discussed elsewhere two different orientations in psychology that can be roughly correlated with the above distinctions (Hunt and Sullivan, 1974). The two orientations we discuss are "psychology as science" and "psychology as understanding," or hermeneutical psychology (cf. Habermas, 1968). Most people who have taken a course in psychology would be likely to say that its definition is "the prediction and control of behavior." As pointed out earlier, this definition is usually associated with the belief that this objective can be accomplished by discovering, or verifying, general laws of behavior (e.g., laws of learning). This conception of psychology has produced a highly organized belief system that implicitly specifies what will be studied and how (Hunt and Sullivan, 1974). Defining "mastery" in psychology as the prediction and control of behavior, Bakan (1965) summarized the features of the "mastery-mystery complex" as follows, and they are appropriate features that characterize "psychology as science":

(1) The scientist-subject distinction.

(2) The definition of psychology as the study of behavior.

(3) The choice of lower animals, particularly domesticated animals, as subjects of choice in research.

(4) The specification of the aim of research as the discovery of "laws."

(5) The cultural norm that research consists of is testing of preconceived hypotheses (p. 187).

When this orientation departs from the animal world for research subjects, it has shown a preference for the more docile populations of children and the poor (Braginsky and Braginsky, 1974). Finally, adding one more feature to Bakan's five, there is the belief that laws are discovered through "randomly-assigned-to-treatments" designs. In these designs persons or animals are randomly assigned to different experimental groups in an effort to eliminate individual differences (Hunt and Sullivan, 1974). The last feature I would venture to say is ultimately an exercise in depersonalization and therefore dehumanizing. The "psychology-as-science" conception has led, therefore, to inquiry and research with fairly simple human characteristics that can be predicted and controlled, to the almost total exclusion of research that takes individual *personological* differences seriously (Hunt and Sullivan, 1974). As with mastery over nature, mastery over man is aligned to the development of technology. Control through psychological *technology* is just beginning to raise profound human issues for our society (London, 1971). The nondialogical character of a *tech-*

nological orientation is now being severely criticized in circles that see "scientism" as a unreflective ideology. Jurgen Habermas (1970) of the Frankfort School of "critical social theory" sums up what we are trying to develop thus far in our critique of "psychology-as-science":

> Technocratic consciousness reflects not the sundering of an ethical situation but the repression of "ethics" as such as a category of life. The common, positivist way of thinking renders covert the frame of reference of interaction in ordinary language, in which domination and ideology both arise under conditions of distorted communication and can be reflectively detected and broken down. . . . Technocratic consciousness makes this practical interest disappear behind interest in the expansion of power of technical control (Habermas, 1970, pp. 112-133).

"Psychology-as-Understanding" is an orientation that systematically attempts *dialogue* and *interpretation*. From another perspective it might be termed "hermeneutical psychology" (cf. Habermas, 1971). Bakan (1965) brings out the dialogical nature of "psychology-as-understanding" by emphasizing that the psychologist is not intrinsically different from other people. All people seek to understand themselves and others in the course of their lives; and all people continually attempt to bring to bear such generalizations in the management of their lives. The special character of the psychologist inheres only in the intensity and systematic nature of his search.

From the perspective developed above, it would follow that a counseling relationship should be based on dialogue and understanding rather than manipulation and control. For the most part the counselor's role is defined in quite different terms by the institutional demands of the school. His job is to help in the administering of persons, the engineering of souls (Seeley, 1974). I would contend that as an institution, notwithstanding exceptions, counseling and its ancillary responsibilities are involved in administering through psychological technology the conventional ethos of the school and controlling deviance from this dominant ethos. The use of psychological technology in this context offers a serious threat to the rights of students. The labeling process that psychological technology has become identified with in the schools is a process for controlling students; hence "administered persons: the engineering of souls." Magnusson (1975) conjectures that these labels, as terms of control, imply the power that educators have over students to direct and shape their lives, a relational movement that follows logically from a psychology based on prediction and control.

The Role of Advocate

The role of the counselor as we have described it thus far has been a reactive one. As part of the school institution the counselor has ordinarily been given the task of providing objective rationales for the school's decision-making process concerning students. Since the role defined is reactive it tends to be *conservative* in nature. For the most part the counselor or school psychologist is not expected to take an active role as a *change agent* in the school. In general he is not expected to change anything at all—with the exception of the student who turns out to be deviant and is not falling in with the school's routine. Specifically, he does testing and counseling, but these roles are simply there to help buffer the ongoing bureaucracy of the school. As a result of this passivity, counseling and school psychologists have found themselves carrying out activities for school administrators that are in direct violation of the student's interests and his rights. Tests were given and results recorded in school records. School records have been released to other parties without parent or student consent. Throughout this process, the counselor's and school psychologist's role has hardly taken the side of the student and in many instances to the detriment of student interests. This passive and conservative role has come under criticism in the last few years and there is an increasing demand that psychologists should change their role in the school system. Part of this changing role is the desire to have counselors and school psychologists taking an active role in school changes in line with the student's best interest rather than that of school administrators or other school personnel. Hyman and Schreiber (1975), for example, maintain that school psychologists must consider their major client, the student, and not the school system, a position consonant with the A.P.A. code of Ethics for practicing psychology. The role of the counselor as an active partner with the students in positively relating to the students' total effectiveness can be described as that of a *"student advocate"* (Linton and Menacker, 1975). The advocate's role assumes that the counselor will support students' interests and needs in a total environmental sense, enabling the student to profit from positive opportunities for personal growth within and outside the school and, in general, combat the negative forces that impede wholesome development (Linton and Menacker, 1975). The importance of a more dialogical relationship becomes apparent since the relationship between counselor and student is more a partnership based on mutual commitment, trust and understanding, forged out of the concerted actions they undertake together, and the results that these activities produce. Moreover, the role of advocate changes the focus of his loyalties. Instead of, as in the past, taking the position of the school bureaucracy by simply implementing its normative procedures (e.g., testing), it would not be unusual to find the counselor in opposition to the school or educational system in which he is employed. Counselor activities will probably span a broader range of skills than presently taught in counseling programs, demanding greater versatility and skill in human interaction and a good deal of innovative ability (Linton and Menacker, 1975).

RETROSPECT AND PROSPECT: EMERGENT ROLES AND VALUES

The future directions of counselor education will demand that the counselor or school psychologist be like the good scribe "who brings out from his storeroom things both new and old" (Matthew 13:52). In looking over some of the points that were made in this chapter, a departure from some aspects of existing programs of training appear to be in order. The separation of theory from practice, the assumed value neutrality and the importance of a psychology based on prediction and control appear to have little moral justification. A psychologist working in the schools is not just simply a psychologist; he must also be an educator. His/her skills should not be simply restricted to psychological testing and psychotherapy. Linton and Menacker (1975) attempt to broaden this role in defining the role of a Counselor-Educator. Five components of this role would be utilized within the school system: 1) child advocate, 2) systems-change agent, 3) direct involvement with children, 4) behavioral objectives to social and academic interests, and 5) reeducation approach to school and social adjustment. Using their framework I would like to briefly conclude with some descriptions of the scope and functions assumed within these components.

(a) *Child Advocate*

Linton and Menacker (1975) see the training of counselors in this context focusing on the developmental needs of children as members of the school system, and the larger social system apart from the school. I would add to this the importance a thorough grounding in the recent literature that has been developing on the "rights of children" (e.g., Haubrich and Apple, 1975). The questions considered under this rubric will be essentially moral and legal questions—an area that psychology up to this point has neglected to oversee. Being a child advocate may demand actions that heretofore have not been assumed by psychologists in the schools. For example, he may be the one person who will be able to identify and report child abuse by parents or teachers. Specifically, his role may be to sensitize other school personnel as to their responsibility for reporting child abuse (Hyman and Schreiber, 1975). The responsibility may also fall to him of seeing that children and their parents have full access to procedures and materials regarding their relationship with the school. These rights include due process and availability of psychological records (Hyman and Schreiber, 1975). In the past, and to a great extent now, psychologists have been the prime violators of these rights.

(b) *Counselor as Systems-Change Agent*

Linton and Menacker (1975) see a counselor's role as a change agent in the school system. For example, when a counselor identifies negative and personally destructive elements in the student's life, he would be equipped to change those aspects of the school and community that are destructive to his client's welfare. This function would demand an understanding of the culture of the school and the problems of change (Sarason, 1971). At this moment, most certification programs do not develop these skills or their knowledge base. Training would not only focus on the development of psychometric and therapeutic skills but also an emphasis on community psychology skills (e.g., Sarason, 1971). The type of training that Sarason (1971, 1974) envisages is virtually unheard of at the moment. Psychologies that systematically divorce themselves from applied settings like the schools, as in the "myth of contamination" discussed earlier in this chapter, are ill equipped to handle the types of skills that are demanded here.

(c) *Direct Involvement with Students*

In most school settings the counselor or school psychologist is seen when something has gone wrong or when some normative test has to be given. At the moment, one would hardly identify the counselor's office as a place where students can find a haven to deal with problems. As a change agent, one would expect that the counselor or school psychologist would initiate contacts with students without interference from other members of the school administration. In keeping with the role of *advocate*, it would not seem inappropriate to find a counselor interfering with some test procedures that may not be in the best interests of the students at that school. For example, in Toronto schools he might object to premature, though routine, testing of immigrant children because these tests are unduly biased against children who do not have English as their first language.

(d) Behavioral-Objectives Approach to Social and Academic Interests

This particular component would demand that a counselor or school psychologist have some training in the area of educational psychology. This part of his training would allow him to provide the student, the teacher and the parent with specific methods for achieving specific goals for a student (Linton and Menacker, 1975). The above authors describe this aspect as a competency approach to academic and behavioral goals for the student and it is in marked contrast to the approach that emphasizes in-depth clinical and therapeutic evaluation of the students presenting problems, an approach which frequently ends up by "blaming the victim." The advantage of this approach is that:

> It requires the identification of specific troublesome areas for the student, and the development of short-term and practical steps essential to lessening the anxiety or concerns of the student. . . . Recent research evidence suggests that many non-productive social and academic behaviors can be positively changed through altering of social and academic stress factors present in the student's life. To make these changes effective with the student, the counselor does not need to provide long-term personality counseling, nor to label the student into a low expectation classroom setting within the school (Linton and Menacker, 1975, p. 4).

This role would prevent the frustration of simply being the labeler of a problem with all of its negative consequences, by encouraging procedures that are involved in the amelioration and transformation of student problems.

(e) Reeducation Approach to School and Social Adjustment

Although I have argued against some of the negative effects of behavioral psychology in this chapter, one should not be blinded to the fact that some of the developments in "behavior-modification" techniques can have a salutary effect when they are developed within the context of the students' needs rather than the needs of the school bureaucracy. I am well aware of the dangers of "behavioral control" when they are designed to foster institutional maintenance. Nevertheless, it seems that some of the skillful techniques developed by "behavior modifiers" can have limited usefulness in a school setting. Some of the "desensitizing techniques" could help students deal with undue and debilitating anxiety in school situations. Reading and speaking skills seem to be facilitated by short-term "behavioral methods," short-circuiting long-term therapy techniques that eventually seem to come around and to "blame the victim." Instead of the counselor's attempting elaborate personality changes through depth-therapy methods, his skills would be confined to short-term therapy procedures that make no pretenses of plumbing the depths of the student's psyche—the latter approach usually ending up to the detriment of the student.

(f) A Moral Educator

Part of the counselor's role as an advocate together with some group dynamics skills from his training may qualify him for the unlikely role of a moral educator if moral education in the schools is broadly conceived. For our purposes let me focus on the high school; a specific example given by De Cecco and Richards (1975) will illustrate my point. Their example involves an issue of "due process" which was raised by a student's complaint:

> It happens on a school day in the cafeteria when the teacher in charge grabbed a student's books and told her to go to class. The girl hesitated for a moment by the way she was told by the teacher to go to class. So the teacher said again for her to go to class. The student went for her books that the teacher had, and the teacher pushed her in the chest. The student tried forcing her books out of the teacher's hands and the teacher reported to the office that the student had punched her and had pushed her.

> Immediately, the student was expended (sic) from school. She didn't have the right to explain herself. She was just kicked out—I feel this was wrong. The administration should have had the teacher and the student in the office to find out just what happened and why.

De Cecco and Richards maintain that an incident like the above calls for school procedures that provide for due process in the form of student courts, teacher-review panels and school conferences where all personnel meet to iron out areas of conflict. A school psychologist or counselor could conceivably take on a vital role in this process.

> The cafeteria incident above struck the student writing about it as involving one teacher and one student. Other conflicts put one group against another group. Sorting out exact parties to a conflict is obviously crucial to negotiations. So is an understanding of the relative status of parties involved, since a conflict between parties of unequal status may require mediation by a third party (De Cecco and Richards, 1975, p. 120).

A school psychologist or counselor could provide the necessary neutrality to mediate in these conflicts that can be considered as morally educative in a broader value context. Moreover, this is only one area of conflict where the counselor could play a helpful role. Other areas of negotiation are even more obvious.

> One source of conflict we have hardly mentioned is the kind that exists within adolescents. Parental values often conflict starkly with the values of teachers and peers. And when it comes to consolidating an individual set of values, a high-school student may experience still more powerful conflicts within himself. Adolescent development makes great demands on teachers, sometimes for unlimited freedom and sometimes for unlimited control. When teachers capitulate to these demands they may avoid conflict, but at the same time deny their students adult models of behavior. When they suppress demands, teachers deny their students the democratic rights they are trying to teach. By listening, however, to student demands without surrendering to them, school adults can negotiate the limits of freedom and control (De Cecco and Richards, 1975, p. 120).

My own addition to the above, is the possible crucial role that a school counselor could play in this process of negotiation. If he is to fulfill a role as student advocate, he would have to have some critical distance from the teachers and the school administration. It might therefore be suggested, where possible, that the counselor's site and supervision be transferred away from the school to a central educational bureau that encompasses very many projects and is open to people of all ages and students at all schools.

CONCLUSION

This chapter started with a critical analysis of the role of the psychologist in the schools. It pictured the conventional psychologist in the school as an unwitting agent for social conformity and convention. Further, in his role as the elite expert in the use of psychological technology, he becomes involved in a decision-making process that is oppressive in nature. The technology of testing has been a sorting devise that clearly favors a caste and class mentality. What's more, his psychological training has systematically blinded him to the real value implications of his work and role in the society of the school. From the perspective developed in this paper, the school psychologist and counselor would do well to avoid carrying out this school-assigned role. We have suggested some new roles and images that psychologists should aspire toward which can be considered counter-cultural as far as the culture of the school is concerned. At present there is very little support for sustaining this new type of "advocate" role either in the psychological or educational profession. The advocate role of the type that I have described will probably attract a special kind of "person." As a psychologist he will have to have a deeper humanism than is illustrated by most of his professional peers. In addition he will have to have the courage to maintain the development of new roles for psychologists in the schools even when these roles are not actively encouraged by other school personnel. Obviously, there are inherent dangers for a person involved in the development of new professional images. This ultimately demands at least two major virtues: prudence and courage.

Reaction to Sullivan: HELPFUL RELATION OF THEORY AND PRACTICE *by* Ronald J. Hine

Two sets of ideas in Sullivan's paper are particularly intriguing: first, his insights into the relationships between counseling practice, scientific psychology, and philosophy; and secondly, his notion of the place of moral education in the training and practice of the counselor. This reaction will focus on these two areas.

Philosophy and Psychology

Sullivan alerts us to the domination of psychological practice by scientific psychology and to its divorce from philosophy. While accepting the general tenor of what he has to say on the interrelationship of theory, practice, and meaning, there is another point from which to view such relationships, and this second viewpoint needs to be kept in balance and tension with the first. From this second viewpoint, it is not that scientific psychology dominates practice, but rather that scientific findings are poorly understood and frequently translated into unsound practices. In this regard, one might critique the "behavior modifier" cited from Burger (1972) not just for lack of sensitivity to the social and cultural worlds of Navajo children or for claiming the ascendency of the expert, but also for a poor understanding of behavior modification. The cultural information that he chose to ignore indicated the operative reward system for Navajo children, which as a competent "behavior modifier" he should have tested out and utilized in accordance with the principles of his expertise.

Such a lack of thorough attention to scientific psychology is not an isolated incident in psychological practice. In the area of classroom practice, for instance, one gains the impression that popularizers of Kohlberg's work have oversimplified his theory and findings, thus confusing many teachers and leading them to a misunderstanding of the cognitive-developmental model of moral judgment. Their simplifications have resulted in too close an identification of progressive structural changes in moral thinking with particular typical products of thinking at particular stages, as if, for example, "I'll scratch your back, if you scratch mine" was a complete description of structural processes for Stage Two, and "good-boy mentality," or "law-and-order mentality" were complete descriptions of the structural processes for Stage Three and Stage Four reasoning. Again, teachers have been frequently left with the simplistic ideas of how to "move" a child quickly from one stage to another. They have even been left with the impression that Kohlberg's theory prevented them from being concerned about the opinions, the choices, and the content of moral judgments, and narrowed their role to assisting students to achieve a higher stage of moral reasoning as quickly as possible. None of these ideas are implicit, let alone explicit, in a cognitive developmental approach to moral education. They result not from the dominance of scientific psychology over practice, but from the lack of a proper understanding of the psychological theory as hypothesized and researched.

If this is the danger to which classroom practice has been exposed, perhaps it is important to warn counselors of it, side by side with Sullivan's warning about the domination of scientific psychology. In the relationship between counseling and moral development, the danger is not only that counseling practice may be exposed to the domination of a scientific psychological theory of stage development of moral reasoning, but also that counselors will fail to take seriously enough the real meaning and application of the psychological theory properly understood. These two warnings can achieve some kind of unity if the relationship of psychology to philosophy that Sullivan has examined is more fully considered from another aspect.

Much after the style in which teachers are influenced in their classroom practice by the "hidden" curriculum, every psychological practitioner, researcher, and theorist is influenced by a "hidden" philosophy that provides direction, purpose, meaning, and ethic for his psychological practice. The "behavior modifier" practices and analyzes the control of behavior and in so doing is acting out his belief that it is necessary and good to control behavior. What Sullivan has suggested is the need for a conscious assessment of the philosophy that guides the practice of psychology, so that one's guiding philosophy be not a hidden philosophy, but a consciously articulated one. He speaks strongly for the conscientization of counselors to the hidden purposes and values of the institution within which they work, and to the domination they may exercise over their clients. In this, his strong words echo Freire (1970), Overly (1970), Postman and Weingartner (1969) and others (Mac-Donald, 1973) in their condemnation of the hidden curriculum based on the hidden philosophy of education as domination.

But while recognizing the impact of a hidden philosophy on the practice of counseling, as Sullivan does, it is also important to emphasize the desirability of an interaction between philosophy and psychology. It is not sufficient for a counselor's philosophy to guide his psychological practice. His philosophy needs to be derived, at least in part, from his psychology. This interrelationship is made clearer by the distinction between a descriptive and a prescriptive theory of psychology.

Since a descriptive theory provides a description of the functional relationships among the variables of a system, its formulation is basically a matter of science, though Snow (1973) in his review of theory construction is at pains to point out that even descriptive theories are shaped by metatheories which, in part, represent a hidden philosophy. Prescriptive theories, on the other hand, provide norms and guidelines to bring about optimal or desired psychological states. Their formulation is in some ways as much a matter of philosophy as of preferred psychology. Thus, the cognitive-developmentalist describes higher-stage functions as more adaptive than lower-stage functions, since the capacity for, say, Stage Five moral judgments is a more differentiated and integrated capacity than the capacity for Stage Three moral judgments. The cognitive-developmentalist can also provide the counselor with guidelines and norms that will enable him to present the experiences that will tend to make his client more adaptive in his moral judgments, and so advance him toward a higher stage of moral thinking. But the decision to follow such guidelines is a matter of philosophy, a judgment about the goodness and utility of promoting advances in moral judgment. Someone might argue that the good of society and the best happiness of individuals is achieved by the fixation of citizens at a Stage Four level of moral judgment, and this philosophic judgment will determine which psychological prescriptions guide his practice. This is the interaction of philosophy and practice that Sullivan analyzes.

But while expecting the counselor, as Sullivan does, to take stock of the influences of his philosophy on his psychological practice, one might also expect that the counselor take full account of the findings of descriptive psychology in the formulation of his philosophy. Thus, his understanding of the nature of the common and social good should be fully integrated with the psychological description of a fully developing and fully adaptive person, so that for him any notion of common good that had no room for the full development of an individual's capacities for moral judgment would be a misunderstanding of the common good. That is to say that at least part of the data that goes into the formulation of an adequate philosophy is data derived from an accurate scientific descriptive psychology. Only a psychologically informed philosophy can be used to derive an adequate prescriptive theory for psychological practice.

Of course, assessing the validity of various descriptive theories of psychology is not easy, since the behavioristic, the psychodynamic, the humanistic, and the cognitive-developmentalist approaches provide theories that are fundamentally contrary, if not contradictory to one another. Perhaps it is hardly possible to choose one rather than another with finality. But, in fact, one does choose, at least implicitly, one or other position as a working hypothesis, and consistency requires that such a working hypothesis be included among the considerations that give rise to one's philosophy. If behaviorism is your working hypothesis, then your philosophy has to be one of control and your design for the engineering of the environment should presumably be one that will enable human beings to be reinforced by reward rather than by the avoidance of pain, as Skinner suggests (1971). If cognitive developmentalism is your working hypothesis, then your philosophy has to include the promotion and encouragement of self-regulating processes of individuals, and while an environmental design may grow out of your philosophy, it would be a contradiction if the design were an attempt fully to control and determine individuals. Sullivan has alerted counselors to the danger of a hidden philosophy behind counseling practice, and requested them to consciously formulate the philosophy that guides their practice. But the further request must also be made that counselors take seriously the findings of psychology in the very formulation of their philosophy, so that psychological practice will not be guided by a philosophy ignorant of or inimical to the findings of psychology.

Moral Education and the Counselor

The foregoing comments and elaborations of Sullivan's discussion of scientific psychology, philosophy, and counseling practice flow over into comments on the second set of intriguing ideas presented in his paper, namely, his ideas about the place of moral education in the training and practice of the counselor. He suggests that the study of moral education would help the counselor be more sensitive to the moral issues involved in his functions and alert him to the possibilities of victimizing his client. His forceful words about "blaming the victim" further highlight the importance of psychology in formulating a philosophy and ethic.

If a counselor adopts behaviorism as a working hypothesis, he should take to heart the warning about victim-blaming since the environment is the determinative element in the victim's behavior, cognition, affect, and judgment. If another counselor works from a cognitive-developmentalist hypothesis, the warning is still apt, since the environment is an interactive factor in a client's responses. Whichever philosophy guides counseling practice, it ought to make the counselor willing to be a change agent, an advocate, and a protector for his client. But if the counselor is working out of a cognitive-developmentalist hypothesis, an additional principle should find its way into his guiding philosophy, for in accordance with his working hypothesis, the environment is not the sole determinant of behavior, cognition, affect, and judgment. Moreover, even a socially unsatisfactory environment may interact with a victim's affective-cognitive structures to produce the disequilibration essential for the extension of a structure or for progression to a higher stage of reasoning. In other words, while the victim may not be worthy of blame, simply to right the injustice that surrounds him would not be adequate psychological practice. To be no longer a victim, whether of a just or an unjust environment, requires the victim's development through stages of growth. Only with better perspective-taking and evaluative capacities can the client grow from victim to self-regulating agent. The counselor guiding his practice with an ethic that takes full account of cognitive developmentalism as a working hypothesis, far from blaming the victim, will work not only to remove injustices from the victim, but will interact with the victim in a way that will promote the gradual long-term growth of his capacities to deal more adaptively with the environment. Sullivan, of course, has proposed the need for counselors to practice a dialogical psychology, and this makes sound philosophical sense for a counselor if and when his psychological working hypothesis understands dialogue as the means to encourage a more differentiated and integrated psychological development. It would not be sound philosophy, however, if the only reasons supporting dialogue were cultural fashion, social requirement, or some concept of freedom and dignity unrelated to and ungrounded in the psychological working hypothesis adopted by the counselor.

Better, Not Less, Psychology

Numbers of interesting and provocative ideas have been raised by Sullivan. It would be unfortunate if they were interpreted, or perhaps misinterpreted, to mean a lessening of the importance of a sound psychological basis for the training and practice of counselors. It is undeniably important for counselors to face the alienation resulting from a scientific training, to achieve an awareness of real life settings, to see the dangers of professionalism, to heighten self-awareness, and to clarify their values. But these problems do not demand a divorce from scientific psychology. Rather they are more adequately dealt with by a better understanding of psychological theory, by acknowledging the distinction between descriptive and prescriptive theories, and by a thorough analysis of the interrelationships between the counselor's philosophy and practice.

4
The Research Base of the Cognitive Developmental Approach to Moral Education

James R. Rest

In this country there are currently two major value education programs that have widespread appeal and usage: the cognitive-developmental or Kohlbergian programs and the values-clarification approach (Raths, Harmin, Simon, Kirschenbaum). These two approaches to value education have gained appeal for very different reasons: I think the appeal of the values-clarification approach is that it offers very concrete activities and materials for a teacher. Its attractiveness is its specificity and concreteness in telling a teacher what to say and what to do. The values-clarification approach is criticized, however, for not being based on a well-worked-out theory of psychological development or on a well-worked-out philosophy of what values education ought to be. There is not much research that has tested the basic ideas of the values-clarification approach, nor research that demonstrated its effectiveness. Despite its widespread popularity, I am aware of only about a dozen studies on the values-clarification approach (Kirschenbaum, 1975).[1]

In contrast, the cognitive-developmental approach has several hundred studies of its basic ideas and evaluations of its programs. The appeal of the cognitive-developmental approach is in its basis in psychological research and its basis in moral philosophy—not in its having a lot of concrete curriculum materials or a lot of specific things for teachers to say and do. These things are only beginning to be worked out. Rather than starting with a collection of practices

1. I do not mean to imply that the values-clarification approach cannot be researched—there are many interesting and empirically testable hypotheses. Rather it seems to have been the case that its early developers have been more interested in teaching materials and activities than research, and only lately has there developed an interest in research—see Kirschenbaum, 1975.

or materials, the cognitive-developmental approach has started with philosophy and psychology and is just beginning to work out the implications for pedagogy.

The appeal of the cognitive-developmental approach does not lie in spectacular results of its programs, either. The evaluations are encouraging and promising, but not spectacular. Rather, the appeal lies in its rootedness in research, in having ways of examining itself and in improving itself through self-study. Right now, the cognitive-developmental approach has a lot of suggestions to make about educational programs, but these ideas are in a process of evolution. Furthermore, this evolution is not helter-skelter or left to chance but has the potential of being a systematic program of research that checks out alternatives, and figures out how to gather information on which to base the next round of decisions.

Four Theoretical Approaches to the
Psychological Study of Morality

The aim of this paper is to present an overview of the research of the cognitive-developmental approach that has sought to test out its basic ideas, and how these empirically tested ideas comprise a rationale for conducting moral education. But before moving directly to cognitive-developmental research on moral development, it should be pointed out that there are four major psychological theories about how morality develops, and the cognitive-developmental theory is just one psychological theory. There are also the psychoanalytic, behavioralistic, and the humanistic approaches to the psychological study of morality. Each of these theories emphasizes a different aspect of morality. In order to appreciate the particular character of the cognitive-developmental approach, I'll first make some brief descriptions of the other approaches.

According to the psychoanalytic approach, the psychology of morality is a matter of the superego. Freud's account of the establishment of the superego is most clear for males: the five-year-old boy has sexual desires for his mother; accordingly he comes into competition with his father, but since the father is more powerful and threatening, the boy must inevitably curb his own impulses and accept living life on his father's terms. The resolution of this crisis, the Oedipal complex, comes to be the core pattern whereby an individual regulates his impulses according to some external norm. Freud theorized that the way this works was that the superego would issue its demands (reflecting an authority's demands) and enforce these demands by punishing transgression with guilt or rewarding obedience with a feeling of self-esteem. Freud hypothesized a roughly comparable process for women. The key idea to this position is that a person acquires his values from others, originally on threat of retaliation but maintained by the fear of guilt. This theory suggests that if you wanted to do research on morality, you would look closely at impulse control in young children, at how the parents enforce their demands, at how the child comes to identify with and accept the standards of adults.

According to the behaviorist approach, morality is a learned set of behaviors like any other set of behaviors. We label certain behaviors as "moral" and a person learns those behaviors through the three behavioristic principles: classical conditioning, operant conditioning, and modeling. If one's reinforcement schedule is consistent and frequent enough, moral behavior can be firmly established. The behaviorists seem to say that moral character is getting into such a rut of doing good that you can't break the habit. This theory suggests that to do research on morality you would look at what behaviors were being reinforced, what behaviors were being modeled. How much reinforcement, how often, how consistent would be crucial aspects of a study.

Note that both the psychoanalytic and the behavioristic approaches define morality as a matter of matching an individual's behavior with the standards of a group or with the demands of an authority. Many psychologists accept this definition of morality: "by moral values we mean those evaluations of action as right or wrong held by a majority of members of the individual's group." But philosophers have long noted the deficiency of making conformity the essence of morality. For one, it fails to distinguish between types of nonconformists, thus putting Thomas More and Jack-the-Ripper together into the class of old English nonconformists. Another deficiency is that conformists such as Sheriff Bull Connor of Alabama and Nazi S.S. troopers are classified on the moral side, rather than their victim nonconformists.

The romantic humanists, such as A. S. Neill and Carl Rogers, turn the psychoanalytic and behavioristic ideas about morality completely around. They say children do not learn to be good, children are good when they are born. It is the "education" and "moral instruction" that is foisted upon children that makes them bad. If the child were left alone to develop naturally, the child wouldn't get so neurotic and messed up as so many children do. If children were allowed to be themselves, they would naturally develop into sociable, altruistic, publicly concerned individuals. Whereas the Freudians and behaviorists say it takes pressure from society to make someone inhibit his naturally selfish impulses, the humanists say pressure from society fouls up and corrupts individuals.

The humanists view the paradoxical effects of education and training in this way: parents and society try to tell a child what he ought to value, ought to feel, ought to be doing with his time. They remove the child from establishing and developing his own basis for evaluation and have the child playing so many faking games that he becomes involved in a phony world, pursuing worthless goals, and out of touch with himself. In this condition he is most grasping and ruthless, insensitive to others as well as himself, and most likely to tolerate cruelties like the Nazi concentration camps, the atrocities of the Vietnam war, etc. If the child were allowed simply to become himself, he would not be so sick and so cruel, for the natural state of human self-actualization is to be moral.

Although I find the "live and let live" sentiment of the humanists appealing, I don't see that it inevitably and automatically follows that being in touch and in tune with my own feelings and establishing my values on the basis of my own experience will make me more moral. I would think that moral dilemmas often involve trying to decide between my own personal fulfillment and that of others. Furthermore, this connection between self-actualization and morality is not established by research. I don't think humanistic psychology has given us a very clear account of how self-actualization need not be egoistic nor does it give an account of the psychological processes by which a person comes to see his self-actualization as involving the actualization of other selves, and how people come to judge just what is the proper mix of self-interest with the interests of others.

In contrast to these other approaches, the cognitive-developmental approach starts off with the question, how do people understand what their responsibilities are to others, and what rights can a person claim from others? For a cognitive developmentalist, the essence of morality is not capitulating totally to the claims that others make on the self (or on the demands that society places on the individual). Nor is the essence of morality a matter of turning inward and getting entirely clear about what the self really wants or what would be self-fulfilling. Rather, the essence of morality is to understand social interactions with others who are also selves such that an equilibrium of serving each other's interests is established. Morality is a matter of establishing a cooperative system with other individuals—and in order to do this, a person must understand a lot about how other people think and make decisions, and also must understand how social cooperative arrangements can be set up. Children are not born with this understanding but must develop concepts about the social world just as the child must develop conceptions about the physical world. The title of one of Kohlberg's articles is "The Child as a World Philosopher" (1968). This expresses the idea that cognitive developmentalists start out by viewing the child as someone trying to make sense out of social experience, trying to understand what the patterns of human interaction are and how he fits into these patterns, how he can use these patterns to further his own interests.

Now it is true that a person's cognitive *understanding* of social interaction is not all there is to the psychology of morality. But the cognitive developmentalist says that the first thing psychologists have to do in investigating moral development is to study how the person perceives social reality—what is it the person sees out there? What is it the person believes is involved in social interaction? After psychologists have a picture of what social reality is for an individual, then we can work on the issue of how a person behaves in response to his reality. (For further discussion of the basic ideas of the cognitive-developmental approach, see the Introduction and other papers by Sprinthall, Selman and Sullivan.)

Methods of Identifying a Person's Developmental Progress

The most fundamental research problem of the cognitive-developmental approach is to have a way of identifying what picture of social reality a particular person has—of identifying what conceptions a person uses in analyzing social problems, and how he arrives at a judgment. Kohlberg in the 1950's approached the problem by asking people to discuss how they would solve a number of hypothetical moral dilemmas. An example of one of the most famous of the dilemmas, that of Heinz and the drug, can be found in the Introduction to this book, pp. 1-12. In view of the importance of the dilemma to the pages that follow, readers are urged to recall or reread the details of the Heinz story.

Kohlberg would interview a person, asking for judgments about such moral dilemmas and a person's reasons for making a decision one way or another. Upon examining the discussions of people of these dilemmas, Kohlberg found recurrent themes and common characteristics in what people said. These themes and characteristics seemed to cluster into six basic types, and there are the six moral stages of Kohlberg's scheme (see Introduction, pp. 1-12.) Over the years Kohlberg and his associates have developed a scoring guide for analyzing a person's discussion of moral dilemmas. The process involves matching what a person says with a description of stage characteristics in the scoring guide, and thereby arriving at a stage score for a subject. This method of identifying a person's stage of moral judgment has good independent agreement among trained judges. However, the method is very complicated and requires long training, and is impractical for many research and most educational uses.

Recently, at the University of Minnesota another method of identifying a person's developmental progress has been devised that is derived from Kohlberg's basic theory of six stages but which uses a multiple-choice format and therefore can be objectively and easily scored. The new method, called the Defining Issues Test (or DIT), compares very favorably with Kohlberg's test (Rest, 1975a, 1976) in terms of reliability and validity and correlates .68 with Kohlberg's test, although the two tests are not assessing exactly the same facets of moral judgment.

The DIT is based on the assumption that people at different developmental stages perceive moral dilemmas differently. Therefore if you present people with different statements about the crucial issue of a dilemma, people at different developmental stages will choose different statements as representing the most important issue. E.g., in connection with the "Heinz" story, (pp. 108-9) twelve statements are presented to a subject; the subject is asked first to rate each statement in terms of its importance in making a decision about what Heinz ought to do (on the left-hand side of the page), and secondly, a subject is asked to rank the top four choices in terms of importance (on the bottom of the page).

As the summary below illustrates, it turns out that people rate and rank these twelve statements very differently. Table 1 gives the percent of subjects at different points in schooling who endorse item #3 (a Stage Two item) as a top first or second choice, and also item #8 (a Stage Six item).

As can be seen, the older, more sophisticated groups tend not to choose the Stage Two item, whereas they do tend increasingly to choose the Stage Six item. Six stories are used altogether in the DIT, each with twelve items, thus containing 72 items in all. The way a subject chooses the most important issues in these stories

HEINZ STORY

On the left-hand side of the page check one of the spaces by each question to indicate its importance.

GREAT importance *MUCH importance* *SOME importance* *LITTLE importance* *NO importance*

_____ 1. Whether a community's laws are going to be upheld.

_____ 2. Isn't it only natural for a loving husband to care so much for his wife that he'd steal?

_____ 3. Is Heinz willing to risk getting shot as a burglar or going to jail for the chance that stealing the drug might help?

_____ 4. Whether Heinz is a professional wrestler, or has considerable influence with professional wrestlers.

_____ 5. Whether Heinz is stealing for himself or doing this solely to help someone else.

_____ 6. Whether the druggist's rights to his invention have to be respected.

_____ 7. Whether the essence of living is more encompassing than the termination of dying, socially and individually.

_____ 8. What values are going to be the basis for governing how people act toward each other.

GREAT importance _MUCH importance_ _SOME importance_ _LITTLE importance_ _NO importance_

___ ___ ___ ___ ___ 9. Whether the druggist is going to be allowed to hide behind a worthless law which only protects the rich anyhow.

___ ___ ___ ___ ___ 10. Whether the law in this case is getting in the way of the most basic claim of any member of society.

___ ___ ___ ___ ___ 11. Whether the druggist deserves to be robbed for being so greedy and cruel.

___ ___ ___ ___ ___ 12. Would stealing in such a case bring about more total good for the whole society or not.

From the list above, select the four most important:

Most important ___

Second most important ___

Third most important ___

Fourth most important ___

Table 1

Percentage of Endorsement of Different Academic Groups

on Two Items

	Junior High	Senior High	College	Seminarians	Ph.D.
Stage two item (#3)	48	30	10	8	0
Stage six item (#8)	10	25	70	75	88

yields stage scores (for Stages Two, Three, Four, Five-A, Five-B, and Six).[2] The most useful single index we have found so far in research with the DIT is the combined weighted ranks of items keyed as Stages Five and Six—this is called the "P score" since it represents "Principled Morality" or Level III in Kohlberg's scheme (see Rest et al., 1974). The P is interpreted as the relative importance a subject gives to Principled moral considerations in making moral decisions.

Although an objective, multiple-choice test is obviously easier for the researcher to score, it may appear also easier for the subject to fake or distort. Several features of the DIT help detect and/or prevent this. First of all, several items were written into the DIT to detect the tendency to endorse complex, high-sounding wording rather than choosing items for meaning. Item #7 for instance has a complicated, pretentious ring to it, and it is not keyed to any stage, but is meaningless. If subjects choose too many of the meaningless items, the questionnaire is discarded because it appears that the subject is not paying sufficient attention to the meaning of the statements. These items are included in the DIT not so much to "catch" a subject as to correct a test-taking set to choose items on the basis of their apparent complexity. In fact the instructions to subjects taking the DIT clearly warn beforehand that there are high-sounding but meaningless items in the test and that the subject should choose only items that are meaningful and important. Another feature of the DIT enables the identification of subjects who randomly check off their answers, or who have such a misunderstanding of the test instructions that their questionnaires are useless—the Consistency Check. If the researcher compares the ratings (the checks in the left-hand column) with a subject's rankings (the list at the bottom of the page), there should be some consistency if the subject is cooperating and understands the task. Random checkers show gross inconsistencies, and their questionnaires can be eliminated from data analysis.

McGeorge (1975) conducted an interesting study looking into how subjects could fake high scores on the DIT. He asked subjects to take the DIT twice: on one of the times, subjects took the test under normal conditions. For the other time, some subjects were asked to fake high, and some subjects were asked to fake low. McGeorge found that subjects could fake low but not high on the DIT.

2. No single item or story is a reliable guide to a person's developmental progress in moral judgment, but rather the pattern of responses over 6 stories or 72 items is used.

In short, the DIT has shown itself to be a very useful method for identifying a person's developmental progress in moral judgment.[3]

Major Research Findings and Their Implications for Education

Given that the researcher has a method for identifying types of moral orientation, then what hypotheses about moral judgment does the cognitive-developmental theory lead us to make, and what is the empirical evidence in testing these ideas? In the next sections I will present the major findings of this research,[4] and their implications for educational practice.

1. Age-Trend Studies.

One major hypothesis of cognitive-developmental theory is that people change over time in their moral orientation. One's type of orientation is not a permanent trait, or fixed at an early age, but undergoes successive transformations in a definite, prescribed order. Therefore one would expect that older subjects in general should show a more advanced stage of moral judgment than younger subjects. There should be developmental age trends in the usage of moral stages.

In his 1958 thesis, Kohlberg showed stage differences in 10-, 13- and 16-year-old boys—that is, the older the boy, the greater use of higher stages. Kohlberg has reported similar age trends in other cultures, notably Turkey, Formosa and Mexico (Kohlberg, 1969).

Using the DIT, we have found highly significant differences between junior highs, senior highs, college students, seminarians and Ph.D. students in moral philosophy and political science (Rest, et al., 1974). We could summarize about 20 studies in this way: the P score for junior highs tends to be in the 20's to the low 30's; for senior highs it tends to be in the mid to high 30's; for college freshmen and sophomores, in the 40's; for college juniors and seniors, in the 50's; for graduate students in general, in the 60's; for graduate students specializing in moral philosophy and political science, in the 70's. Another way to portray the age trends of the DIT's P score is to report the percentage of subjects in each of these academ-

---

3. It should be mentioned that the DIT seems to work best with high-school and older subjects, although some researchers report finding it useful for subjects as young as the 6th grade.

4. This overview of the research is very selective and does not mention many interesting studies that have been done. I have chosen studies which bear on major issues of educational significance and in which there is accumulation of results from a series of studies.

ic groups who regard principled moral consideration as preponderantly important (have P scores of 50 or above): from junior highs to Ph.D.'s in moral philosophy, the percentages are 2.5%, 7.5%, 45%, 60%, and 93%, respectively. The P score of adults (nonstudents) tends to be roughly equivalent to the student group representing their highest extent of education—that is, adults who went no further in their education than high school tend to have scores like high-school students, adults who went no further than college tend to have scores like college students.

The studies cited so far are all *cross-sectional* studies in that they make comparisons between different subjects at different ages. A more powerful kind of study but more difficult to do is a *longitudinal* study which compares scores from the same subjects at different times—that is, a group of subjects are followed up over the years and retested at intervals. Kohlberg and Kramer (1969) and Holstein (1973) used Kohlberg's test, and (combining the results of both studies) showed that of 95 subjects tested at three-year intervals, 47 had moved upward in developmental stage, 38 stayed the same, and 10 went down. In a more recent reanalysis of the Kohlberg and Kramer data using a revised scoring system, Kohlberg reports (1975) that of 15 subjects studies at 3-year intervals over 15 years, all subjects show perfect upward and irreversible movement. This later study is somewhat tentative, however, because the data were not scored blind and because the scoring system was derived from the same data to which it was applied.

A recent DIT longitudinal study (Rest, 1975b) of 88 subjects followed up after two years showed highly significant gains in the P score. Junior high subjects were still showing some shifts from preconventional morality to conventional morality, while senior highs were mostly showing shifts out of conventional morality into principled morality. High-school graduates who went on to college showed twice the gains of high-school graduates who did not go to college, even though both groups were indistinguishable in high school.

In summary, there is strong evidence that moral judgment changes with age. One's moral orientation is not simply a matter of what subculture one is born into, where people simply assimilate the values they are exposed to. Rather, the fundamental conceptual structure of a person's thinking develops in a describable and orderly way.

What implication does this have for educational practice? Since moral judgment is developmental, it means that the aims of an educational program can be set forth in a developmental framework. Namely, the goal of moral education is to foster and facilitate the natural, developmental processes—this may mean facilitating movement to the next stage, or preventing fixation from taking place, or extending already acquired concepts across new content.

2. *Correlations of moral judgment with other cognitive variables: I.Q., Comprehension, Formal Operations, Role-Taking.*

Even if we accept the notion that moral judgment does change with age, what evidence is there that upward movement represents greater understanding, better problem solving, or more adequate conceptualization? How do we know that moral-judgment development is *cognitive* development?

The earliest research on this question presented correlations of I.Q. measures with moral judgment (Kohlberg, 1958, 1964). It was argued that significant correlations with I.Q. indicated that moral judgment development was largely cognitive rather than a matter of acquiring mindless habits or conditionings or identifying with parents, or getting in touch with inner feelings, or increasing one's capacity for guilt.

A more direct test of the relation between moral judgment (as assessed by Kohlberg's method) and the cognitive comprehension of stage characteristics comes from a series of studies (Rest, Turiel, Kohlberg, 1969; Rest, 1973) in which subjects were asked to paraphrase statements written to exemplify various stages of moral judgment. A subject was presented with a card on which an argument at some stage was written; the subject was asked to discuss the statement and to put it in his own words; then a judge examined the discussion to determine if the subject gave evidence of understanding the stage distinctive reasoning of the statement—if so, the subject was credited with comprehending that stage characteristic. The whole procedure involved presenting subjects 60 cards, each exemplifying characteristics from various stages.

The major findings from these studies are: (a) Comprehension of stage characteristics is cumulative—that is, if a subject comprehends Stage Four statements, he also tends to comprehend Stage Three, Two and One statements. (b) Subjects comprehend statements at stages up to the stage at which they produce arguments themselves; then comprehension tends to drop off sharply at stages above their own. (c) When subjects were asked to express a preference for the statements, they tended to prefer statements at least as high as their own stage, and often higher.

There are several important implications from the comprehension and preference studies. One is the demonstration that the moral judgments that one produces are highly related to one's capacity to comprehend that level of concepts. In other words, the developmental order of the stages is also an order of increasing cognitive complexity, and that as people *can comprehend* certain concepts, they tend to *use* them. Another implication is the demonstration that comprehension is poor of statements two or three stages above one's production—comprehension places an upper limit on what one can assimilate. Therefore educational programs that pitch a program at too high a conceptual level cannot be assimilated. At the same time, another implication is that subjects reject thinking which is developmentally less advanced than they are. Therefore educational programs that pitch a program at too low a level will be rejected.

Research with the DIT has also confirmed the close relationship between comprehension and moral judgment (Rest, et al., 1974; Coder, 1975).

Studies relating Piagetian Formal Operations to moral judgment, or role-taking to moral judgment, attempt to clarify the basic cognitive components involved in operating at various stages of moral judgment. Studies by Keasey and Keasey (1974), Kuhn et al. (1973), and others show relationship of Formal Operations with moral judgment; a study by Cauble (1974) shows the relationship with the DIT. Studies by Selman (1971, 1973) and others show relationships of role-taking with moral judgment—since this line of research is more fully discussed in Selman's paper, I won't go into this here except to say that this work suggests some basic operations and cognitive capacities a child must master in order to attain higher levels of moral judgment. If an educator is aware of the components, teaching strategies can emphasize preparation of parts that lead to mastery of larger systems of thinking.

3. *Correlations of moral judgment with noncognitive variables: values, guilt, cheating, sharing, moral reputation, and delinquency.*

Even accepting that moral judgment is both *cognitive* and *developmental*, we still might say, so what? What difference does it make to have people with highly developed moral judgment? Is moral judgment anything more than an intellectual skill or sophistry?

The cognitive-developmental view is that one's cognitions affect how one perceives reality, how one is aware of options and of possibilities for organizing one's actions, and how aware one is of the implications of those actions. Accordingly it is expected that cognitive development will have a large interplay with one's affect and behavior—and therefore moral judgment should relate to non-cognitive variables.

The most consistently powerful noncognitive correlate of moral judgment has been a measure of one's value position on a number of controversial, public-policy issues. The P score of the DIT has been shown to relate highly with a person's stance on punishment of criminals, civil disobedience, free speech, inner-city riots, wire-tapping, etc. (Rest, et al., 1974). Therefore moral judgment is not a value-neutral, only-cerebral variable, but has a lot to do with how one perceives the world and one's value positions in it.

Kohlberg (1969) has reviewed several studies relating his test to cheating in a classroom, to helping a person in distress, to political participation, to resistance to a cruel authority, to guilt for wrong-doing, and to reputational ratings of a person's fair-mindedness and considerateness. These types of relationships are usually statistical-ly significant, but the power of the relationships are usually mod-est, indicating that other factors besides moral judgment (at least as measured in these studies) are probably involved.

Recently there has been a good deal of interest in the relation of moral judgment to delinquency and criminality. McColgan (1975) has reviewed eight of the studies using Kohlberg's test that reports significant differences in moral judgment between delin-quents and nondelinquents. Finding that delinquents are retarded in moral judgment has led to the hope that raising delinquents' moral judgment would remediate their delinquency—the rationale being that if a distinguishing characteristic of delinquents was removed (low moral judgment), then these subjects would no longer be de-linquent. Some rather extensive intervention programs have been developed on this rationale (Hickey, 1972; Kohlberg and Hickey, 1972; Kohlberg and Freundlich, 1973). McColgan (1975) himself did a very precise study in which predelinquents were carefully matched with nondelinquent controls on IQ, age, sex, race, socio-economic status (S.E.S.), testing and scoring conditions, neigh-borhood and school. Previous studies have not employed such rig-orous control of other factors when comparing delinquents and nondelinquents on moral judgment. McColgan found that Kohl-berg's test did not discriminate these groups; however, the DIT's P score did. Since McColgan's study is a more adequate study than the previous studies, it raises the question of whether the difference between delinquent and nondelinquent samples on Kohlberg's test are really due to some other factor, such as I.Q. or S.E.S. At any event, the causation and remediation of delinquency is certainly a multifaceted and complicated problem, and seems to be related to (if not caused by) moral-judgment development.

The research discussed so far under the headings of age trends, cognitive and noncognitive correlates of moral judgment is primarily addressed to clarifying the nature of moral judgment, to demonstrating basic tenets of cognitive-developmental theory, and exploring the place that moral judgment has in total personality organization. I would capsulize this research by saying that moral judgment is one of the best established variables in social-personality research, it has great theoretical richness, is related to real-life behavior, and has potential for practical and educational applications. A great deal of work has been done in formulating the ideas of cognitive-developmental theory into precise and testable propositions, and much work has been done in putting these ideas to empirical test.

4. Experimentally and Educationally Induced Change.

Can moral judgment be affected by experimental or educational intervention? The answer to this question is closest to home for the educator, because if no one can do anything to change moral judgment, then it is hardly worth developing programs for that goal.

The early work of Turiel (1966) seemed to give an unambiguous "Yes!" to the question of whether change was possible, and many subsequent researchers and educators cite this study as giving the green light to intervention efforts. The conclusion that many drew from this study was that change was possible by modeling for a subject the stage of thinking directly above his own ("+1 modeling"). In retrospect, I think this study posed intriguing questions, explored them in an ingenious way, and offered many provocative ideas—however, the results of the study are really very ambiguous (see Hoffman, 1970; Kurtines and Grief, 1974). Subsequent studies have contradicted the conclusions (see Turiel, 1973), and many researchers now (including Turiel) have second thoughts about the meaningfulness of attempting to change a subject's moral judgment stage by a half-hour intervention. Some researchers continue to do short-term (an hour or less) intervention studies but the results are confusing and inconsistent. Is it reasonable to expect that mild interventions that last an hour or less can alter the fundamental way a person thinks about moral issues, especially considering that it takes over five years on the average for one of Kohlberg's longitudinal subjects to move one stage?

The first longer intervention programs (9 to 12 weeks) were conducted by Blatt (1969; Blatt and Kohlberg, 1973). Blatt's first study was with 30 children in a Jewish Sunday School, ages 11-12 years, meeting for an hour a week over 12 weeks to discuss controversial moral problems based on biblical situations. Using Kohlberg's test, 9 out of 11 subjects tested showed upward movement between the pre-test and the post-test (a gain of 66 points on the Moral Maturity Scale, or the equivalent of 2/3 of a stage) in contrast to several comparison groups drawn from other studies which did not show significant gains. Furthermore, on a follow-up testing one year later, Blatt's discussion group had essentially stabilized their gains made during the intervention.

Blatt's second study was an expansion and replication of his first. Variations explored in this study included two age levels (6th grade and 10th grade), two socioeconomic groups (lower middle class and lower class) associated with race (white and black), and different "curriculum" (a teacher-led discussion group versus a peer-led discussion group). In addition, the study contained a comparison group from the same schools and much more adequate sample sizes (about 46 subjects in the teacher-led treatment, 41 in the peer-led treatment, and 40 in the control condition). Blatt met with subjects in the teacher-led condition in groups of 8 to 12 subjects, over 18 sessions held twice a week for 45 minutes each. Again, the format was the discussion of moral dilemmas (see Rest, 1974b, for critique of programs). The teacher-led discussion group showed average increases in Kohlberg's Moral Maturity Score of 34 points (1/3 of a stage) while the other groups showed a 7-point gain and a 15-point drop, respectively. In follow-up one year later the teacher-led group maintained its lead over the other groups.

Blatt's findings have created a great deal of enthusiasm in educational-researcher circles because they indicate that educational intervention programs can be devised to produce significant shifts in an important variable, moral judgment. A large number of educational programs have followed Blatt's lead, although not always replicating Blatt's findings. See, for example, Kavanagh's study reported in this book. Hickey (1972) conducted a discussion group with 20 prison inmates, 19 years old, and found an increase of 17 Moral Maturity Score points over a period of 12 weeks. Sullivan and Beck (Sullivan, 1975) conducted a moral-education program somewhat differently than Blatt's, but found that in these programs (one in elementary school, two in secondary school), none of the experimental groups showed significant increases from pre- to post-testings; however, two experimental groups had advanced beyond the comparison groups at a year later follow-up. Schaffer (1974) attempted to replicate Blatt's study but found a nonsignificant gain (8 points on Kohlberg's Moral Maturity Scale). Sprinthall (see his paper in this book) reports results on five Deliberate Psychological Education programs which were not specifically focused on moral education but used moral-judgment development as one measure of more general psychological development: a study of college juniors and seniors (Hurt, 1974) showed significant increases on the DIT, three other studies with high-school subjects approached significance (showing 34-, 31- and 32- point gains in Kohlberg's Moral Maturity Score), and one other of college students showed no gain on Kohlberg's test. Two studies using the DIT with older groups found significant changes. The first study by Panowitsch (1975) compared college students in an ethics course with students in logic, art, and world religion courses, and found that the ethics students gained significantly on the DIT but the students in the other courses did not. In the second study, Coder (1975) conducted a moral education class with adults, and found that adults gained significantly on the DIT while adults in the other religious education classes did not.

What can be concluded from all these studies? Certainly there are many more studies that have not been reported here and that I do not know about, many of these never getting into the literature because they did not obtain significant gains in their experimental groups. Of the 14 studies cited above, Blatt's first study was the most dramatic in terms of amount of change, but this study is hardly representative of them all, and it is a little suspicious because of lack of proper controls and small sample size. I think that about all one can safely say is that some educational interventions seem to promote significant moral-judgment development and others don't. Beyond that statement, things get muddy. It is still important, however, that some studies have found significant results, for this promises that the whole educational enterprise in moral-judgment development can be effective, if only we single out the crucial ingredients.

What might some of the ingredients of effective programs be? Blatt's second study suggests that having an effective group leader is important. Panowitsch's study found that the below-20-years group was much more responsive than the beyond-20-year-old group. Schaffer's study indicates that "+1 modeling" cannot be identified in an ongoing classroom discussion, and that "+1 modeling" may be more rhetoric than an actual condition that can be supplied in an educational program or that is crucial to an educational program (see Rest, 1974b). A study by Holstein (1972) suggests that engaging children and youth in active controversy and discussion—giving them practice in problem solving—may be the essential ingredient in facilitating moral judgment development. Formal education seems to be powerfully associated with moral-judgment development (Rest, 1975b).

Currently there is much effort in devising richer curriculum materials and in exploring various educational settings and formats. While these efforts as yet have not fully demonstrated their effectiveness and usefulness, the enterprise is grounded on a psychological variable that has demonstrated empirical reality, and preliminary results of program evaluations indicate that educational intervention in this area is possible. Furthermore, by being grounded in a research base, various ideas and innovations can be tested—they need not depend solely on their surface plausibility or the salesmanship of their proponents. Hopefully new program ideas will keep apace with ideas about how to gather information on program effectiveness, such that successive rounds of decisions will be self-correcting and make optimal use of intuition as well as empirical data.

Reaction to Rest: AMBIGUITIES IN THE RESEARCH BASE OF THE COGNITIVE-DEVELOPMENTAL APPROACH TO MORAL EDUCATION *by* Robert Hogan and Wayne Bohannon

James Rest's review of the empirical support for a cognitive-developmental approach to moral education raises a number of debatable issues, making it hard to respond to his paper in an organized fashion. There are, in addition, some important related issues that Rest does not discuss—e.g., the evidentiary base for the central assumptions of a cognitive-developmental approach to education (i.e., whether development is stepwise or continuous; the meaning and existence of formal operations; the definition of the term "moral education"; and the merits of a constructivist versus a tutorial approach to education). Looking at the paper he actually has written, there are some positive and negative aspects of his review, as well as some important meta-issues that warrant discussion. We will begin with some critical remarks, raise two meta-issues, and then describe what seem to be the most important contributions of the paper.

At the outset of his discussion, Rest presents a selected overview of alternative theories of moral development. Here he misrepresents certain aspects of these alternative perspectives. For example, the psychoanalytic approach does not claim, as Rest suggests, that obedience is rewarded with a feeling of self-esteem (there is no self-concept in psychoanalysis); the social learning theory analysis of self-control is much more sophisticated than simply "getting into such a rut of doing good that you can't break the habit"; and behaviorists do not say that "it takes pressure from society to make someone inhibit his naturally selfish impulses"; they make no motivational assumptions at all. In addition to these misrepresentations, there are several equally important views that he fails to mention; e.g., those of Mead, Durkheim, Hoffman, and Rawls.

Secondly, the age-trend studies that Rest reviews are subject to criticism or alternative interpretation. For example, Kohlberg's (1968) cross-cultural data seem to exist only in the form of a single uninterpretable table in a popular magazine. Nor do the studies Rest cites strongly support the notion of progression through developmental stages, i.e., that there is structural wholeness, necessary sequence, and hierarchy to cognitive development. And the age-trend studies of his own, showing, for example, that graduate students in philosophy have higher "P" scores than an unselected sample of junior high-school students, are obviously confounded with I.Q., social class, and education.

Finally, there is the problem of the nontest meaning of scores on Rest's DIT and Kohlberg's moral-judgment scale. The research results to date are compatible with the interpretation that these two procedures assess a person's level of moral education and the sophistication and adequacy of his thinking (i.e., his ability to produce or endorse philosophically sophisticated analyses of moral dilemmas) but not his stage of moral development as reflected in actual behavior; these results further suggest that training programs improve a person's moral education but have as yet no demonstrated effect on overt moral conduct. This interpretation is in accordance with Rest's findings that people with higher I.Q.'s and more education get higher scores on the DIT, and people educated in moral philosophy get the highest scores of all. This interpretation is also compatible with the findings from programs designed to induce change in moral judgment—i.e., that practice and feedback

in the analysis of moral dilemmas sometimes produce greater sophistication and adequacy in moral *thought.* With the exception of
the decidedly encouraging study by McColgan (1975), however, the
only important external correlations Rest has established are between moral-judgment scores and two attitude measures. But the
critical question for the cognitive-developmental tradition is, will
people with Stage Five or Six scores act differently in real-world,
moral-choice situations than people with "lower" scores? On this
question the jury is still out, and after 17 years of research.

At the level of meta-issues, one consistent claim of cognitive-
developmental writers is that it is necessary to distinguish between
the structure and the content of moral reasoning, that the same
structure can produce a range of contents, and any single content
can arise from several different structures. The Kohlberg moral-
judgment scale and the DIT are alleged to assess "the basic conceptual frameworks by which a subject analyzes a social-moral problem and judges the proper course of action" (Rest, 1974, b, p. 4-1).
These basic conceptual frameworks are usually defined as structural, perfectly formal concepts representing universal thought forms
that characterize reasoning at various points in human development, regardless of the socio-historical context of the thinker. It
comes then as something of a surprise to discover that structure
and content are confounded in both Kohlberg's and Rest's measures, and this raises a serious question regarding the universality
of the stages they have discovered and endeavor to assess. Two examples will make this plain. In the first case Rest (1974, b) tells us
that principled morality is associated with an anti-law and order,
pro-civil libertarian ("Libertarian Democracy") view on social
issues. Although Jerry Rubin and Hubert Humphrey might be
pleased to know that their personal political attitudes are considered
the most moral humanly possible, others (e.g., anti-authoritarian
conservatives) might regard Rest's finding as an example of the
degree to which his measure reflects the dominant values of the
American Intellectual Establishment of the mid-1970's. A second
example of the parochial (as opposed to universal) values bias informing the cognitive-developmental tradition is the Kohlberg-Rest
claim that a social contract (i.e., Utilitarian) morality represents a
"level 5" morality, whereas "level 6" represents a (Kantian) morality of universal and ideal social forms. There is absolutely no logical,
empirical, or historical evidence to support their claim that an ide-
alistic, universalistic Kantian system of ethics is more moral than a
pragmatic, positivistic Utilitarian system. The Kohlberg-Rest claim

here rests entirely on personal preference that is then asserted as fact (cf. Simpson, 1974).

A second, and more interesting meta-level question regards the relationship of Rest's work to that of Kohlberg. This can be determined by examining what Rest actually does and how this compares with Kohlberg's approach. When this is done many of the foregoing criticisms of Rest's paper lose their force. Specifically, Rest departs from the Kohlberg model in three critical ways. First, in working with the DIT he makes little use of the notion of a stage (indeed, the concept of a stage in cognitive development is problematical in itself); as Rest (1974, b) observes, "I have not found stage-typing useful." Rather he scores his test dichotomously (levels 1-4 versus levels 5-6) and relies almost exclusively on the "P" score derived therefrom. That is, in Rest's model people are classified not in terms of their position along a hypothetical and *discontinuous* stage continuum, but in terms of the relative importance they give to ". . . principled moral considerations in making a decision about moral dilemmas" (Rest, 1974, b, p. 4-3); thus persons are placed along a *continuous* distribution of percentage scores. Rest also departs from Kohlberg in his unwillingness to describe an intuitive, universalistic ethic (Stage Six) as intrinsically more moral than a Utilitarian relativistic ethic (Stage Five). Here then he contradicts the cognitive-developmental assumption of hierarchically upward development. Finally, Rest implicitly assumes that the structure and content of moral thought are confounded. Thus we have a cognitive-developmentalist who doesn't find stage typing useful, who doesn't believe that "higher" levels of thought are necessarily more moral; and who doesn't believe cognitive structures are content free. We applaud Rest's conclusions on these issues but wonder how he is able to remain strictly identified with the cognitive-developmental tradition.

Concerning the strong points of Rest's paper, three warrant particular mention. First, his criticism of the humanistic perspective on moral development is very well taken. The facile Romantic assumption that man is basically good and that children will develop in a spontaneously healthy and moral fashion is empirically unsupported and has pernicious consequences. Without the restraining effects of culture implanted by firm parental control, children turn into unsocialized horrors of no use to themselves or the society they tend to prey upon. Self-actualization depends on prior socialization, otherwise the term self-actualization becomes a rationalization for narcissistic, self-aggrandizing, egoistic conduct (see also, Campbell, 1975; Hogan, 1975).

Second, in the careful development and standardization of the DIT, Rest has produced one of the most interesting and original contributions to the assessment of the psychological substructure of moral conduct in nearly 30 years. He has moved the study of moral judgment away from its reliance on interviews and projective techniques and has begun to develop a firm, reliable psychometric base for its study.

Finally, his review of the implications of existing research for the possibilities of training up moral judgment scores is even-handed and judicious. Any single moral judgment reflects a number of covert influences (education, intelligence, desire to make a good impression, true feelings about the issue, competence). The problem is to determine what features of a moral judgment are reliably associated with what forms of nontest behavior, what the determinants of these features are, and how they may be modified. Thus the relationships between moral education, moral judgment, and moral conduct are exceedingly complex, but in principle amenable to rational and empirical analysis. Although we have a long way to go in terms of understanding how to do moral education, the path if not easy is at least open.

5.
Moral Development in a High School Program*

Harry B. Kavanagh

In the previous chapter, Rest, quoting from Blatt and Kohlberg (1973) pointed out that Blatt's findings created a great deal of enthusiasm in educational-researcher circles because they indicate that moral-education programs can be devised to produce significant change in moral judgment. Rest further pointed out that some studies promote significant results, others do not.

In this chapter, the relative effectiveness of three different approaches in raising the levels of moral judgments of high-school students will be described. The three different approaches were based on cognitive-developmental theory described by Rest in the previous chapter. The three approaches were: 1) A peer-led group, 2) a counselor-led group, 3) a writers' group. There was also a control group.

1. The approach in the peer-led group was based mainly on Piaget's theory where there is an emphasis on the role of peer interaction as distinct from adult interaction in bringing about upward change in moral judgment during the preadolescent and adolescent period. Piaget says, "It is in the clash of wills among equals in the context of mutual respect in the peer group that judgments get changed." This group was exposed to the interaction of peers in a classroom setting after viewing a movie.

2. The approach in the counselor-led group placed emphasis on the role of the adult interaction while at the same time acknowledging the power of children's contact with one another. This approach was supported mainly by Kohlberg's view. He sees the young person's search for values as stimulated by the adult because the adolescent is interested in joining adult society and, therefore, wants to learn the values of that society. Furthermore, it is a search that involves adult values mainly, necessitating contact with adults

*Taken from the author's Ph.D. dissertation at the School of Education, Fordham University.

as well as peers. In this group, adult-guided peer discussion was stressed. The adult was a counselor and he led group discussions following the viewing of a movie which depicted a moral conflict.

3. The approach in the writer's group was the author's preferred technique (a written reflective analysis of the problem). Students were asked to express in writing their innermost thoughts and feelings aroused by the moral conflicts in the movies viewed. The students were asked to express themselves freely, to give insight to self-concerning self, thereby increasing the understanding of their perspectives on life in their own writing.

The author's choice of personal writing as an approach was supported by Allport (1942) who saw personal writing as preoccupied with conflict with what he called "personality-making situations." In personal writing, peaceful experiences tend to be passed over, while turbulent experiences that have wrecked or seriously altered expectations are treated as episodes. In articulating moral-cognitive conflicts in their personal writings, some of our greatest artists clarified issues and dilemmas of a very personal nature, e.g., Augustine in his *Confessions*, Ignatius Loyola in *The Spiritual Exercises*, Pope John XXIII in *The Journal of a Soul*, Anne Frank in *The Diary of Anne Frank*, Thomas Merton in *Conjectures of a Guilty Bystander* and James Joyce in *A Portrait of the Artist as a Young Man*.

Allport explains it this way: "Personality . . . does seem to be a succession of organization—disorganization—reorganization" (p. 78). Allport enumerates as many as 12 possible motives or reasons that may underlie personal writing. Among these motives he considers desire for order, securing personal perspectives, and relief from tension as forces in the making of personality. Personal writing is also seen as ego-involved focusing upon the central organization of personality and involving both the cognitive and affective elements of human behavior (Allport, 1942).

It was hypothesized that writing could facilitate moral development, since moral development is an important aspect of personality development. The students in the writers' group were excluded as far as possible from peer-group influences and counselor influences as these occurred in a classroom setting.

Research Questions

The investigator addressed himself to the following questions:
1. Were younger students more amenable to moral-judgment change than older students on the high school level?

2. Were high-school girls more amenable to moral-judgment change than boys?
3. Did high-school boys and girls with higher I.Q.'s change more in moral judgment than those with lower I.Q.'s?
4. Are peer discussions, counselor-led discussions, or writing experiences more effective than a control condition in increasing moral judgment?
5. Is one of the training experiences more or less effective with seniors versus freshmen or boys versus girls?
6. Did students with high interest and participation gain more in moral judgment than those who were low in interest and participation?

Procedures

The students for this moral-education program were chosen from four different Catholic high schools in the New York suburban area. The students were all Catholic and of white, middle-class background. There were no obvious socioeconomic differences among the students, nor did any of the groups differ from each other on group levels of I.Q. Four different high schools were chosen to protect against contamination of the different approaches to teaching moral education.

Volunteers were requested for the program through a memorandum distributed in all homerooms. From approximately 400 volunteers, 96 students were randomly chosen on the basis of age and sex. The students consisted of 48 freshmen and 48 seniors; 48 were boys and 48 were girls. The students were further divided into the four groups: a peer-led group, a counselor-led group, a writer's group and a control group. In each of the four different groups (which were in four different high schools), there were 12 seniors (6 boys and 6 girls) and 12 freshmen (6 boys and 6 girls).

During the first meeting each student responded in writing to four hypothetical moral dilemmas taken from the Kohlberg Moral Judgment Scale. A program of 18 sessions, with 50 minutes in each session, twice a week, over a period of 9 weeks followed. At the end of 9 weeks, the same dilemmas from the Kohlberg Moral Judgment Scale were given as a post-test.

Three different approaches to moral education were used, but all students received the same stimulus for each session which was a specially selected film, frequently an excerpt from a longer film, that presented a moral conflict. The same films were viewed by all the groups but each group viewed them separately.

The peer-led group was basically a self-directed group. Leadership of the group was rotated according to alphabetical order from session to session except where a student did not wish to be a leader, in which case leadership passed to the next volunteer. The student leader was responsible for presenting to the group the moral conflict and the questions on resolving it. He invited discussion, personal opinion, argument, identification and resolution of the conflict. He encouraged students to introduce their own dilemmas. No adult participated in the process. At the end of every session, each student rated himself or herself on a rating scale on the amount or extent of his or her interest and participation in the topic under discussion.

The counselor-led group was directed by a counselor. He led discussions and kept attention on the moral conflict to be resolved. After presenting the conflict situation, students were asked to respond to questions on resolving it. Students were encouraged to compare their ideas with those of their peers and those of the counselor. The counselor introduced current controversial issues when they seemed related. He attempted to challenge the students' thought on a stage or half-stage above the dominant stage of the group. Sometimes he tried challenging individual students a stage above their thinking. He encouraged students with higher levels of moral judgment to point out inadequacies in thinking at levels below their own. At the end of every session, each student rated himself or herself on interest and participation in the topic discussed.

The writers' group differed from the two described above in that they had no discussions but responded in writing to questions concerning the moral conflict in the films that they viewed. Students varied in the length of their responses, but all spent the same length of time in the classroom regardless of when they finished writing. A teacher was always present during the sessions to give out the materials and collect the completed work.

The control group followed the regular school curriculum. They did not view the films, engage in discussion or writing about moral conflicts. They were given the pre-test and post-test at the same time as the other three groups.

The reader may wish to read a description of one of the films used to generate cognitive conflict among the students. An outline of a film follows. The film was *Trouble with the Law* and it was edited from the motion picture *Pursuit of Happiness*. It has as its theme the laws of society, justice and the individual. A college student involved in an auto accident rejects the standards by which the court finds him guilty, and decides that justice has not been served by the legal process. William Popper is accused of vehicular homicide for the death of an old woman, Mrs. Conroy. He tells the police, his father and his uncle, a lawyer, that it was an accident. It was dark and raining, and the old woman had come out of nowhere, stepping off a curb into the street. He had slammed on the brakes and swerved to avoid hitting her, but it was too late. William's uncle impresses upon him the importance of his actions and appearance subsequent to arraignment and during the trial. He coaches him on how to behave in court, but William's attitude is that his behavior is irrelevant. Hitting Mrs. Conroy was an accident, and he thinks the facts of the accident should be the only basis for judgment, not how he looks or expresses himself in court. William is sentenced to one year at hard labor. The judge's decision is based largely on William's poor driving record—unpaid parking tickets, an expired driver's license, faulty brakes and bald tires. William, on impulse, escapes from the courthouse before he can be escorted to jail.

The discussion questions were:

1. William had 22 traffic violations, bald tires and no insurance, but he chose to report his accident, despite the fact that there were no witnesses. What does that reveal about William's character? Does William believe he is guilty of a crime? Why or why not?

2. Do you judge William to be guilty? Why? Do you judge the legal system as guilty? Why?

3. Have you ever had an accident where you damaged a person or property? What were your feelings afterward? Did you consider what you did to be a crime?

4. It was clearly established that William was from an influential and wealthy family. What effect did this have on William's attitude? Did it affect the way he was treated by the law?

5. How would you define the difference between law and justice? What is "natural law"?

Some freshmen responses were as follows:

1. "I think William was spoiled by his father and was slip-shod in his ways. He was honest, though."

2. "William wasn't guilty, but the legal code was. No one wanted to know the truth, they only wanted to make an example of William to scare other kids."

3. "Yes, I hurt someone. I was fooling around on my bike and

knocked my friend down. I felt bad because I fool around too much."

4. "If William was poor and from a minority group the judge would have been more careful, because he would fear being called a racist pig."

Some senior student responses were as follows:

1. "It may be contradictory but William reported the accident either because he was afraid or he respected the law which says it is wrong to leave the scene of an accident. I think his reason was the second because he seemed to respect major laws but not minor violations like bald tires, no insurance, etc. Since he felt it wasn't a crime, he unfortunately put his faith in the law."

2. "No, he wasn't guilty. The legal system was guilty in giving a wrong judgment. They accused him of being guilty because of other traffic violations and because he was a college kid with long hair and, therefore, irresponsible."

3. "I was in an accident, I damaged someone's cars. Afterwards I was upset, because my father yelled at me, but I was definitely not guilty of any crime."

4. "If he was poor, the sentence would have been stiffer. However, William's attitude was one where he thought he could do anything in society because he would have someone to get him out of his mistakes. A poorer person would have panicked and drove off because they wouldn't have an uncle, a lawyer, to run to. If William was black, he would get five years for killing a white woman."

5. "Laws are rigid rules and don't consider justice for individuals only for the society. Justice is an abstract idea that stands for truth. Natural law is the law of the jungle which we all follow because we want to survive."

6. "Law is a written set of rules one must follow. Justice is whether you are guilty of wrong or not and that's up to the judge and police."

The Results

In an analysis of covariance on post-test moral maturity scores, with I.Q. and pre-test moral maturity scores covaried out, there was a significant difference between the treatment groups and between freshmen and seniors. The graph in Figure 1 shows the gains made by the four different groups of freshmen and the graph in Figure 2 shows the change in moral-maturity scores for the four different groups of seniors. There was no significant difference between boys and girls. The interaction effect of treatment groups and age was not significant.

There was a drop in the level of some moral-maturity scores from pre-test to post-test, especially in the control group. This condition was also found by other investigators (Turiel, 1965; Blatt, 1970). This regression could possibly be a re-test effect because of the use of the same four dilemmas. The repetition of the dilemmas may have caused a lower interest level, resulting in fewer judgments and, therefore, thinner data on which to base scoring decisions.

In an analysis of variance for subjects rating themselves high in interest and participation versus those rating themselves low in interest and participation, there was significance at the .01 level.

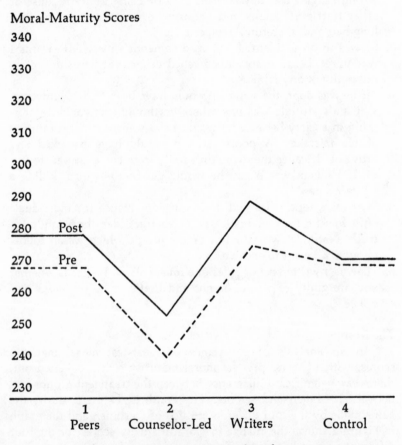

Figure 1. A graph of the relationship of pre-test to post-test for freshmen.

Moral-Maturity Scores

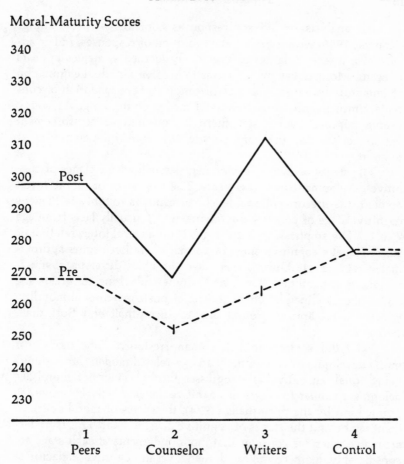

Figure 2. A graph of the relationship of pre-test to
post-test for seniors.

Discussion of Results
1. Were younger students more amenable to moral-judgment
change than older students on the high-school level?

In this study seniors made more significant change than freshmen. Yet the changes made were consistently less than one whole
stage. The change was always within the same stage. For individual
students the change range was from half a stage downward to
something less than one stage upward. Growth among the seniors
was characterized more by a decrease in usage of lower-stage thinking than by a progression to a new and higher stage. The growth
was more horizontal than vertical.

An analysis of subject responses confirms earlier findings (Kramer, 1968) with regard to the evolution of responses. In late adolescence a recapitulation of previously learned strategies appears to occur. Moral development seems to involve a gradual elimination of immature responses and a clarification and consolidation of concepts aimed mainly at conventional modes of thinking. As young people approach adulthood there is considerable reinforcement within society for the conformistic and conventional modes of thought.

The stages of moral development lag behind the stages of cognitive development by a few years. The first stage of moral development, the preconventional level, corresponds roughly to Piaget's cognitive stage of concrete operations, which usually lasts from age 7 to 11. The emphasis in both stages is on a literal interpretation of rules. Piaget's cognitive stage of formal operation begins approximately at age 11. During this stage the child develops abstract-reasoning capabilities that eventually enable him to grasp the higher moral principles characteristic of postconventional morality, which should appear around age 16 (Sprinthall and Sprinthall, 1974).

Why did seniors do better than freshmen? The model for moral development is essentially an age-related model. Other things being equal, an individual progresses through stages of moral development similar to stages of cognitive development. However, as pointed out by the Sprinthalls (1974), the stages of moral development lag behind the stages of cognitive development. This is understandable when we consider that moral judgments at each stage are considerably more complicated than overall cognitive capacity at each stage. For example, it is one thing to be able to recognize and understand abstract thought during adolescence but it is more difficult to take an abstract concept like the Golden Rule and apply it to a difficult human dilemma, such as that represented in the film *Trouble with the Law*.

Most seniors in high school have passed through Piaget's four stages of cognitive development, i.e., they are able to use some formal operations (abstract thinking) but few of them ever reach principled moral thinking (Stages Five and Six) according to Kohlberg's stage theory. No subjects reached the level of principled moral thinking (Stages Five and Six) in this study. Though most seniors are capable of abstract thinking on leaving high school, many do not even reach the third or fourth stage in moral development (Sprinthall and Sprinthall, 1974). So the question is: can we educate students during the elementary and high-school years so they can reach higher levels of moral maturity than is now the case? The findings in this study point toward some hopeful possibilities.

2. Were high school girls more amenable to moral-judgment change than boys?

The findings from this study do not indicate any difference in moral-judgment change between girls and boys. However, in view of the obvious sex-role differences of females and males and the different experiences to which each is exposed, some discrepancy would be expected between the sexes in their rate of moral development, but this discrepancy would emerge at a later age when roles and occupations become more diversified. The present finding that there is no significant difference in moral-judgment change between girls and boys at the high school level is in agreement with a previous finding by Holstein (1969).

3. Did high school students with higher I.Q. change more in moral judgment than those with lower I.Q.?

Although the exact nature of the relationship between cognitive and moral development is not known and although a time lag may intervene between them, the theoretical framework of moral-judgment change indicates that there is a relationship between the cognitive and moral dimensions of development. In view of the above it appeared important to see if a relationship did exist between measured intelligence and moral-judgment change.

There was no significant difference in moral-judgment change when the three I.Q. groups (upper, middle and low) were compared. According to previous investigations by Kohlberg (1966) and Holstein (1960), categories of I.Q. above 100 do not differentiate stages of moral judgment. However, it should be pointed out that measured intelligence, using the traditional forms, in this case Otis-Lennon, cannot be regarded as precise indicators of intelligence as defined by Piaget and Kohlberg. Especially with regard to the student's conception of justice, measures other than the traditional I.Q. would appear to measure more adequately what Piaget understood by intellectual development.

4. Is one of the treatments more or less effective with seniors versus freshmen or boys versus girls?

The three different approaches were not more or less effective with any special group: seniors, freshmen, boys or girls. Since the interaction effects of treatments, age and sex were not significant, it follows that the treatments that were effective were so regardless of age or sex. In view of this finding, attention must focus upon the two approaches that were significant, which will be discussed in response to the next question.

5. Are peer-led discussions, counselor-led discussions, or writing experiences more effective than a control condition in increasing moral judgment?

Peer discussions and writing experiences were more effective than counselor-led discussions or control group in this research program. The peer discussion treatment was supported by the theory of Piaget (1932) who sees the clash of wills among equals in day-to-day exchanges as the chief catalyst for growth.

6. Why did the peer group do better in moral judgment change than the counselor-directed group?

The theory in support of the peer groups was taken from Piaget. For Piaget, cognitive development, in which moral development is contained, involves presenting the students with situations in which they experiment; that is, they manipulate symbols, pose questions, and seek their own answers, reconciling what they find at one time with what they find at another, and comparing findings with peers (Sullivan, 1967). Piaget plays down the teacher- or counselor-directed interaction in the direct verbal sense. These prescriptions stem from Piaget's notion on how stage transition takes place. Specifically, the mechanisms for transition from concrete to more abstract stages of development or from conventional to post-conventional moral development occur as a result of maturation, interaction with the social environment, interaction with the physical environment, and finally equilibration or self-regulation. It appears that equilibration or self-regulation subsumes the other three mechanisms of transition. Hence, for human development, the importance of moral-cognitive conflict is evident. Almy, Chittender, and Miller (1966) note that the concept of equilibration or self-regulation means that students should be allowed a maxium of activity of their own, and should be directed by materials that permit their activities to be cognitively useful. It is noted that students have real understanding only when they invent the structures themselves through their own activities rather than have them imposed by others.

Piaget's equilibration or self-regulation is not only directed toward the physical environment, the model is also seen in social interchange, especially in the clash of wills among equals, namely in the peer group. Peer-group interaction is an essential factor in cognitive and moral development, since it is a factor in the students' move from what Piaget calls "egocentric thought" (Stages One and Two) to more "sociocentric" (Stages Three and Four) types of thinking. In his explorations into the moral judgments of students, Piaget notes that peer-group solidarity and mutual respect among equals leads to the transition from what he calls "heteronomous morality" or morality based on consequences and external orientation, to more "autonomous morality" where intentions are considered.

7. Why did the writers do better in moral judgment change than the peer group or the counselor-directed group?

Although the writers did not formally discuss moral-conflict situations in the classroom, there is no guarantee that informal discussion did not occur at other times. In view of the fact that a warning to a particular group of subjects could set off an additional reaction not shared by all groups, it was decided that no stipulation concerning discussion outside the classroom would be given. Therefore it is possible that informal-peer interaction outside the classroom could have influenced the writer group.

It is also possible that the act of writing calls into play a discipline not required in group verbalization or group responding. In other words, it is quite possible that writing causes a cognitive organization or reorganization that would not occur in the case of vocalization. When one writes the intent is not only to understand but also to synthesize and communicate as effectively as possible the critical aspects of the message. As can be seen when verbal communication is compared with written communication, there is a conciseness and depth in the written word that is often lacking in the spoken word.

It must also be pointed out that the measure which is used in this study presupposes adequate writing skills. This would mean that the literacy of subjects and their ability to express themselves in writing could bias their scores. The writing group did gain considerable practice in writing about moral dilemmas and the gains from practice could have contributed to their significantly greater change.

Recommendations

Historically, a conclusion had existed that morality was outside the field of scientific investigation. The studies of Hartshorne and

May in the 1920's and 1930's appeared to confirm this belief. In recent times, however, mainly because of the effort of Piaget and Kohlberg, certain aspects of morality have been researched and there are indications that the techniques now being used are promising.

Thus a beginning has already been made in the scientific and systematic study of natural morality. The present study has used the theoretical framework that presently exists. However, no complete formulation in which to anchor a study of moral development does now exist. The magnificent contributions of Piaget and Kohlberg represent only one segment of a possible comprehensive theory of moral judgment.

The existing framework relies heavily on cognitive-development theory which by virtue of its history and evolution emphasizes the intellectual aspect to the exclusion of other aspects. What is called for is a theory that would embrace not only the intellectual or cognitive aspect, but also the affective and the spiritual working together with the genetic and maturational. In this way the totality of influences on moral development could be taken into consideration.

The present system reflects knowledge and judgment rather than behavior. In other words, a comprehensive theory of moral behavior is lacking. Since the time of Socrates it has been abundantly evident that the man who knows about virtue is potentially virtuous but does not necessarily act virtuously. It is also obvious that people of the highest intellectual caliber can be and sometimes are immoral. True moral development involves all human powers and behaviors, not just a judgment system. In view of the above, the Kohlberg system would be more correctly labeled moral judgment rather than moral development.

Similarly the present formulation of stages in moral development needs to be expanded in line with a more comprehensive theory. Rest (1974) expressed it this way:

> By knowing a person's moral judgment stage do we really know his moral values? . . . The scoring characteristics of moral judgment are very basic, highly abstract aspects of thinking . . . Perhaps if we knew both the basic structure (i.e., stage of moral judgment) and the more concrete beliefs, images and constructs of a person's moral thinking then more meaningful relationships with behavior could be established (p. 73).

In a stage sequence of this kind, the interaction of basic structure with cultural and personal values could be given the required emphasis.

There is a general consensus in all presently existing theories of learning that the earliest stage of human development is also the most critical for later adjustment and indeed adjustment throughout life. This idea is fundamental to the theories of Freud, Adler, Erikson and Piaget. Perhaps the most fruitful and yet untried approach to developing morality would be a strategic use of the best known child-rearing techniques. For example, a judicious use of indirect or psychological forms of discipline as distinct from direct or physically punitive forms of discipline could be expected to induce more reasoning at earlier stages, stronger interpersonal relationships and more independence in decision-making (Bronfenbrenner, 1972). In a similar vein there is considerable evidence pointing to the unique value of discovery as a mode of learning, especially in the early years, and the possible transfer of this learning to a variety of situations, including moral decision-making. Piaget (1932) explained it simply: "In the moral as in the intellectual domain we really possess only what we have conquered by ourselves" (p. 382).

In the 9-week period of treatment described in this paper, a few students gained a stage in the Kohlberg Scale, some gained a half-stage, some showed no gain and some regressed. We need the factors that influence the manner in which transition is made between stages for different types of students. An in-depth longitudinal study of these students might help clarify stage transition. When the manner of transition from one stage to another is understood for different students, then the optimum conditions under which change takes place needs to be translated into curricula.

Interest and participation was a strong variable in this study. Different movies and different dilemmas in movies aroused varying degrees of interest. Even when students had the same conceptual understanding of a moral conflict, they seemed to differ in the degree of intensity they felt about it.

Conclusions

The goal of moral education ought to be the stimulation of development, step by step, through the stages. According to Kohlberg, very few people reach the highest stage. The educator should be interested in faciliting moral development as far as possible, even with people who may never reach the higher stages. The educator should strive to facilitate "horizontal" development as well as "vertical," that is, not only to push for new structures but to extend the full use of an acquired structure to new domains of activity and problem areas.

The teacher should "meet the student at the student's level of development" and this axiom can be given precise and operational meaning if the course of development is defined and the student's level can be assessed. Understanding the course of development enables a teacher to optimize the match between student and curriculum and also serves as a guide for sequencing curriculum. Lockwood (1974) has questioned whether the new social studies and the structure-of-the-discipline approaches (those inspired by Jerome Bruner) to curriculum revision are to be faulted because the level of reasoning presupposed by these curricula is inappropriately high for most students for whom it is intended. According to Kohlberg, many new curricula often presuppose Piaget's stage of Formal Operations or his own Stages Five and Six, and high-school students typically are not there yet.

The contributions of curriculum developers are needed to furnish a complete pedagogy and curriculum materials. It will take much research to determine what works best with what students under what conditions. This kind of advance requires collaboration on educational-research enterprises whereby the researcher and practitioner share each other's problems, perspectives and ideas.

Reaction to Kavanagh: OBSERVATIONS ON METHODOLOGY, MALES AND RELIGIOUS SCHOOLING *by* Maureen Joy

Kavanagh's study of Moral Development in a High-School Program illustrates a variety of problems and questions about the conduct of research in the development of moral education and the current process of moral education in the Catholic high schools.

The moral-development experiment described is similar to the Blatt-Kohlberg studies—short-term intervention to stimulate moral reasoning. The investigation includes comparisons of growth of younger and older adolescents, boys and girls, response to peer discussions, counselor-directed groups, personal writing sessions, I.Q. and interest variables.

The work with students was limited to 9 weeks. Within that brief time, and in the restrictions of the three types of groups, Kavanagh finds no significant difference between the growth rate of boys and girls, or those with different I.Q.'s. He does find evidence that older students increase their moral reasoning power more rapidly than younger students. The treatment that seems most effective of the three interventions is the writing group. The peer-led group ranks second, and the counselor-directed group third.

To understand the inconclusive results concerning boy/girl growth and the apparent success of the writing groups over the peer-age and counselor-directed groups, one must examine more closely the structure and content of the group sessions.

Trouble with the Law is cited as a typical film presented to all groups. I assume that other films from this series *Searching for Values* (Guidance Assoc.) were used in the 9-week course. The same questions were asked of all of the students. They are, I believe, highly structured and possibly limiting to the student's thought. The low rating given to the counselor-directed group might result from an authoritarian approach—need for a right/wrong answer assumption by students. In fact, a counselor/teacher director for students should encourage awareness of a variety of moral issues in the film: conscience, law, justice, property, power, responsibility. Each of these themes can be examined with regard to Mrs. Conroy (the victim), Billy's father and his uncle, the judge—as well as to Billy himself. A skilled teacher would want several sessions for the study of this film.

The peer-led group in the post-test session receives higher scores than the counselor-directed group. Since both groups are dealing with the same questions, one can assume that without adult imposition, the students feel freer to examine issues. They possibly take a broader view; they also will probably tend to listen to one another rather than channeling ideas through an adult intermediary. The small group of 12 students facilitates interaction and individual participation. Exposure to more than one style of reasoning will encourage new thinking.

The writing groups showed the most growth in the study. The writers worked alone, it seems, simply under silent supervision. Interaction is a condition for moral growth. The student writers were responding to a film episode and to a set of questions. I suggest that all of the subjects in the study (counselor-directed, peer-group and writers) were responding individually to the powerful stimulus of the film. The questions posed to all groups invite an individual response (e.g., "Have you ever had an accident where you damaged a person or property? What were your feelings?"). The responses cited do not indicate give-and-take among students. There are no comments referring to other students' ideas. One might expect il-

lustrations such as: "I agree with Mary's idea that ... but disagree with her statement that ...." In brief, the greater gains
of the writers' group should probably be attributed to the fact
that students had greater opportunity to think out various conflicts
in the brief time allowed all students for dealing with complex
issues. The greater gains made by the writing group do not necessarily indicate that writing is better. Rather the gains made by this
group possibly indicate weaknesses in both content and conduct of
the other groups. The writing group may be the winner by default.

The study gives no new information on the possible differences between moral development in boys and girls. As Kavanagh indicates, some discrepancy should be expected. He concludes
that the discrepancy will emerge at post-high school age "when
roles and occupations become diversified." I suggest that the moral
development of both men and women will be fostered in youth and
all of life when roles and occupations are not expected to diversify.
The role models presented to boys and girls in *Trouble with the
Law* and *all* other films of the *Searching for Values* series presents
man as central to moral decision-making, woman as victim or servant in the enterprise. *Trouble with the Law* actually dramatizes expectations for men and women. The woman dies at the outset of the
film; her daughter-in-law is a pathetic semicomic figure; the judge
speaks of her life as servant; Billy's mother is a shadow in the
background. Question #3 of the session discussing this film allows
boys and girls to discuss their own actions and reactions to personal
acts. Study of responses to this question might give some clues to
the differences of thinking among boys and girls.

Kavanagh's positive conclusions about the significance of the
writer's group and his inconclusive findings on boy/girl development must be questioned. Long-term, not brief interventions, are
required for an adequate program of moral education. Kavanagh's
work points up the value of including a writing component. As he
suggests, writing allows an individual to clarify ideas, to gain skill
in argument. However, studies, such as the OISE Pickering
study (Beck et al., 1972), indicate that a variety of experiences extended over at least a year produce significant results. The teacher's
role is that of understanding students' level of development, encouraging through instruction, questioning, designing activities
leading to a higher level of thinking.

The boy/girl differential aspect of Kavanagh's work is inconclusive possibly due to the nature of the pre- and post-test
questioning. Despite claims that content is not central to testing of
moral reasoning, it must be noted that the episodes are male-orient-

ed. The classic Kohlberg questionnaire is a series of moral dilemmas where man is the decision-maker. In the most famous of these, a woman (unnamed) is a victim suffering from cancer. The husband (Heinz) is the decision-maker. The questions focus on Heinz ("Should he have done that?" "What makes a good husband?"). Other episodes describe the following: a boy's response to giving money to his father for a fishing trip, money the boy had saved to go to camp; two boys stealing, one from a store, another from an old man. The conflict episode provides a tool for understanding students' thinking. The content of the episodes should include situations involving women as well as men in central roles.

The most important issue for me, however, that is not discussed in Kavanagh's report is the fact that all of the subjects in the study are students in Catholic high schools. It can be assumed that the majority of these students have attended parochial schools. In all probability the ninth-grade students (half of those studied) had 9 years of religious schooling, while the remainder of the students had 12 years of religious training. As a Catholic educator, directing or approving the study, I would seek some evidence of the impact on these students of their religious education. Although one can argue for the incorporation of moral instruction within religious instruction, most programs of religious education present moral issues as needing examination in their own right. Eventually they are placed in a religious content. It is not unusual to find civil rights, political responsibility, law, justice, war, poverty, etc., as topics of study among Catholic students in religion classes from seventh grade through senior high school. Students who have had regular exposure to the dilemmas involved in such issues can be expected to demonstrate stronger power in moral reasoning than those who have had a public-school experience. This assumption suggests new areas for research: a comparative study of Catholic-school students and public-school students to investigate the possible differences as a result of religious schooling, an examination of the content and approaches used in individual classrooms in Catholic schools. Kavanagh recommends an in-depth longitudinal study to gain understanding of the growth-transition process in cognitive-moral development. Catholic schools provide a unique setting for such work. Catholic educators are receptive to Kohlberg's theory. Many are eager to examine the implications of his work for their schools. Study of students in an elementary/secondary school complex from sixth through twelfth grades would provide important data for religious educators and all those concerned about the process of moral education for young people today and tomorrow.

6.
A Developmental Approach to Interpersonal and Moral Awareness in Young Children: Some Educational Implications of Levels of Social Perspective-Taking*

Robert L. Selman

The search for knowledge applicable to moral education brings researchers into important related areas. Some concentrate on a topic such as empathy, the focus on the feelings of the other persons. Others like myself have worked in the area of perspective-taking where the ability of a person to perceive the other person's thinking and feelings is encouraged and measured. Perspective-taking is viewed as an aspect of social development that is basic to moral development. Indeed, especially with young children, social and moral development are often inseparable to the mind of the child. Yet use of the term "social development" is often more acceptable to parents and educators who often fear sectarian pressures in the moral-education movement.

The close relationship between moral reasoning and perspective-taking is demonstrated in the research that we cite in the paper, particularly in the type of dilemmas that are discussed and in the approach taken by the children in their responses. Yet perspective-taking embraces a wider area than moral reasoning and it is possible to produce perspective-taking problems where moral aspects are seldom adverted to. Ultimately we believe that the child's social—

*This research was partially supported by a grant from Guidance Associates, a subsidiary of Harcourt, Brace, Jovanovich, Inc.

We would like to express our appreciation to Dr. Elizabeth Boyce, Assistant Superintendent for Social Studies, Cambridge, Massachusetts, and to the faculty of the Tobin and Peabody Schools for their cooperation in making this research possible.

Parts of this paper were first presented at the American Montessori Society—1974 National Seminar in Boston, Massachusetts, June 20, 1974.

and moral—development will be stimulated through the activities we suggest in the paper.

This paper is divided into three sections. The first offers our views on the structural-developmental approach and explains how perspective-taking fits into this approach. The second section describes the educational implications and methodology of perspective-taking. The third section explains elements of a pertinent pilot research project and suggests educational implications from analysis of the results.

I. A Structural-developmental Approach to Understanding Social Thought in the Young Child.

Piagetian or structural-developmental theory considers together both the intellectual and the social or emotional aspects of the child's life. It does not focus on the intellectual domain to the exclusion of the social or emotional elements. Instead, it considers as false the dichotomization of the intellectual and social or emotional aspects of the child. Indeed, recent research indicates that children's social understanding develops according to systematic sequences of stages which parallel awareness of logical and physical concepts. For example, Lawrence Kohlberg's research in the area of moral development (1968) indicates that moral judgment develops through a sequence of universal stages.

Although it has been commonly assumed that moral values and beliefs are acquired through some process of cultural transmission, or of identification with the beliefs and values of parents and members of adult society, the research of Kohlberg and his associates indicates that children pass through an invariant sequence of stages of reasoning about values and beliefs, and that the *mode* or *way* of moral reasoning is as important in understanding moral behavior as the content of the beliefs themselves.

My own research falls within this structural-developmental framework and is in part related to research in moral development. My colleagues and I have been studying the development of a basic process that underlies interpersonal cognition—social perspective-taking. Levels of social perspective-taking refer to the developing awareness of a *uniquely* human property and characteristic—*subjectivity*. People as objects are different from other objects of experience for the child because 1) people can think, and 2) people can think about each other and each other's thoughts, feelings and emotions. In other words, people are the only class of objects with the capacity for reflective subjectivity. How the child comes to know about these uniquely human abilities, how knowledge of these abilities manifests itself in the child's interpersonal conceptions, and how this new knowledge relates to his conception of fairness and justice are the foci of our research.

Just as Piaget's stages describe the ways in which the child reasons about physical objects and logical relations, levels of social perspective-taking describe the way the child at a given level understands human subjects and social relations. This analysis emphasizes the structure of social understanding rather than the content, the ability to conceive of subjective perspectives rather than the accuracy of person perception. Let me try to clarify the distinction, as it is basic to all research within the Piagetian framework.

It is common to note people who are particularly insightful into the psychological nature of others, or people who are particularly empathic. These abilities, however, are not the direct focus of my research. My research is more directly concerned with when and how the child realizes that another person can consider his point of view, not what that other person thinks his specific thoughts or feelings are. What is in other's mind is the content. That other is conceived of as having a perspective, and what the nature of the relation between perspectives of self and other is conceptualized to be is the structure of social thought. These two aspects of social thought, content and structure, are obviously related, but for theoretical purposes, we focus on the structure.

Very young children, even as they begin clearly to distinguish the self from other, and the self's *visual* perspective from others, still lack a conception of persons as having subjective viewpoints, as having "minds," or as having "reasons" behind their actions. Thus "why questions" which demand an understanding of psychological causation, such as, "why did you do that" are often meaningless to two-year-olds. For example, when my eldest boy was about two and one-half, we began to have verbal exchanges of which the following is just one example:

Son: I want to go down the hill.
Father: You can't go down. No one will be able to watch you. Stay here.
Son: I don't want to stay here. I want to go down.
Father: No, son, you can't.
Son: *Don't say no*, Daddy, say yes.
Father: But I don't want you to go.
Son: (emphatically) *Say yes*, Daddy.

My interpretation of this interchange may help to clarify what I mean when I say that young children do not conceive of others as "subjects," as having covert psychological existence. My son's command to change my response (no to yes) implies an unawareness that even if my words were changed, my *mind* would not be changed. At a slightly older age children begin to become aware that by "saying no" I would "mean (intend) no." My son was at a presubjective level of social perspective-taking.

My evidence for this level rests mainly on anecdotes such as the above. However, we have begun some systematic research on children as young as four and this research has led to *definitions* of higher levels of perspective-taking ability. These studies of children from four years of age through young adulthood show that each perspective-taking level stems from the preceding level and paves the way for the next one. Children may go through the levels at different rates, but always in the same order.

Our research has made use of a program of audio-visual film-strips to study perspective-taking within the context of both interpersonal and moral dilemmas. To exemplify levels of social perspective-taking, I will draw upon responses of children to the following interpersonal dilemmas:

Two boys are trying to figure out what to get a friend for his birthday. Greg has already bought some checkers for Mike, but Tom can't decide whether to get Mike a football or a little toy truck. The boys see Mike across the street and decide to hint around to see what he'd like for his birthday.

Greg and Tom ask Mike about trucks and football, but nothing seems to interest him. He's very sad because his dog, Pepper, has been lost for two weeks. When Greg suggests that Mike could get a new dog, Mike says he doesn't even like to look at other dogs because they make him miss Pepper so much. He runs off home, nearly crying.

Greg and Tom are left with the dilemma of what to get Mike. On their way to the toy store, they pass a store with a sign in the window—"Puppies For Sale." There are only two dogs left. Tom has to make up his mind whether to get Mike a puppy before the last two are sold.

After the child views a sound filmstrip depicting the above dilemma, we present the child with questions concerning his conception of persons (e.g., motivation, personality) and his conception of relationships between persons (e.g., friendship, trust). In our analysis of children's responses we find the following levels of perspective-taking. Table 1 summarizes the nature of the child's developing conceptions at each level.

TABLE 1
BRIEF DESCRIPTION OF SOCIAL PERSPECTIVE-TAKING LEVELS

Level	Description
0	*Egocentric perspective-taking* Although the child can identify superficial emotions in other people, he often confuses other's perspective with his own. He does not realize others may see a social situation differently from the way he does.
1	*Subjective perspective-taking* Child begins to understand that other people's thoughts and feelings may be the same or different from his. He realizes that people feel differently or think differently because they are in different situations or have different information.
2	*Self-reflective perspective-taking* The child is able to reflect on his own thoughts and feelings. He can anticipate other's perspective on his own thoughts and feelings and realize that this influences his perspective on other.

Level	Description

3   *Mutual perspective-taking*
           The child can assume a third-per-
           son point of view. He realizes
           that in a two-person interaction
           each can put himself in the
           other's place and view himself
           from that vantage point before
           deciding how to react.

4   *Qualitative-system perspective-*
           taking
           The adolescent conceptualizes
           subjective perspectives of persons
           toward one another to exist not
           only on the level of mutual ex-
           pectations, but also on deeper
           levels. Perspectives between per-
           sons are seen as forming a net-
           work or system. There are mul-
           tiple levels of perspective-taking
           and multiple systems of perspec-
           tives.

5   *Symbolic interaction perspective-*
           taking
           Perspective-taking is seen as a
           method for the analysis of inter-
           personal and social relations.
           Owing to the nature of human
           subjectivity itself, one does not
           necessarily "know" the other's
           perspective as content. Mutual
           understanding occurs through the
           use of similar *processes* of social
           reasoning.

Level 0 Egocentric Perspective-taking
     Social perspective-taking at level 0, though primitive, has its

positive aspects. At this level, the child separates the attitude or viewpoint of self and other. For example, the child may realize that another may be sad even if he, himself, is happy. But even though the child separates viewpoints, he assumes that in similar situations, others will feel or act as he would in that situation. Prior to level 0, there is no differentiation of perspectives. At level 0, although the child recognizes there are more than one perspectives on a situation, they are assumed to be identical. A beginning conception of subjectivity emerges, but it is contaminated by a *confusion* of the self's subjectivity with the subjectivity of other. Social perspective-taking at level 0 was predominantly found in our data in the reasoning of children from ages four to six. Here is an example.

> Abby (five years, one month): Do you think Tom will get Mike a new puppy? *Yes. He'll be happy. He's sad now but he'll be happy.* But Mike says he never wants to see another puppy. *Dogs are fun. I like puppies.* And so why will Tom get him a puppy? *Puppies are fun. I like puppies.*

Abby does not seem aware of the possibility that Tom might possibly not share her attitude toward a new puppy but she does seem aware that he has a perspective.

Level 1 Subjective Perspective-taking

At level 1 social perspective-taking comes clear recognition that the self's perspective is separate from other's, and thus is unique. At this level the child realizes that self and other may view the same social situation in very different ways, and that similar actions might reflect disparate reasons. The child focuses on the uniqueness of the covert, psychological or subjective nature of others, rather than on others' overt actions. Social perspective-taking discovery involves a new awareness of the thoughts, feelings and intentions of others as distinct from the self's.

> Brenda (six years, two months): Do you think Tom will get him a dog? *No. If he says he doesn't want a dog, that means he doesn't want a dog. Just because Tom thinks he wants a dog doesn't mean Mike wants one.* Will Mike and Tom be friends if Tom gives Mike a puppy? *Well, Mike will be kind of angry; he doesn't want a dog.*

Brenda is able to differentiate the subjective perspectives of the two boys, to focus on the viewpoints underlying their actions. However, her belief that Mike will be angry at Tom implies that she is *unable* to realize that Mike might understand that Tom *was* thinking about Mike when he bought the puppy. This marks the limiting characteristic of level-1 reasoning.

Level 2 Self-reflective Perspective-taking

The major advance of level 2 social perspective-taking is the child's ability to see the viewpoints of persons (who may, of course, be self and other) in relation to one another. The perspectives are now seen to exist in a state of reciprocal influence, rather than as independent assessments of objective information in the world. For the first time the child recognizes that his judgments and actions are open to the scrutiny and evaluation of others, and his view of other is influenced by the realization that others (or the self as other) can view the self as a subject just as the self can view others as a subject (hence self-reflective perspective-taking). Level-2 perspective-taking usually emerges after age eight.

> Carl (eight years, three months): *Mike doesn't know what he's talking about. He just says he doesn't want the puppy, but he doesn't mean it.* How do you know that? *Well if I were Mike, I would feel bad too, but later I'd realize that I really want the new puppy.*

There is a big conceptual leap between the "I like dogs; (therefore) he likes dogs" logic at level 0, and "If I were he, I would want a dog" at level 2. This latter statement implies that the self can consider the self's subjective viewpoint from a separate other's point of view. When Carl says, "If I were Mike I would feel bad too," we infer that Carl can view his own subjective reaction from outside of himself, hence, self-reflection.

Level 3 Mutual Perspective-taking

At level 3, the child is newly aware of the infinite regress (I know that you know that I know that you know, etc.) characteristic of dyadic relations; that each person is simultaneously aware of his own and other's subjective abilities. At this point (about ages 10 to 12), the child leaps to a new level of awareness; he begins to view his own interactions with others from a third-person perspective.

He begins to see interpersonal relationships in terms of abstract mutuality, rather than concrete exchange.

> Alex (eleven years, two months): Will they still be friends if Tom gets Mike the puppy? *Well if Tom gets Mike a puppy and Mike doesn't like it, Tom still knows that Mike will understand that he was only trying to make Mike happy. They are good friends and good friends understand each other.*

At this level the child begins to understand that each subject can be simultaneously and mutually aware of the other person's subjectivity, his thoughts, feelings, and motivation. More complex levels of awareness emerge in adolescence.

The levels that I have described are best viewed as *idealizations*. Very rarely does one find a child whose responses across a range of measures fall only within the framework of one particular level. In fact, insofar as levels really represent new levels of conceptual development each should probably be seen as representative of the final *consolidation* or clarification of a structure, not its *emergence*. This may help to explain why certain aspects of the levels I have described seem to appear at earlier ages in natural situations than on the measures we use. However, although accurate normative age data for each level is of practical importance, it is the *qualitative* nature of the *order* of changes in social understanding that I wish to stress.

Our present research focus is on how perspective-taking levels relate to and influence moral and interpersonal conceptions (conceptions such as personality, motivation, friendship, peer and sibling relations, and parental and authority relations). However, we have also dealt with the implications of a sequence of perspective-taking levels for social and moral education in the elementary grades. It is to this topic that I will now turn.

II. *Educational Implications of Perspective-taking Levels.*

Ironically the educators who deny that the structural-developmental approach has any direct or meaningful implications for education focus only on the theoretical assertion that there are universal, lawful, consistent, and invariant stages in the development of reasoning. Often these educators ask, why teach something which will develop whether I teach it or not? In fact, they ask whether one can teach developmental concepts or abilities at all. Overlooked, however, is the role of variability in the theory. Three observations are in order. *First*, universality of sequence does not imply biological invariance such as a biological theory of intelligence might. Experience plays a critical part in conceptual stage development. One way to understand educational implications within a theory of universal stage development is to understand that in theory, certain intellectual and social experiences are also universal, such as the observation that a dropped ball falls or that people become angry. Each child needs to "experience" these experiences if he is to develop through the entire sequence. The number and kind of experiences have a more or less facilitating effect on development. *Second*, there is a wide range of individual differences in the *rate* of development through the hypothesized invariant sequence of stages. For example, much research (Selman, in press) supports both the hypothesis of universality of the sequence of social and logical thought and the hypothesis of fixation or retardation of rate of stage development in some children. *Third*, even *within* the individual there is variability of level of reasoning depending upon the concept or domain reasoned about. These aspects of structural developmental theory bear directly on education.

My own educational interest within the structural-developmental framework has been social development and has been guided by the conceptualization of social perspective-taking levels I discussed in the first part of this paper. For the past several years my colleagues and I have worked to develop paradigmatic methods of social education based upon a structural-developmental approach to understanding and stimulating children's perspective-taking. The cornerstone of our approach is guided peer-group discussion. We have developed audio-visual filmstrips which portray open-ended social and moral dilemmas typical of the lives of children of elementary-grade age. Each filmstrip leaves the ending to the dilemma open. Arriving at a solution is up to each child. Development occurs through the *exercise* of the child's reasoning and the *exposure* to the reasoning of peers. Children at different levels of social reasoning may decide on the same alternative, but the reasons they use to justify their choice may differ. Although final choices are important, the emphasis is on the reasoning offered for the preferred choices.

The filmstrips we use to promote and stimulate the exercise of social reasoning and judgment are basically the same as the dilemmas we have used in our research to study the social reasoning of each child individually.[1] Of course, interviews with individual children are essential to the psychological description of stages of interpersonal and moral reasoning. However, according to structural theory, the discussion and role-playing of dilemmas by peers within a group is the basis for meeting the educational criteria of developmental change. Discussion and other techniques such as role-playing are essential because optimal movement to more adequate social reasoning is seen as occuring through two basic developmental principles: (a) social-conceptual conflict and (b) exposure to reasoning slightly above one's own level. Social-conceptual conflict refers to the rethinking of one's own theory of the nature of the social world and social relations. In this respect, Flavell (1968) writes:

> In the course of his contacts (and especially, his conflicts and arguments) with other children, the child increasingly finds himself forced to reexamine his own precepts and concepts in the light of those of others and by so doing gradually rids himself of cognitive egocentrism.

In addition to presenting a natural environment for this kind of conflict, peer-group discussion is also the most natural vehicle for exposing the child to reasoning slightly higher than his own in the developmental sequence. Here are two excerpts from typical discussions of the lost-puppy dilemma among third-graders that exemplify these principles:

1. Conceptual Conflict

Bill: Get him a dog to replace Pepper.

Bob: But remember, Mike said he didn't want to see anybody else's dog.

Bill: Yeah, but that *would* be *his* dog.

Bob: Yeah, but it wouldn't be Pepper [a view one level above Bill's].

Bill: Name him Pepper.

Bob: Still not the same thing.

In this exchange, Bob challenges Bill to reflect on his own reasoning. What does Bob mean when he says, "Still not the same thing"? If Bill thinks about this idea in juxtaposition to his own

1. The filmstrips, *First Things: Values* (developed with L. Kohlberg) and *First Things: Social Reasoning* (developed with D. Byrne) are published by Guidance Associates, a subsidiary of Harcourt, Brace, Jovanovich, Inc., New York, N.Y.

concepts of social relationships, it may provide the mechanism for social-concept development.

2. Dialogue Between Children at Two Different Levels
Alex (level 2):

> I think it's important because like um, if you buy something ah, something for the other person, that he doesn't like, he might get mad at you or something and not be your friend or something and then you'd just be down one friend and if you hadda have very many friends besides the ones in school. So if I did that I'd be in trouble.

Jane (level 3):

> Yeh, but that's not gonna make them not friends. His friend will understand. Besides, I think that um, he should buy the puppy because in a month or two he's going to be wanting one. He just said that because he lost his dog and he's sad. I think he should buy it and he'll start to like the dog and after a few days he'll stop thinking about Pepper once he gets another thing he loves a lot.

In this example, Alex has a very concrete and moment-to-moment conception of friendship. Jane rejects Alex's reasoning based on her awareness that friendship is based on expectations of each person toward each other, not on specific acts such as the gifts that one person gives the other. Her reasoning represents a level one above Alex's and provides stimulation for him, as well as for herself. This discussion exemplifies another aspect of stages of reasoning: children at higher levels usually reject lower-level reasoning as immature or inadequate.

Our aim has not been to accelerate development through social perspective-taking levels. Rather it has been to devise a peer-oriented developmental program whose aims are (a) the stimulation and exercise of the child's social perspective-taking across a range of social judgment and behavior, and (b) the prevention of retardation of social understanding.

We stress stimulation and prevention of retardation rather than acceleration for the following reasons. *First,* research indicates that movement from stage to stage is a long-term process. Findings indicate that complete transition from one level to the next may take several years or more. Teachers, therefore, should not expect to see great leaps from level to level in the space of a few months. Stages refer to the qualitatively new ways of thinking, not to overnight change. Furthermore, the ages given for our research are only averages. A child may move into a level earlier or later than the guidelines suggest. And sometimes a child can be in transition between two levels. *Second,* only when the child has a firm command of one level of reasoning does the next level begin to be accessible to him. In other words, over the long haul, rapid development may not be optimal development.

Just as children need to exercise their reading and math skills, they must also exercise their social and logical abilities across a wide range of situations. Perhaps the most important point to make with regard to educational practice, is that the application of the child's social perspective-taking level to the child's performance across a range of social behaviors is not an automatic process. For example, in the application of perspective-taking to moral development, our research points to the fact that each perspective-taking level is necessary but not sufficient for a parallel moral level (Selman, in press). This means that a high level of perspective-taking does not guarantee equivalent mature moral thought. As a case in point, recent research indicates that although delinquents have adequate perspective-taking compared to their peers, they do not apply this process to their moral judgment. Our basic educational goal is to help children apply the perspective-taking they have to various areas of social behavior. We speculate that in the long run, such applications will eventually facilitate forward stage movement.

In addition to moral and interpersonal contexts, two other overlapping areas of social development are dealt with in our work:

Solving social problems. Examples of this activity follow. When two people get separated in a busy store without having planned where to meet, each person must think about what the other is thinking. If a person plans to meet someone else at the park but forgets to specify which park, both people must do some perspective-taking. Many games of strategy also depend on a player's ability to figure out his opponent's potential behavior. In social problems of cooperation, coordination, and competition, an essential element for success is the ability to take another's perspective.

Communication and persuasive skills. Parents are familiar with the problem of trying to understand what a young child means when he refers to "this" or "that" while on the other end of the phone or in another room. The child has not taken into account the fact that the listener cannot see what is meant by "this" or "that." The ability to communicate one's point of view is important in a child's attempt to persuade others when he believes he has a good idea, or when it is necessary for him to clarify his ideas in a social situation that has become confused. To communicate or persuade effectively, the child must be able to take into account the needs and wishes of his listener.

While these distinctions among areas may be conceptually useful in pointing out the need for the application of perspective-taking, in the "real world" each social area is inextricably intertwined with the others. For example, in one of our educational interpersonal conflict dilemmas, a young girl, Jane, truthfully tells her friend Brian that she cannot go to the rodeo with him because her aunt is coming to town. Brian takes the rejection personally, and claims Jane does not really want to go with him. When Jane finds out she can go after all, she calls Brian but he has already left. Jane goes with another friend and, of course, runs into Brian. What will Jane do, what will she tell Brian? To think maturely about the problem demands sensitivity in many social areas. It demands application of perspective-taking to interpersonal problems (awareness of Brian's feelings and attitudes toward Jane—he thinks she does not like him). It demands persuasive and communication abilities (Jane must consider Brian's perspective as she explains her presence at the rodeo). And it demands value judgment. (It may be easier to lie rather than present a truthful but unlikely story, but is that really being fair to everyone involved?)

Our educational assertions are in keeping with the implications of structural-developmental theory and evidence from research. Direct short-term *vertical* training of higher levels is relatively unsuccessful. But the horizontal application of a structure of thought to a wide range of content areas lays the groundwork for subsequent vertical development.

Furthermore, education based on social-developmental stages should not be viewed as a "Band-Aid" approach. It is a theoretical misinterpretation to assume that stimulation of a stage of social or moral reasoning will repair *specific* classroom management problems. Rather, structural theory has implications for a *general* educational approach to be built into the fabric of the daily class activity. Let me clarify this point with reference to two final topics: first, the developmental conception of the teacher's role, and second, some pilot research evaluating our educational procedures.

The teacher within our framework has two major functions: a) to arrange the optimal conditions for open discussion, and b) to help keep the discussion relevant and stimulating. The most challenging problem for teachers, particularly in the elementary grades, is to help children to focus on reasons and reasoning rather than on right answers. The teacher must encourage the child to give reasons for their opinions and to demand them of others in the group.

Although we emphasize peer discussion, occasionally the teacher must intervene in the discussion to keep it focused. Children, like adults, can wander from the main issues designated in the original dilemma. The teacher must use his judgment in guiding the discussion back to the main issue. For example, in the puppy story a discussion of the types of dogs that the children in the class have would be considered somewhat off the track. However, some digressions may be very valuable in that they explore important areas of social reasoning and may relate to the underlying social concerns of the dilemma. Here is an example:

Andy: This story reminds me of when my dog was killed by a car and we got another one later on.
Karen: How'd you feel?
Andy: Well, um, I when I got it for a Christmas present and everybody was all excited about it and um, so I, so there was a lot of pictures being . . . so I didn't have any time to feel happy or sad or mad or glad.

The teacher can use such a situation to encourage further probing into social reasoning and to bring the child's relevant personal experience into the realm of discussion. Furthermore, by conceiving of the filmstrips as a model, the teacher can begin to take natural classroom and life experiences as the basis for peer-group discussion.

The second implication of structural theory regarding a general educational approach is discussed in the following section.

III. *Implications From a Pilot Intervention Program*

Elementary-grade children readily discuss hypothetical dilemmas when presented audio-visually. And, with practice, children are just as capable of using the methods I have described to discuss the real-life events of their own parental, peer, and authority relations. In fact, in the first pilot study which we have undertaken to evaluate the effectiveness of our peer-discussion approach on the moral reasoning of second-graders, there was evidence that the greatest advance in reasoning occurred when teachers used our curriculum as a paradigm for "natural" moral discussions to resolve classroom conflicts the rest of the school year (Selman and Lieberman).

In this pilot study we compared three groups—two experimental and one comparison group. The two experimental groups participated over five weeks, in 30 to 40 minute, twice-a-week discussion of the filmed moral dilemmas of our social-development program. One experimental group was led by trained developmental discussion group leaders, the other by the classroom teachers. All children's moral reasoning was assessed prior to the experimental intervention, just subsequent to the intervention, and 5 months later, at the end of the school year.

The evaluation consisted of a comparison of the reasoning of children exposed to the filmstrip program in sections run by classroom teachers versus those run by developmentally trained discussion leaders, as well as a comparison of these groups with a control group receiving no intervention. The two hypotheses entertained in this study were:

1. Intervention in the form of a filmstrip dilemma presentation and discussion will cause significant change in moral concept level compared with a comparison group that does not receive the treatment.

2. Although the amount of change may be greater with a teacher familiar with the stage theory (expert-led) using the material than when used by a classroom teacher who has only read the manual and instructions, it was hypothesized that both the "expert-led" and the "teacher-led" groups would not differ significantly from each other but their mean amount of change would differ from that of the control group.

Subjects were 68 second-graders, half from an integrated blue-collar and half from a middle-class school district in the Cambridge, Massachusetts, public school system. Subjects were divided equally by sex. Six classrooms participated in the experiment. While entire classes were exposed to the program, random samples of children within each class were selected to be interviewed as subjects.

Three schools were represented to increase the generalizability of the results. In School 1, one class of the three was randomly assigned to one of the three treatments: expert-led, classroom teacher-led, and control. In School 2, one class of the two was assigned to either an expert-led or a classroom-led group. To estimate and control for carry-over effects from the children in the experimental group who communicate casually with children in the control group, a second control group was drawn from a third school geographically but not demographically separate from the second.

The design is summarized as follows:

Table 2
Experimental Design

	Expert-led group	Classroom teacher-led group	Control group
Middle-class	School 1 6 female 6 male	School 1 6 female 6 male	School 1 5 female 5 male
Working-class	School 2 6 female 6 male	School 2 6 female 6 male	School 3 5 female 5 male

Interviews were conducted three times: once in the fall before the instructional program, once in the winter immediately after the program, and at the end of the school year (to determine long-term effects).

The filmstrip presentation to the group was only a small part of total instruction. The remaining portions involved asking the children what should be done to resolve the dilemma, reasons for each choice, and debate about whether some reasons are better than others. Children discussed the dilemmas in small groups or role played the dilemmas, and teachers acted as guides, keeping the discussion on the topic.

The experimental groups began after the pretesting of all subjects. They met twice a week, each session running for approximately 30 to 40 minutes. Each week both dilemmas from each of five units were presented to the class, one at each session. The units covered the following moral concepts: Truth Telling, Sharing and Taking Turns, Promise Keeping, Property Rights, and Rules.

The "expert teachers" had training in cognitive-developmental theory as well as experience with primary-grade children. The classroom teachers simply used the teacher's training guide. The control-group teachers were told to conduct the classrooms in their usual manner.

Three types of moral dilemmas were used to evaluate the intervention program: one based directly on situations in the filmstrip series, one analogous to those of the filmstrip situations but not identical with them, and one adapted from standard dilemmas used in previous research on moral development. There were no differences in performance across the different measures.

The subjects were given the age-appropriate moral dilemmas, and a series of questions probing for moral conceptions. The dilemmas were illustrated on picture cards or presented through audiovisual filmstrips. Each sociomoral dilemma posed the subject with a problem concerning either punitive or positive justice. In each case, the subject was asked for his judgment of what constitutes a good solution to the dilemma. This response was then extensively probed in order to obtain as full a sample of his social and moral reasoning as possible. A typical dilemma follows:

Holly is an eight-year-old girl who likes to climb trees. She is the best tree-climber in the neighborhood. One day while climbing down from a tall tree, she falls off the bottom branch but doesn't hurt herself. Her father sees her fall. He is upset and asks her to promise not to climb trees any more. Holly promises.

Later that day, Holly meets Sean. Sean's kitten is caught up a tree and can't get down. Something has to be done right away or the kitten may fall. Holly is the only one who climbs trees well enough to reach the kitten, but she remembers her promise to her father.

As a change measure, we analyzed the development of a single moral concept over the course of the intervention; the child's conception of moral intentionality. This concept was used for two reasons. First, it is often difficult to interview children at this age for the extended period necessary to assess a complete stage of thought over a wide range of concepts. Second, we felt that this one specific moral concept might be more amenable to change through a short-term (five-week) intervention than a complete restructuring of moral stage.

Furthermore, as our research indicates that perspective-taking plays an important part in the moral reasoning of young children and as our intervention involves techniques closely related to this process (e.g., role-playing), we wished to assess an aspect of moral development that was closely aligned with the perspective-taking process. Conceptions of intentionality require that the child be aware of another person's reasons or motives and use this awareness in his moral justification. Hence it meets the third requirement. Three levels of conception of moral intentionality were defined in the study.

Level 0—Moral Judgment Which Disregards or Confuses Intentionality

At level 0, the concepts of psychological and physical causality (intentions) are often confused. Other's actions are sometimes seen to be based on underlying reasons or motives and sometimes on the physical event or its consequences. Thus, the child's understanding of intentions is wavering and uncertain.

> Julie (four years, one month): What should Holly Do? *Save the kitten.* Why is that right? *Kittens are nice. She doesn't want it to get hurt.* What will Holly's father do when he finds out? *Be angry.* Why? *She broke her promise.* Was it right to climb the tree? *No.* Why not? *Because her father could punish her.*

In the above example, although Julie initially considers intentions (she doesn't want it to get hurt), when asked to make a judgment of whether it was right to climb the tree, she focuses on her own assumption as to the father's actions—certainly not to the father's understanding of Holly's intentions.

Level 1: Simple Moral Intentionality

At level 1 the child is able to conclude that the intention behind an act cannot be inferred directly from the act itself. In the making of moral judgments the child can now reason that acts are not morally right or wrong in themselves, but rather that acts intending good are right, and those intending bad are wrong. The understanding of the subjective nature of persons coupled with the process of moral evaluation generates the concept of simple moral intentionality.

Tom (six years, eight months): Should the father punish her for climbing the tree? *He could, but it wouldn't be right.* Why not? *Because she didn't mean to do anything wrong. She was trying to save the kitty.*

Sarah (seven years, four months): Do you think Holly's father would understand if she told him why she climbed the tree? *Yes. Because she got the kitten down instead of just climbing it for fun.*

Level 2: Reciprocal Intentionality

The concept of reciprocal intentionality is distinguished by the child's beginning ability to coordinate the perspectives of two persons (his own and another's, or those of two others), and to view those perspectives in their relation to each other. The child now begins to see that his moral judgment is in part a function of his own subjective attitudes and that his intentions are open to evaluation by another. Thus, if the child expects his judgment to be accepted by another, it is necessary for him to anticipate potential conflicts. This anticipation is accomplished when the self's intentions are considered *from the other's point of view.*

Ann (eight years, one month): Do you think that Holly should climb the tree? *No.* Why not? *She might think she should because she's saving the kitten but she is afraid her father would think she didn't care about him.*

Allan (nine years, two months): Do you think Holly will climb the tree? *Yes.* Why? *To save the kitten.* Won't she be worried that her father will punish her? *No. She knows her father will understand why she did it.*

In the above examples the children are not only aware of intention as the basis for judgment, but also of the fact that the self's actions are judged on the basis of other's awareness of the self's intentions.

For purposes of data analyses, the qualitative level of conception of moral intentionality across each of the three dilemmas was transformed into a mean moral concept score (MMC) where 100 represents pure level-1 conception of intentions, 200 represents pure level-2 reasoning, etc. To arrive at MMC, each subject was given a qualitative score across dilemmas that represented a predominant and a minor level of moral concept development (e.g., a score of 1(2) indicates that level-1 reasoning was predominant but some level-2 reasoning was evident). Qualitative scores were transformed into quantitative scores (e.g., in the above case 1(2) transforms 133, a score of 2(1) would transform to 166). The MMC was the average of scores across dilemmas for each child.

An estimate of the test-retest reliability of the moral dilemma interviews was found by correlating control groups' pre- and post-testings with a five-week interval between administrations. Filmstrip dilemmas correlated .67 and standard dilemmas correlated .62. These results were judged adequate for test reliability, given the small number of subjects (20) and the narrow range of possible scores.

To determine interjudge reliability, 18 protocols were picked from each testing session, three protocols randomly picked from each class (six classes). Correlations between two trained scorers were as follows: Pretest, $r = .844$; Post-test, $r = .900$; Post-post-test, $r = .816$.

MMC scores for social class and treatment groups on the three administrations of the interview are presented in Table 3.

Table 3
Mean Moral Concept Score

	Controls	Expert-led	Classroom Teacher-led	
Mixed Middle	103.6	109.1	116.7	Pretest
and	110.7	125.0	125.0	Post test
Working-class	117.9	163.6	147.2	Post-post test
	116.7	112.5	122.9	Pretest
Middle-class	122.2	137.5	135.4	Post test
	130.6	156.2	189.6	Post-post test

Since post-test and post-post test scores were highly correlated, with pretest scores ($r = .67$ and .46 respectively), and regression lines were not significantly nonparallel, an analysis of covariance was performed on the data.

Orthogonal contrasts among treatment groups showed significant differences between the control group and the mean of the two intervention groups on both the post and the post-post testings (p = .012 and p< .0001 respectively) and no difference between the expert-led and classroom teacher-led groups (p = .155 and p =< 494). One interaction, that of treatment by social class, was significant on the adjusted post-post testing (p =<.024) mostly due to a classroom teacher continuing to use the classroom discussion method during the remainder of the school year and producing the highest score of any group.

Analyses of the change in scores from pretest to post-test and pretest to post-post tests adjusted for pretest scores produced identical results.

The most interesting result was the differences in level of moral concept development between control and both experimental groups at the time of the post-post testing, i.e., at the end of the school year. Taken across both types of treatment, expert and classroom teacher, and across both social classes the mean quantitative amount of change was about "one-half a level of concept development" for the experimental groups over the control group.

In effect these results most likely reflect the fact that the four teachers whose classes defined the experimental group continued to use the methods of small-group discussion to resolve interpersonal and moral conflicts that arose in the classroom throughout the school year.

It is obvious that in our experimental design it is impossible to sort out "teacher effects" from "intervention techniques." In other words, we cannot tell how much of the difference in level of reasoning at the post-post test is attributable to the competency of the teachers involved, how much is a function of the curriculum technique, and how much a function of some interaction of the two. For this reason alone, this program should be regarded as a pilot study. It is very possible that such post-post test gains would not have been obtained without a certain level of teacher competence or cooperation.

In fact, the biggest gains occurred not in an expert-led class, but in the group of the classroom teacher who showed the greatest interest in the program, its techniques, and the underlying theory. The treatment X social class effect on the post-post test is largely a function of the change in this one classroom.

The most compelling evidence for the effectiveness of the developmental discussion-group model are the protocols themselves, the record of the actual reasoning of the children in response to the assessment procedures. Below are excerpts of the pretest and follow-up post-test responses of a second-grade boy, Peter, age eight, who participated in the experimental group of the intervention study.

Pre-test (October)
What would you do if you were Holly?
Well, I would keep my promise I guess.
Why would you keep your promise?
It would be better.
Why would it be better?
Because my daddy said not to climb trees and I might get hurt and it's not a good idea.
It is not a good idea to break your promise?
No.
Why isn't that a good idea?
Because her daddy doesn't want her to. It is nicer to do what your parents say.
If she climbs the tree, should she tell her father?
No. He might yell at her.

Post-post-test (May)
Do you think Holly should help Sean by climbing the tree to get the kitten down?
I guess so.
Why?
Well, the cat is a living thing and I am sure Holly's mother wouldn't mind or Holly's father.
Sean says he will keep it a secret if Holly climbs the tree, is that a good idea?
No.
Why not?
It is better to tell your father what you did because he might get worried anyway. I think it is much better to tell what you promised your father, then he won't get so upset maybe.
Would you help Sean get the kitten down?
I suppose so.
Why?
Because as I said, the cat is a living thing and Sean must like it.
What about the promise to your father?

The promise to my father I think, well, I would wait until my father came home to tell him what had happened and then if he said yes I could climb the tree, I could climb it.

The kitten might fall before your father gets home and he is away on a business trip and won't be home for several days.

Then I would get the kitten and when my father came home I would tell him what I did.

On the pretest, Peter chose not to climb the tree. His choice is based on an orientation to authority ("it is nicer to do what your parents say") and to consequences ("I might get hurt"). However, this orientation to consequences also effects his belief that it is a good idea to keep the wrongdoing a secret to avoid the consequences of the father's anger.

There is a major change in both content and structure on Peter's post-post test. Here he thinks Holly should help Sean (content) because the parent will consider Holly's reason ("Holly's father or mother wouldn't mind") (structure) and although he would climb the tree, he would not keep it a secret (content) from Holly's father because the act of keeping a secret is worse than the promise-breaking itself in the father's viewpoint ("Then he won't get so upset") (structure).

It is not so much that Peter changed the content of his choices from one time to the next which is educationally salient here, but that the basis upon which he justifies his choices have changed. *On the pretest, Peter did not consider intentions. None of his responses indicated an awareness that the father would consider Holly's motives. On the post-test this awareness is clearly evident. That Peter now considers that one person can base his actions on the awareness of the intentions (subjectivity) of another rather than only on the actions of another, is an example of social development from a structural-developmental point of view.*

The fact that the most significant educational change occurred not immediately after the intervention, but six to eight months later supports the finding of others (e.g., Sullivan, 1975) that structural change is not an immediate reaction. Apparently this form of intervention requires some time for students to think over their own reasoning and to construct for themselves more adequate levels of conceptualization. This requirement of time supports our contention that relatively immediate short-term vertical into another level or stage movement is not an educationally sound expectation.

There are major limitations to this study; for example, we used only one evaluation procedure, the assessment of moral concept development. There was no evaluation of whether the children who participated in the intervention gained moral-judgment stage, perspective-taking level, or in other abilities. Some questions that we refrained from researching follow. Were children better able to communicate with one another after the group-discussion experience? Were they more aware of what moral conflicts are? Were they better able to articulate their own reasons to others both in hypothetical and real-life situations? Informal reports of the teachers involved in both types of treatment conditions indicated improved communication and transfer to personal problems. In fact, in many ways, development was not specifically "moral." As we noted previously the acquisition of the conception of intentionality is pertinent to social relations in general, not only to moral judgments. Our own conclusion is that moral intervention techniques at the early stages primarily make children more socially aware of other's ideas and better able to integrate other's thinking and valuing with their own. In effect perspective-taking training in the elementary grades can be thought of as a basis for later moral education in junior and senior high school.

Given the amount of moral concept development that occurred over the October-May period, it seems worthwhile to design and carry through research that takes teacher factors into consideration and that looks systematically at other social behavioral objectives which might be influenced by this type of program. Such studies are currently underway (Cooney and Selman, 1975).

I have spoken from the perspective of a *developmental psychologist* interested in psychological interventions and assessment methods for young children's social reasoning which also are relevant to educational psychology. The task of *educators* is to coordinate this approach with their own theories and practical experience. I do not expect one approach to explain all there is to know about the behavior or education of children. However, in seeking to define basic characteristics of each level of social interpersonal, and moral thought, and in seeking to understand the mechanism of change from one level to the next, I believe structural-developmental psychology has great potential for a meaningful contribution to education.

In summary, we have reviewed the Piagetian, structural-developmental theory, emphasizing the basic social-cognitive process and the levels through which this process appears to develop. We focused on the perspective-taking element of the social process and included in this process the ability to come to know the nature of the relation between one's own and the other's perspective in thinking and in social or emotional living. The levels of perspective-taking were described and viewed as a more adequate social conceptualizing as one went from a lower to a higher level. The educational implications of this approach were described, especially the use of filmstrips, peer discussion and role-playing to stimulate discussion and expose the child to thinking at a level slightly above his own stage. The content material used in the stimulating discussions was usually of a moral nature. The researcher concentrates not on the content of the thinking but rather on structure, though obviously structure and content are related. Finally, we examined research on children's growth regarding dilemmas such as that of Holly, the tree and Sean's kitten. The classroom teacher's continued use of our methodology showed her grasping the point that perspective-training in the early years may be the social-cognitive foundation for future developmental moral and psychological growth in junior and senior high school.

Reaction to Selman: SOCIAL PERSPECTIVES AND THE DEVELOPMENT OF MORAL JUDGMENT *by* Robert J. Havighurst

My own interest in the development of moral character goes back to my first study and teaching of child development, when I came across Piaget's early books on the *Moral Judgment of the Child,* and on the development of thought and reasoning in children. In the summer of 1936, I was attending a meeting of the International Bureau of Education in Geneva and I took the opportunity to have lunch in a garden restaurant on the shore of Lake Geneva with Professor and Mrs. Piaget. At the University of Chicago several of us started a 10-year study of children and youth in a midwestern county-seat, commencing in 1941 and continuing into the 1950's. This community has had several pseudonyms—Prairie City, Elmtown, and Jonesville.

We developed a theory of the development of moral character, with five character "types" which form a sequence in the lives of people, though some stop at an early stage, displaying throughout their adolescence and adult lives the "expedient" form of character, which is the second of our five types, while others progress to the highest type, the "Rational-Altruistic," in which a person behaves in accord with a set of moral principles that he believes have universal validity and that are as fair and just to other persons as they are to him. This theory of character types prepared us to understand and accept and work with the theory of moral judgment developed by Lawrence Kohlberg. His six stages of moral development were easy for us to comprehend and to work with (Peck and Havighurst).

We secured data on the personality characteristics of the youth we were studying, and we noted among other things that the more mature character types were characterized by a number of personality traits, three of which had to do with "perception of other people." These we defined as:

    a. Observation: accuracy of perception of how people behave
    b. Insight: accuracy of recognition of what other people want, and how they feel
    c. Empathy: degree of ability to "feel with" others' emotions, aims, and behavior from their point of view. (Peck and Havighurst, p. 217)

Thus we were prepared to accept and to use Selman's concept of levels of social perspective-taking. Selman states explicitly that his research deals with "the structure of social understanding rather than the content, the ability to conceive of subjective perspectives rather than the accuracy of person perception." Our personality variables were *insight* and *empathy*, and these develop in a personality structure which moves up through a series of stages defined by Selman from "egocentric perspective-taking" at the lowest level to "symbolic interaction perspective-taking" at the highest level.

Selman usefully stresses the value of the child's development through several stages or perspective levels, in which the child becomes aware that other people have their own points of view, and then becomes able to put himself in the other's place, and thus to analyze the behavior of others and to relate his own behavior to that of other people in a way that is useful to both parties.

Moral behavior is essentially interpersonal or social behavior. If there was no social interaction between persons, there would be no morality. And the development of the ability to see how and why other persons think and behave the way they do is essential to the development of moral judgment and of moral character. Selman published an important paper on "The Relation of Role-Taking to Moral Judgment" in 1971 (Selman, 1971). His current paper on

"Levels of Social Perspective-Taking" carries on his thinking and that of his readers by defining a sequence of six "social perspective-taking levels," and showing how a child of seven or eight years of age can be assisted to move up through the earlier stages.

An example of growth in role-taking or perspective-taking ability at adolescent ages has been given by Richard Graham in his chapter on "Youth and Experiential Learning" in the 1975 Yearbook of the National Society for the Study of Education entitled *Youth* (Graham, 1975). Graham gives a chart showing in parallel columns the stages of moral judgment as described by Kohlberg and the related stages of role-taking or social perspective-taking described by Selman. He describes Kohlberg's Stage Three as follows:

> The right is defined as the Golden Rule: Do unto others as you would have others do unto you. One considers all points of view, reflects on each person's motives, and tries to come to some agreement among all participants. Good behavior is what pleases or helps others and is approved by them.

The equivalent Stage Three for Selman is stated as:

> One realizes that both Self and Other can view each other mutually and simultaneously as subjects. One steps outside of the two-person dyad and views the interaction from a third-person perspective. One can have each participant take the other's role (reciprocity) and simultaneously consider self and other's position (inversion).

Graham then describes several examples of "action-learning" that facilitate behavior at this level, as follows:

> Group work as at some hamburger stands, secretaries in a pool, some kind of sales work, some shared production work or group bench work, some responsibilities for helping others, e.g., child care. One's desire is to do one's share and be liked by peers, employers, or the persons served. Loyalty is to the "group" whether it is viewed as peers or employers. One's concern is for self and others.

This is important to me, because it illustrates another method of teaching or learning in the service of growth in moral judgment and moral character—another method than the one which Selman and Kohlberg use, which is to present the child or youth with a dilemma—a moral or an interpersonal dilemma—and to guide them into a discussion of what is appropriate behavior in this dilemma. They propose that thinking about this dilemma, and discussing it with others, when guided by a teacher or someone who is operating at a more mature level, will lead the child to grow in his ability to understand the situation and the problem, and therefore to move more surely in the direction of a more mature stage.

Both Selman and Kohlberg give useful examples of discussion and consideration of moral and perspective-taking dilemmas, with children being guided to more mature verbal solutions of the problem. Both argue that experience in thinking about the problem-situation or the dilemma under expert guidance helps to speed up the moral growth of the person. And they also argue that the more mature stages may never be reached by young people who do not have this kind of educative experience. They point out that the average adult hardly gets beyond Stages Four or Five of Kohlberg's six stages of moral development and of Selman's six levels of social perspective-taking.

The tremendous interest in the work of Kohlberg and his colleagues at the Center for Moral Education at Harvard University is evidence both of the importance of this aspect of education in the minds of educators, and of the effectiveness of the research and documentation of the Harvard group.

Words versus Deeds?

The one question that seems to persist in the minds of some experienced educators has to do with the method of education used by Kohlberg and Selman—which is a central element of their *cognitive-developmental* approach. Do they overemphasize cognition—thought and understanding—as against action? Put in oversimple terms, do they permit words to stand for deeds? Critics of Kohlberg's theory are concerned about his apparent assumption that, if a person responds verbally to a description of a moral dilemma, his words describing the "best" behavior or solution of the dilemma are a reliable indication of the action he would take if he were placed in a similar situation in his personal life, and were forced to act. There is ample evidence that many people talk about a moral problem in more "liberal" or "mature" terms than they act when placed in a real-life situation of the same sort. For example, studies of race prejudice have shown that many people state their attitudes as more liberal than their actions when they are faced with the responsibility of accepting people of other races as guests, or of sending their children to the same school with children of other races.

But Kohlberg has at least some preliminary observations of behavior that support his methods. For instance, his educational work in New England reform schools seems to have resulted in less recidivism or parole-breaking and subsequent arrest for the youth who took part in his program, compared with control groups of youth who did not participate in his program.

The arenas in which experience may lead to higher levels of moral judgment and of social perspective-taking are school, family, peer group, and work-place. Selman and Kohlberg emphasize the school, and they are in a strong position here, because they can influence educators, and educators have the school situation pretty much under their control and supervision. The family has an important set of functions, as the Peck and Havighurst research clearly indicated. Levels of moral character were closely related to the quality of family relationships. The peer group can readily be seen as a training and proving ground for character development, and those who have ready access to youth peer groups (athletic coaches, Boy and Girl Scout leaders, etc.) can see the possibilities.

The work-place may seem more limited in its possibilities since a youth must generally work at rather simple jobs under supervisors or employers who have no interest in the possibilities of the job for moral character beyond very simple and routine habits of honesty, punctuality, etc. But if the work possibilities are expanded to the broader area of experiential or action-learning, generally done without pay but for academic credit in high school, the student may become a kind of intern working with a mature supervisor who is interested in the student as a person, and willing to give time to discussions and demonstration of the social and broad moral significance of the work. Graham's chapter on Experiential Learning in the NSSE Yearbook on *Youth*, previously described, shows some of the possibilities in this kind of activity for adolescent youth.

The Value of Variety of Experience

Selman makes a vigorous and effective case for the values of the classroom or small-group discussion of moral dilemmas under the guidance of a mature leader. He stresses the necessity of discussion over a wide range of moral dilemmas as a means of extending the grasp of the student over the behavior that is appropriate for a given stage of social perspective-taking. He says, "Direct short-term *vertical* training of higher stages is relatively unsuccessful. But the horizontal application of a structure of thought to a wide range of content areas lays the groundwork for subsequent vertical development." In other words, a child or youth cannot move securely from one stage or level of development to a higher level with only one "lesson" in the consideration of a moral dilemma. He needs to go over this ground again and again with a variety of somewhat similar moral dilemmas, so as to fix them in his mind, and to understand the application of the principles he is learning.

In Selman's experiments with second-grade children, it was found that the changes in children of the experimental group developed gradually, over almost a whole school year, though the actual intervention by the teacher or group leader came at the beginning of the year, for a five-week period, and was not continued explicitly after that. Selman concludes: "The fact that the most significant educational change occurred not immediately after the intervention, but six to eight months later, supports the finding of others that structural change is not an immediate reaction. Apparently this form of intervention requires some time for students to think over their own reasoning and to construct for themselves more adequate levels of conceptualization."

7.
Stages in Faith: The Structural-Developmental Approach[1]

James W. Fowler

INTRODUCTION

During the twentieth century students of human thought and culture have been flooded with overwhelming amounts of new data in the areas of their interest. This accumulation of data has both necessitated and made possible a method of analysis that enables us to take a comparative look at the development of human mind and culture. Called the *structuralist* point of view, this method has attempted to focus on the underlying *structures* or *operations* of human thought and belief. It tries to understand and define the *laws* or *patterns* the mind employs in constructing the ideas, concepts and beliefs that constitute the *contents* of thinking and valuing (Gardner, 1974; Piaget, 1970, 1973).

Jean Piaget began more than four decades ago to observe that the thinking of children systematically differs in important ways from the thinking of adults (Piaget, 1926; 1928; 1929; 1930). Through years of ingenious research Piaget developed and substantiated an explanatory theory of human mental development. Taking a structuralist viewpoint, he was able to add to it a *genetic* or *developmental* viewpoint. Piaget has shown us that human thinking develops according to certain uniform patterns or *structural stages*. These stages are *universal*. That is, they seem—on the basis of many experimental verifications—to occur in all cultures and human groups. Moreover, they occur in the same *sequence* everywhere, and that sequence is *invariant*. The growing person cannot skip over a stage. The stages build upon each other, and each more

1. The research on which this paper is based is supported by a grant to the author and the Harvard Divinity School from the Joseph P. Kennedy, Jr. Foundation of Washington, D.C. For the genuine interest of the officers and staff of the Foundation the author and his research team have deep appreciation.

advanced stage includes within it the transformed and integrated structures of earlier stages. (It should be remembered that we are speaking of the *structures underlying or constituting thought*, not of the *content* of thought, which of course is quite variable.)

Professor Lawrence Kohlberg of the Harvard Graduate School of Education has developed, across 20 years of research, a structural-developmental theory of moral development (Kohlberg, 1969; 1973). He has shown that though there are many different human cultures with highly diverse values, there seems to be a uniform sequence of structurally definable stages—invariant in order—by which persons develop in the capacity for making moral judgments.

Long before I knew about Piaget or Kohlberg I had become interested in faith and its development. During a year as Associate Director of Interpreters' House (1968-69) my work required that I listen to over 250 lay persons and ministers talk in some depth about their pilgrimages in faith. As I listened to these stories I began to see and expect certain recurring patterns and themes. Erik Erikson's eight-stage theory of psychosocial development proved immensely helpful in ordering and sorting out what I was hearing (Erikson, 1959; 1963). When I began to teach at Harvard Divinity School in 1970 I offered a course in which I tried to reflect systematically with students about certain uniformities in the patterns of development in religious orientation and awareness. As I became aware of the theories and research of Piaget and Kohlberg I was able to add more rigor to my own thinking and research.

Over the past three years I have devoted much of my time to an effort to see if we can empirically establish and refine a structural-developmental theory of what I have called "faith development" (Fowler, 1974 a, b). The present chapter represents a provisional description of such a structurally defined sequence of stages. The detailed description offered here is a preliminary result of the empirical research and reflection carried out by the author, his students, and the research staff of the Project on Faith and Moral Development.[2]

FAITH AS A VERB: A PRELIMINARY DEFINITION

Faith in English can be employed only as a noun. The modifiers "faithful" and "faithfully" are derived from it, but none of the three forms denotes the *activity*, the *state of being*, or the *quality of*

2. Members of the research staff who made special contributions to the research on which this paper is based are: Norene Carter, Ronald Marstin, Robert G. Kegan, Romney M. Moseley, and Lawrence Cunningham.

participation which we need to associate with faith. At the outset, then, we need to begin to think of faith as a way *of knowing, of construing,* or *of interpreting* experience. In short, we need to begin thinking of faith as a *verb.*

In a sense, faith is a knowing, a construing, or an interpreting that fixes on the relatedness of a person or a community to those sources of power and values which impinge on life in a manner not subject to personal control. In theological language, faith is the knowing or construing by which persons apprehend themselves as related to the transcendent.[3]

Understood as a verb, faith has another distinguishing quality: it is a knowing or a construing in which cognition (the "rational") is inextricably fused with affectivity or valuing (the "passional"). In faith, one holds a disposition over against the transcendent. That is, one may trust, give loyalty, have love or admiration for the transcendent; or one may fear, resent, distrust or revolt against it. Thus, faith qualifies and gives tone to one's entire way of understanding, reacting to, and taking initiatives in the world.

Moreover, faith is always *relational.* It is one's *sense of relatedness* to the ultimate conditions and depths of existence. Faith is *bi-polar* in the sense that it is the binding of the self and the transcendent. It is the awareness, the intuition, the conviction of a relatedness to something or someone more than the mundane.

But faith is relational in another sense as well. Perhaps it is more accurate to say faith is *tri-polar.* In addition to the transcendent, there is a binding of the self with *community.* In this sense, there is a relatedness to the ultimate conditions of existence which simultaneously informs and qualifies our relations and interactions with the mundane, the everyday, the world of other persons and things.

This leads to the observation that faith has both an *outer* and an *inner* structure. Though our empirical research will primarily focus on understanding the form of the inner structure of faith-knowing, it is important to point out that faith always has a social or an interpersonal dimension. It is to this outer, interpersonal, or covenantal structure of faith we now turn.

---

3. At the risk of some confusion I am using the term "transcendent" here as a collective construct representing a person's way of taking account of, or paying deference to, some kind of pattern or coherence in the welter of being, value and power that impinges upon the self from beyond the self. The term, as used here, may be filled with theistic or monistic content—as it would have to be for some persons. But it need not necessarily be thought of or be made to function in those ways.

The Outer Structure of Faith: World Maintenance

A few years ago Gerhard Ebeling, a German Luther-scholar and theologian, preached a memorable sermon in Harvard Memorial Church. His title was a question: "What Happens if God Is Removed?" Preaching in the midst of the "Death of God" spasm in the United States, Ebeling tried to depict a world in which any and all awareness of transcendence is expunged. If you picture that circumstance radically, as the expunging of *every* human vision, revealed and otherwise, of excellence of being, you perhaps get at least an intellectual sense of what faith is by imagining its absence. Many of us have known those times when the transcendent was experienced as illusory, a void, or at most a spiteful and arbitrary enemy. We may have been members of communities in which faith was present more by its negation than by its acknowledgment of any vision of excellence of being. If so, we know something of the quality of life the Bible has in view when it speaks of "faithless generations."

World maintenance, the holding together of a shared vision of reality in human communities, requires interpersonal faith and faithfulness. It also requires a common awareness of relatedness to the transcendent. It involves a tri-polar or covenantal relationship among persons, and among them and shared visions of excellence of being. In a real sense the answer to Ebeling's question, "What Happens if God Is Removed?" is that the world of interpersonal faithfulness collapses. Solipsism sets in, both *epistemological* solipsism, in which each person construes the world and the ultimate conditions of existence after his or her own fashion, and *moral* solipsism, in which each person acts solely out of an ethics of maximizing one's own survival, security, and significance.

H. Richard Niebuhr, writing nearly two decades ago, offers a disturbingly contemporary observation:

> Questions about faith, faithfulness or fidelity, trust or confidence arise in an urgent and tragic form as we view the massive and petty betrayals and deceptions of our time —the propaganda of the "big lie," the cultivation of mutual distrust in society as measures of party and national policy, the use of pretended loyalty in conspiracies against state and civilization, the enlistment of men as faithful followers of causes that depend for success on practices of deception. Here the question of faith appears in negative form as the problem of the meaning of treason. The experiences of the twentieth century have brought into view

the abyss of faithlessness into which men can fall. We see this possibility—that human history could come to its end neither in a brotherhood of man nor in universal death under the blows of natural or man-made catastrophe, but in the gangrenous corruption of a social life in which every promise, contract, treaty, and word of dishonor is given and accepted in deception and distrust. If men no longer have faith in each other, can they exist as men? (Niebuhr, 1957)

The maintenance of "reality," therefore, requires constant renewal and transformation. Trust and loyalty to one another—and to one another in a shared vision of excellence of being—must consistently be developing and re-vivifying. The principal contribution of institutional religions in cultures is their generation of renewing power and passion in the mainly tacit covenant which sustains a people's interpersonal trust and their shared visions of excellence of being. A society's covenantal maintenance and continual renewal of "reality" requires faith in a transcendent source and center of being, value and power. It requires the continual emergence of *fresh apprehensions of excellence of being.*

In turning our attention to the inner structure of faith, it is well to remember that in the study of faith development we must hold in view a *dynamic, dialectical relationship* between the outer and the inner structures of faith.

The Inner Structure of Faith: Faith as Knowing

The reality of faith has often been gauged by what it produces in terms of initiatives and responses, heroic sacrifice or leadership, consistent commitment and the like. Scriptural endorsement for this process abounds (viz., James: "Faith without works is dead" and Matthew: "By their fruits you shall know them"). But faith as a *doing* or *being* includes and flows from faith as a kind of *knowing.*

Initiatives and responses arise out of interpretation—*an act of knowing or construing.*

Moral action and responsibility depend upon interpretation and the weighing of norms and values—*acts of knowing or construing.*

Faith as orientation to the ultimate conditions of existence, and as orientation to the neighbor and to everyday life in light of relatedness to the transcendent, involves interpretation—*acts of knowing or construing.*

When we ask "What kind of knowing is faith?" we focus

first on the *content*, i.e., on *what* it is that faith knows. Faith, we have said, is a knowing by which we construe our relatedness to the limiting boundaries or depths of experience. In this knowing, cognition and affection are interwoven. In faith we are rarely indifferent to the transcendent. The total self is involved. It may be disposed negatively and hostilely, distrustfully and rebelliously; or, it may be disposed positively—with love, trust, and loyal responsibility. According to Whitehead, "Religion is the transition from God the Void to God the Enemy, and from God the Enemy to God the Companion" (Whitehead, 1960, p. 17). Faith, which often comes to expression in religion, may apprehend the transcendent and one's relation to it in terms either of the Void, the Enemy, or the Companion. No one of those interpretations is purely cognitive or rational. Each of them, whether positive or negative, is a *valuing* apprehension, a knowing in which passion and care are invested. Faith-knowing, therefore, is simultaneously orientation and arousal, perspective and motivation, indicative and imperative.

On the other hand, we must also look at faith as *a way of knowing and construing* as well as *that which is known and construed*. This involves looking at knowing and valuing as *patterned processes* rather than as *knowledge and values*. This means looking at the inner structure of faith.

This focus on the structural character of faith-knowing has its parallels in theories of cognitive and moral development. Piaget's research has concerned itself, not primarily with the child's knowledge of mathematics, physics and logic, but rather with the patterns of thinking and reasoning which the child has developed to organize its experience of the world, and which therefore underlie its knowledge of the physical environment. Similarly, Kohlberg's studies of moral development have focused not primarily on the content and outcomes of moral decisions, but on the forms or structures of thinking evidenced in the justifications or explanations of moral choices.

Faith-knowing has its own structural core. Now undoubtedly it is the content and concreteness of a particular person's faith that most makes it interesting and powerful in its effects on others. It is the beliefs, the values, the symbols and cultic allegiances of a person which in principal measure give faith its determinativeness for his or her behavior. But that does not give the whole picture, for the same or similar content of faith may be appropriated in quite different ways by persons whose faith-knowing is structurally at different stages. There also exists some correlation between structu-

ral stages and the possibility of grasping or being grasped by particular beliefs, ritual practices, and socioethical imperatives. Certain
types of beliefs, symbols, and ritual practices may vary greatly, but
there is evidence that the structural patterns of faith-knowing show
constancies that may not be so variable with respect to form or the
sequence of development within individuals.

Summary
    Content—the actual images, values, beliefs, symbols and rituals
—of a person's or community's faith is of central importance in informing their behavior and shaping personality. We are interested
in this content of faith in its richness, individuality, and concreteness. The interviews we conduct are designed precisely to try to
bring this out. The stage theory, however, focuses on that which is
less variable and more constant and capable of comparison between
persons and communities, namely, the inner form or structure of
faith-knowing.[4]

RESEARCH PROCEDURE

    Our way of investigating faith development makes use of what
Piaget called a "semi-clinical" interview (Piaget, 1929; Elkind,
1964). With adults we generally spend a half-hour or so taking
preliminary data on life history. Here we ask for decisive events
and relationships, work and marital history, and some indications
of their own ideas about their development. This part of the interview is not recorded. It helps interviewer and respondent become
comfortable with each other, and helps the interviewer to become
acquainted with the vocabulary, frame of reference and self-percep-
tions of the respondent. After this preliminary exploration is complete the taped interview begins. The goals of the interview—which
may last one to three hours, are: 1) to elicit the content of the
respondent's thinking, valuing and feeling about a set of issues
with which faith must deal, and 2) to get and clarify the respondent's sense of the path of his or her development of outlook. The
set of issues, which we will discuss below, is uniform from interview to interview. The order in which they are brought up and the
language in which questions about them are formulated, however,
vary with different respondents. A good interviewer conducts the

4. This section is a modified version of parts of an earlier article (Fowler, 1974
a). For a fuller discussion of these matters and for the author's distinction between
faith, religion and belief see Fowler, 1974 b.

conversation within the frame of reference and vocabulary of the respondent. In an almost conversational manner the issues are introduced in a natural flow. But in order to gain access to the structural characteristics underlying or organizing the person's thinking and feeling the interviewer must probe and question in a much more rigorous way than is usual in everyday conversation.

With children from 4 to 10 or 11 our efforts to elicit their thinking and valuing focus on the same issues. Our modes of approach, however, combine doll-play and story completion with the question-and-answer approach. Children vary greatly in their ability and interest for conversations of this sort. Children's interviews vary in length from approximately 30 to 50 minutes.

With both children and adults our interviewers make an effort not to introduce specifically religious terms or questions during the first half to two-thirds of the interview. We are interested to see if religious ideas, beliefs or symbols are spontaneously drawn upon by the respondent in discussing the issues of faith. Toward the latter half to one-third of the interview explicit questions with reference to religion are introduced if they have not, by that time, entered the conversation through the respondent's initiative.

The following list of issues were generated in our research approach to enable us to deal with two difficult problems. First, having tried to define faith as a human universal rather than strictly as a matter of religion or belief, how were we to gain empirical access to it? How could we elicit the content and structure of a person's "faithing" without biasing their responses by the use of the language of one religious tradition or another? The answer to the first question carried us toward the open-ended, semi-clinical approach already described. As much as possible we wanted to provide a blank slate or screen on which the respondent could project his or her own distinctive manner and content of thinking and feeling. But this brought us up against the second problem. How, while respecting the uniqueness of each person's faith, could we achieve comparability between interviews? How could we assure enough continuity between interviews to make comparative analysis possible and useful? Our solution to these problems led us to try to define a set of existential issues with which faith as a human universal must help persons deal. This set of issues may in fact be the best practical indicator of the focus we have in mind in faith-development inquiry. Informing each interview, they constitute the topics or problems which we ask people to address. In their constancy they provide the basis for making comparisons between the faith contents and processes revealed by our respondents. Remember that in an interview these issues may come up in any order and in terms that are "natural" to the respondents. Here is the list:

Death and afterlife
The limits of knowledge
Causation and effectance in personal and historical life
Evil and suffering
Freedom and determinism
Power and agency
Meaning of life
Ideal manhood or womanhood
The future
Grounding of ethical or moral imperative
Communal identification and belonging
Bases of guilt and shame
Loyalties and commitments
Locus of transcendent beauty, value or power
Grounds of terror or dread
Beliefs about what is sinful or a violation
Beliefs and ideas about religion and specifically religious symbols
Images of male and female; sex-role images and religious symbols

In relation to each of these issues an effort is made in the interviews to test espoused beliefs and values against examples of actual patterns of behavior and action as offered by the respondent in reply to the interviewer's probing.

In our 1974-75 interviews, in addition to following the procedures just outlined, we have administered a Kohlberg moral dilemma in the interview so as to give us some bases for clarifying relationships between stages in moral and faith development. Interviews are transcribed verbatim. Analyses are based on the transcriptions.

RESPONDENT SAMPLE, 1972-74

The stage descriptions that are offered in this chapter are the most complete and comprehensive which we have published to date. They corroborate and extend the descriptions offered in earlier published statements (Fowler 1974 a, 1974 b), and serve, for the time being, as the basis for scoring faith interviews. The descriptions offered here grow out of the analysis of 118 interviews conducted by the author and his associates over a two-year period from 1972-74. Since the present descriptions were written the author and his research team have completed 109 additional interviews with subjects selected so as to correct the biases in the original sample of 118. Preliminary analysis of the 1975 data in principle confirms the ·stage descriptions offered here. However, the present account should be regarded as provisional until our analyses of the more recent data are complete. (A monograph on the project and its findings will appear in September, 1976.)

Table I provides a profile by age, sex, and religious background of the 118 respondents interviewed from 1972 to 1974.

TABLE I

Age	Prot. M	Prot. F	Cath. M	Cath. F	Jew M	Jew F	Other M	Other F	Total M	Total F	Total M&F
4-7	1	2	2	2				1	3	5	8
8-12	6	4	3	4		1		2	9	11	20
13-20	8	8	4	10	2	3			14	21	35
21-30	4	4	5	6		4	4		13	14	27
31-40	2	4	2	6				1	4	11	15
41-50		3		1						4	4
51-60	1	1	1	2	1				3	3	6
61-	1		2						3		3
TOTALS	23	26	19	31	3	8	4	4	49	69	118
	49		50		11		8				

The reader will note the relative paucity of interviews in the age ranges of 4-7 in both sexes, in men from 41-50, and in both sexes 51 and above. While there is substantial representation of Protestants and Catholics from 8-30, Jewish and "Other" subjects were not adequately represented in this age range in the sample. Our spring 1975 data rectifies these imbalances. It also provides a richer diversity in ethnic, social-class, and educational backgrounds. Our preliminary analyses give us confidence that the new data, while clarifying some ambiguities in the present stage descriptions, confirms the presence and validity of the stages we have identified and tried to describe here and elsewhere.

Table II provides a graphic profile of the number of respondents found at each stage. We have plotted male and female respondents separately and then have given the composite curve. Because of the imbalances mentioned above, any hypotheses or conclusions about the meaning of the relative shapes of the curves should wait until we take account of later data. Transitionals are included in the previous stages except at the 2-3, 3-4 and 4-5 transitions, where the numbers are significant and are therefore plotted separately.

TABLE II

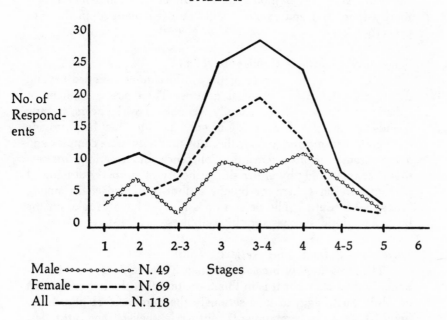

Male ○○○○○○○○○○○ N. 49   Stages
Female — — — — — — N. 69
All ——————— N. 118

THE STAGES: A BRIEF OVERVIEW

In our effort to give a structural-developmental account of faith we have identified *six stages*—moving from more simple and undifferentiated structures to those that are more complex and differentiated. Faith manifests growing self-awareness as you move through the stages. The ages given with each of these stages represent an average *minimal* age. Many persons attain them, if at all, at later chronological ages. Stage attainment varies from person to person and equilibrium of a stable sort may occur for different persons or groups at or in different stages.

Stage one—Intuitive-Projective Faith

The imitative, fantasy-filled phase in which the child can be powerfully and permanently influenced by the examples, moods, actions and language of the visible faith of primal adults (age 4).

Stage two—Mythic-Literal Faith
The stage in which the person begins to take on for himself/herself the stories and beliefs and observances that symbolize belonging to his/her community. Attitudes are observed and adopted; beliefs are appropriated with literal interpretations, as are moral rules and attitudes. Symbols are one-dimensional and literal. Authority (parental) and example still count for more than those of peers (6-1/2-8).

Stage three—Synthetic-Conventional Faith
The person's experience of the world is now extended beyond the family and primary social groups. There are a number of spheres or theaters of life: family, school or work, peers, leisure, friendship, and possibly a religious sphere. Faith must help provide a coherent and meaningful synthesis of that now more complex and diverse range of involvements. Coherence and meaning are certified, at this stage, by either the authority of properly designated persons in each sphere, or by the authority of consensus among "those who count." The person does not yet have to take on the burden of world-synthesis for himself/herself (12-13).

Stage four—Individuating-Reflexive Faith
The movement or break from Stage Three to Stage Four is particularly important for it is in this transition that the late adolescent or adult must begin to take seriously the burden of responsibility for his/her own commitments, life-style, beliefs and attitudes. Where there is genuinely a transition to Stage Four the person must face certain universal polar tensions which Synthetic-Conventional faith allows one to evade:

individuality	v. belonging to community
subjectivity	v. objectivity
self-fulfillment	v. service to others
the relative	v. the absolute

Often Stage Four develops under the tutelage of ideologically powerful religions, charismatic leadership, or ideologies of other kinds. It often finds it necessary to collapse these polar tensions in one direction or the other. Stage Four both brings and requires a qualitatively new and different kind of self-awareness and responsibility for one's choices and rejections (18-19).

Stage Five—Paradoxical-Consolidative Faith

In Stage Four the person is self-aware in making commitments and knows something of what is being *excluded* by the choices he/she makes. But for Stage Four, the ability to decide is grounded, in part at least, on the fact that one set of commitments is overvalued at the expense of necessarily viewing alternatives to it in a partial and limiting light.

Stage Five represents an advance in the sense that it recognizes the integrity and truth in positions other than its own, and it affirms and lives out its own commitments and beliefs in such a way as to honor that which is true in the lives of others without denying the truth of its own. Stage Five is ready for community of identification beyond tribal, racial, class or ideological boundaries. *To be genuine, it must know the cost of such community and be prepared to pay the cost.* A true Stage Five requires time and testing and regard for those who are different and who oppose you which Stage Four does not have. In a true Stage Five *espoused values and beliefs are congruent with risk, and action taken* (30-32).

Stage Six—Universalizing Faith

Stage Five's commitment to inclusive community remains paradoxical. To affirm others means to deny oneself. Defensiveness and egocentrism make the affirmation of others' truth difficult and threatening. One's own interests and investments in tribe, class, religion, nation, region, etc., still constitute biasing and distorting loyalties, which have to be struggled with and overcome continually.

Stage Six Universalizing Faith *is rare.* At this stage what Christians and Jews call the Kingdom of God is a live, felt reality for the person of faith. Here one dwells *in* the world as a transforming presence, but is not *of* the world. The sense of the oneness of all persons is not a glib ideological belief but has become a permeative basis for decision and action. The paradox has gone out of being-for-others; at Stage 6, one is being most truly oneself. Stage Six's participation in the Ultimate is direct and immediate. Their community is universal in inclusiveness. Such persons are ready for fellowship with persons at any of the other stages and from any other faith tradition. They seem instinctively to know how to relate to us affirmingly, never condescendingly, yet with pricks to our pretense and with genuine bread of life (38-40).

Stages Described by Variables

A faith stage is a structural whole. To break open the metaphor a bit we may say that a stage is organismic—a flexible organization of interrelated patterns of operation. When one analyzes a faith interview one wants to read or hear "through" to the structural whole underlying the beliefs, values, attitudes and actions described in the linear prose of the respondent. The problem is to read or hear and comprehend in such a way that the content becomes clear, at one level; but on another level one wants to let the structures of the person's faith "precipitate" out of the content that has been offered. Here it is important to distinguish two possible kinds of "wholes" that might be thought of in this connection. One kind might refer to the organic whole, consisting of the themes, beliefs, ideas and propositions, of the content of a person's faith or worldview. That focus would lend itself to viewing each person's faith as a more-or-less adequate *systematic theology*. The structure—if one used that term—would really refer to a system of ideas. When we use the term "structure" here, however, we are referring instead to the pattern of operations or modes of thinking and valuing which are constitutive of the person's ability to use and give form to beliefs, values, ideas and propositions. Structures in this second sense could not be translated into systematic theology, but rather into a kind of *epistemology of faith*.

As an aid to "precipitating" structures of faith we have identified a series of what we call *variables*. These may best be thought of as windows or apertures into the structures underlying faith. Presumably, if our claim that a stage is a structural whole is correct, one will see the same essential structures, only from several different points of vantage, through these variables. Since the next several pages will present the stages in terms of an articulation of these variables it will be useful now to characterize each of the variables briefly. Each variable has its own developmental pattern across the stages. To really master this theory one must develop a grasp of each stage as a structural whole—the variables in their interrelatedness; but one must also understand the developmental-stage sequence of each of the variables. Thus we find that both "horizontal" and "vertical" readings of the stage-variable presentation are essential for getting hold of the theory.

Variable A: Locus of Authority

This variable focuses on the question "Who or what is the reference by which the person gains or validates reliable orientation toward the ultimate conditions of existence?" Overall, the developmental sequence in this variable is from external authority to internal; from authority inhering in other persons, to authority in custom, institution and law, and on to authority based on one's own more critical experience, judgment and loyalties.

Variable B: Criteria and Modes of Appropriation

This variable fixes on the implicit or explicit criteria employed by a person in weighing and appropriating insights, claims or (his/her own) intuitions as regards faith orientation. Developmentally these range from unconscious characteristics of bodily and instinctual rhythms, to felt but not self-aware affinities and dependencies, to more-or-less self-aware adherence to the implicit norms of one's most primary communities, and to criteria growing from one's increasingly individuated sense of identity, commitment and purpose.

Variable C: Symbolic and Conceptual Functioning

In this variable we see the development of cognitive capacities as they focus on the matters with which faith deals. This variable traces the precursors and development of self-critical awareness and the ability to utilize symbols and concepts in an increasingly self-conscious way. Terminally it characterizes a post-critical capacity to dwell-in but also to transcend religious symbols in a direct participation in Being.

Variable D: Role-Taking and Extensiveness of Identification

In this variable the work of Piaget, Kohlberg, Flavell, and Selman on the development of role-taking has been supplemented by the work of Kegan and Fowler on construction of community. This variable focuses on the person's way of constructing the inner motivations, intentions and feelings of other persons. It begins with initial egocentrism. Then, developmentally it leads through mutual role-taking and eventually to the ability to take the role of other groups and of their world-views. This development is correlated with a gradual expansion in the inclusion of other persons and groups in one's reference community, and moves toward a meaningful sense of membership in a universal commonwealth of being.

Variable E: Prototypical Challenges with Which Faith Must Deal

Informed by Erikson's work on the developmental crises of the healthy personality, this variable seeks to clarify the typical existen-

TABLE III

EXPECTED PARALLELS BETWEEN DEVELOPMENTAL THEORIES

PIAGET (Cognitive)	KOHLBERG (Moral)	FOWLER (Faith)	ERIKSON (Psychosocial)
(0-2)—Sensory-Motor	0—The good is what I want and like	0—Undifferentiated	1—Trust v. Mistrust
			2—Autonomy v. Shame and Doubt
(2-6)—Intuitive or Pre-Logical [Pre-Operational]	1—Punishment and obedience orientation	1—Intuitive-Projective	3—Initiative v. Guilt
(7-11)—Concrete Operations	2—Instrumental hedonism and concrete reciprocity	2—Mythic-Literal	4—Industry v. Inferiority
	3—Orientation to interpersonal relations of mutuality	3—Synthetic-Conventional	
(12-) Formal Operations	4—Maintenance of social order, fixed rules and authority		5—Identity v. Role-Confusion

PIAGET (Cognitive)	KOHLBERG (Moral)	FOWLER (Faith)	ERIKSON (Psychosocial)
		4—Individuating-Reflexive	6—Intimacy v. Isolation
	5—Social contract, utilitarian, law-making perspective	5—Paradoxical-Consolidative	7—Generativity v. Stagnation
Piagetian stages are taken to be necessary but not sufficient for corresponding stages of moral and faith development	6—Universal ethical principle orientation	6—Universalizing	8—Integrity v. Despair

tial challenges we find correlated with each stage. Less structurally definable than the other variables, this one tries to show how structural gains are interrelated with the rise and eventual solution of existential challenges.

In the pages that follow you will find descriptions of the structural features of each of our stages. These descriptions are given in terms of the variables that have just been characterized. The sequence of discussing the variables at each stage will remain consistent to facilitate cross-stage comparisons.

These descriptions have an inevitably formal or abstract quality. The reader is invited to make imaginative use of personal experience or the experiences of others in giving "flesh" or content to the stages as described.

"Average ages" have been given for each of the stages. In a sense, as was explained earlier, these are average *minimal* ages—ages below which we have not found a given stage. Remember that persons may attain structural stages at varying rates; stages are not necessarily tied to biological maturation or chronological age. Persons of normal or above intelligence may reach a stable equilibration or an apparent "arrest" at any stage from Two on. Stage development is not automatic or inevitable. It depends upon biological and neurological givens, the contents and "the modal developmental level" of the cultural milieu,[5] and the idiosyncratic life experiences, challenges and social-role opportunities of a given person. Occasionally we have found adult persons whose faith outlook is best described by Stage Two, but in this society that is rare. Many more adults, however, seem best described by Stage Three. It is not uncommon to find adults whose faith has reached and maintained an equilibrated pattern which is best described by a combination of Stage Three and Stage Four features. And then we find that a significant proportion of our adult respondents are most aptly described by Stage 4. Stage Five is much rarer. Stage 5 we so far know about primarily through such sources as autobiographies, biographies and journals.

We believe that what we are describing here are true stages in the Piagetian and Kohlbergian sense. That is, we believe they do constitute *integrated structural wholes*, which are *hierarchically related* (each successive stage incorporating the capacities of all the previous ones). We believe that the order is *sequential* and *invariant*. We are not, however, prepared to claim *universality* for

5. For a stimulating discussion of this useful concept see Keniston, 1974, pp. 160 ff.

these stages at this point. (See Greenfield and Bruner, 1969.) Cross-cultural studies are projected for the late 1970's that will provide a basis for clarifying the degree to which our stages are culturally relative. Within the cultural and social milieu in which we have conducted research, however, we have growing confidence that these stages begin to approximate a developmental sequence that is universal.

We prefer to think of stage descriptions as lenses or filters through or by which to look at the person's faith as we come to know it through our interviews. Thinking of the stages as heuristic lenses or filters helps to avoid reification into a pigeonhole mentality. The stages are tentative efforts to "model" a sequence of certain wholistic patterns of feeling, valuing, thinking and committing. We believe they are helpful across the range of variables or dimensions they describe. As with any lens or filter system, however, while they clarify in some areas, they blur or obscure or are useless in others. Above all we want to avoid the nefarious misuse of this stage theory that would make of it a value scale to determine the relative worth of persons or groups. Each stage may be *the* most appropriate stage for a particular person or group. Each stage describes a pattern of valuing, thinking, feeling and committing that is potentially worthy, serene and "grace-ful."

STAGE ONE—INTUITIVE-PROJECTIVE FAITH
(Average ages: 4-7)

A. Locus of Authority

Fundamental dispositions and their expression depend principally on relations to "primal" other (parents, family or surrogates). These persons represent power, nurturance and security. The child's dependence on and affectional ties with them makes them prime authorities or references in his/her construction of a meaningful world. They convey both consciously and subliminally their own basic outlooks and commitment toward the ultimate conditions of life.

Where the faith of primal others is expressed congruently in the language, symbol, and ritual of a religious tradition, those media may take on a character of authority for the child, though the child's reliance on them is derivative and secondhand.

B. Criteria and Modes of Appropriation

Manifest interest in a child and the possession of visible (surface) qualities that attract the child's imagination and interest are required to qualify adults as faith models at this stage. Children attend to and imitate the moods, gestures and visible practices of such primal persons. The "forms" so observed stimulate and give channels for the children's own projections of numinous intuitions and fantasies with which they try to come to terms with a world as yet unlawful, magical and unpredictable. Cognitive understanding of the language and actions of commitment of significant others is limited, but affective investment in such often give them formative power in the child's normative awareness of ideal responsibility or adulthood.[6]

C. Symbolic and Conceptual Functioning

Thinking is *pre-operational* (Piaget), marked by egocentrism, and by the use of symbols and concepts (or pre-concepts—Vygotsky) in labile and fluid fashion. Typically there is little concern to separate fantasy from fact. Narrative ability is limited. Causal relations are vague to the child and notions of effectance in the world tend toward magical explanations.

Symbols of deity, where used, are frequently preanthropomorphic with an effort to use such ideas as invisibleness, soul and air to depict a God who nonetheless acts physically and substantially on the world.

D. Role-Taking and Extensiveness of Identification

There is little ability as yet to take the role of others. The child is not yet able to construct and interpret the inner feelings, intentions or reasoning of other persons. Interaction with others therefore is largely a matter of moment-to-moment parallel behavior, as in playing.

Prime identity and attachment are to family or caring group. While there is little consistent awareness of one's differences from other persons or groups, a sense of sexual, racial and perhaps ethnic identity *is* already forming.

E. Prototypical Challenges with Which Faith Must Deal

A self-system is forming that begins to have both a conscious present and a vague futurity. With growing clarity about the self as separate from others comes a new kind of anxiety rooted in the awareness of death. Now the child knows that death threatens.

6. For a dramatic illustration of this see my discussion of the childhood of Malcolm X in Fowler, 1974 b, pp. 11-13.

Those on whom one is so vulnerably dependent can be removed by death. Faith, largely a matter of reliance on these others, needs to find a ground of hope and sustenance beyond them in order to "contain" the anxiety of possible abandonment through their death.

This is not to claim that the child is obsessed with these concerns. There are moments, of course, when they are obsessive, and for some children, actual. But they constitute an unavoidable shadow, an underside of life, which has to be dealt with in some fashion.

There must be some dim but potent locus for authority and forces beyond the immediate, tangible presence of parents or other significant adults. Death, sickness, bad luck as well as their opposites are not totally under control of those who "control" the child. Parents or their substitutes often give evidence of acknowledging power(s) and authority(s) beyond themselves. Some sort of deference must be paid to these powers that transcend and hold even parents in their grip and sway.

STAGE TWO—MYTHIC-LITERAL FAITH
(Average ages: 6-1/2—11)

A. Locus of Authority

The realm of worthy authority now extends beyond primal others to include teachers, religious leaders, customs, traditions, the media, books, and the ideas of peers. The mythic lore, the ritual, the music and symbolism of a religious tradition can make powerful impressions on persons at this stage. As regards matters of perceptual experience the child's own logic and judgment are coming to be relied upon in a kind of empiricism.

Unless they have disqualified themselves, the primal-familial group, now extended to take in others "like us" (in religious, ethnic, social class and/or racial terms), typically still provide the most important models and validating sanctions for the form and content of faith.

B. Criteria and Modes of Appropriation

New role-taking ability enables one now to evaluate and respond to qualities in authorities that are no longer merely surface (as in Stage One). Potentially authoritative persons or sources for faith insights tend to be weighed by criteria like the following: (1) "Fit" with the values, style, tastes and commitments of those with whom one feels greatest emotional affinity and identification. (2) Consistency in expressing real regard for the person. (3) Appearance of competence and/or interesting qualities that promise access to a vaguely aspired to futurity. (4) "Orthodoxy" (the way "we" do it) as regards the style of religious action. The operation of such criteria is not self-conscious or self-aware at Stage Two, but is an implicit function of the person's belonging to a familial or extended-familial group.

C. Symbolic and Conceptual Functioning

Concrete operational thinking has developed. Fluidity of concepts and symbolism has diminished. The child is concerned to understand lawfulness and predictability in relations between persons and in conditions affecting one's life. There is a strong empirical bent fostering an experimental approach as regards the tangible world.

Symbols for deity, where used, are typically anthropomorphic. They have power to cause and make; but they also have feelings and will and are attentive to the intentions of humans.

Narrative ability is now well developed. There is interest in myths and heroic images. One-dimensionality and literalism mark efforts to "explain" that which myth and symbols try to convey.

D. Role-Taking and Extensiveness of Identification

The ability to take the perspective of the other has developed, though mutual role-taking (i.e., seeing myself as others are seeing me as we interact) is not yet possible. The person can take the role of the group, but does not see self through the eyes of the group. Interaction with others is now *cooperative* (H. S. Sullivan) in contrast to Stage One's parallelism.

The person's identity and faith still derive their parameters largely from ascriptive membership in the primal group and its ethnic, racial, social class and religious extensions, which now have considerable clarity for the person. Those who are "different" are characterized in Stage Two thinking by fairly undifferentiated stereotypical images.

E. Prototypical Challenges with Which Faith Must Deal

The person's world now has a kind of order and dependability about it which results from the experience of continuities and from new cognitive abilities (inductive and deductive logic, capacities for classifying and seriating, understanding of causal relations, and a sense of time as linear). No longer does the person experience the world as potentially so capricious, arbitrary or mysterious as before. The person operates with a more dependable understanding of the dispositions, intentions, motives and expectations of others—and of oneself. The orderliness or dependability of the (cognitively available) world makes possible a projection of order and intentionality onto a more cosmic theater. Reciprocity and fairness, lawfulness and respect for intentions characterize ideas of God at this stage.

There are still, however, arbitrary elements and forces impinging on life beyond the ordering capacities of the child. Death, illness, accidents, and the unfolding of the person's own physical characteristics and capacities come as contingent elements of experience.

Faith helps sustain a sense of worth and competence by investing in ideal self-images which, though largely private, do include identification and affiliation with ideal persons and groups. Religious symbols, myths, ritual, music, and heroic figures can provide (where accessible) important vehicles of identification and affiliation. Where effectively offered they can become means of evoking and expressing the child's or person's faith in a transmundane order or meaning, as well as being guarantors of present and future promise.

STAGE THREE—SYNTHETIC-CONVENTIONAL FAITH
(Average ages: 12-adulthood)

A. Locus of Authority

Conventionally or consensually sanctioned authorities are relied upon in the various different spheres of one's life. Criteria for valid authority continue to be a blend of requirements of interpersonal virtues and competence, but now add credentialing by institutions, by custom, or through the ascription of authority by consensus. Authority tends to be external to self, though personal responsibility is accepted for determining the choice and weighing available sources of guidance or insight. Dissonances between valued authorities are solved either by compartmentalization or hierarchical subordination. Feeling tends to dominate conceptual reasoning.

B. Criteria and Modes of Appropriation

Criteria for truth are generated from what one feels or thinks on the basis of conventionally validated values, beliefs and norms.

The examples and expectations of "collective others" constitute important sources of criteria. Stage Three differs from Stage Two in that there is now a "collective other" which includes institutional and civil doctrines and law (as well as significant persons) which constitute an implicit value system against which authorities and insights can be evaluated. But there is no ground for other criteria by which one's own most deeply felt and held commitments can be critically evaluated. There is implicitly a continuing reliance on a community (or communities) which sponsor or nurture one's beliefs, attitudes and values.

C. Symbolic and Conceptual Functioning

Early Formal Operational thinking is characteristic. Symbols are employed as having multiple levels of meaning, though there is little self-consciousness about this. There is a limited use of abstractions.

There is a tacit system to one's world-view, but this system is legitimated by external authorities and inner feelings and is not a matter of critical reflection *qua* system. The person's beliefs and concepts that are expressive of faith function not as theoretical ideas but as existentially valued orientations.

The person is prepared to make do with rather global and undifferentiated ideas and symbols. A penumbra of mystery and deference to qualified authority compensate for the lack of conscious internal linkages and integration.

D. Role-Taking and Extensiveness of Identification

Mutual role-taking has developed in interpersonal relations. One can now see himself/herself through the eyes of a group or groups. Interaction with others now can be collaborative (H. S. Sullivan), involving full mutuality of role-taking with each other and with groups to which there are common loyalties (though such loyalties as yet are not matters of critically self-conscious choice).

Role-taking or identification with individuals beyond one's group(s) shows a limited development, but the inability to take the role of *groups* different than one's own is marked. Their world-views are likely to be assimilated to one's own. Identity derives from *belonging* (family, ethnic groups, sex-role, work unit) and/or *possessing* (respectability, competence, children, etc.).

E. Prototypical Challenges with Which Faith Must Deal

The existential challenges dominating Stage Three derive primarily from new cognitive capacities underlying mutual interpersonal role-taking. The person, now able to see himself/herself *as being seen by a variety of significant others* who occupy a variety of disparate standpoints in his/her world, has the problem of synthesizing those mirror images. Moreover, congruence must be found between his/her own feelings and images of self and the world and those held by others.

An amalgam of conventional images, values, beliefs and attitudes is fashioned to orient and provide boundaries for an as yet incompletely differentiated faith. In theistic expressions of faith at this stage, God is often the bearer of the role of the "collective other" who sums up the legitimate expectations and the individual loyalties of the significant others and groups in one's life. Faith is *derivative* at this stage as is identity—a more or less promising variant of a larger group style. (*Group* may here be defined by any or all of the following: ethnic-familial ties, social-class norms, regional perspectives and loyalties, a religious system, a techno-scientific ethos, peer values and pressures, and sex-role stereotypes.)

Faith, so expressed and buttressed, serves to provide a kind of coherence and comprehensive unity to one's experience of a now much more complex and ambiguous world. It also functions to sustain ideal self-images and bonds of affiliation with those significant others or sources of values and insights whose expectations, examples and teachings provide orientation in a potentially overwhelming and chaotic world. By appropriating mainly *vicarious* solutions to life's besetting tensions, and by screening out a fair amount of dissonant data, this stage of faith can provide powerful sustenance and a basis for decisive initiatives and action in life. But it has little way other than denial or oversimplifying assimilation to meet and take account of world-views and life-styles different than its own.

STAGE FOUR—INDIVIDUATING-REFLEXIVE FAITH
(Average ages: 18-adulthood)

A. Locus of Authority

Charismatic representatives of ideological options, intensive (if selective) attention to the personal experience of oneself and peers, and/or the ideological consensus of intentional (as opposed to ascriptive) groups, are typical loci of authority for this stage. Authority has begun to be internalized and criteria for its acceptance are no longer matters of convention. Loyalties are committed on the basis of the self's felt and ratified affinities of valuing, beliefs, style and need-fulfillment.

B. Criteria and Modes of Appropriation

Appropriation of truth or insight is guided by criteria of existential resonance and congruity with what one is becoming or has become. While previously one's world-view was part of a matrix of experiencing, authority and an implicit and assumed coherence, now there is awareness that one holds (as do others) a point of view. The reference point for validating explanations has shifted from assimilating them to a nurturing ethos (Stage Three) to measuring them and that ethos against one's own experience, values, and critical judgments.

C. Symbolic and Conceptual Functioning

Full formal operations are employed. The ability to reflect critically on one's faith has appeared. There is awareness that one's outlook is vulnerable and can shift, and also of the relativity of one's way of experiencing to that of others whose outlook and loyalties are different.

There is an awareness of one's world-view as an explicit system. There is a concern for inner consistency, integration and comprehensiveness. Stage Four typically has an ideological quality. There is an excess of assimilation over accommodation, of subjective over objective content. Differences with other world-views are sharply recognized and often dichotomized.

D. Role-Taking and Extensiveness of Identification

Subject has the ability to treat other groups or classes as objects of mutual role-taking. The continued existence and integrity of one's own group becomes an issue of concern, and conscious commitment is possible not only to other individuals (as in Stage Three) but also to norms, rules, and ideological perspectives that underlie groups or institutions.

Concern with group boundaries, exclusion and inclusion is typical. Purity and consistency are matters of both personal and group concern. Ideal patterns of relation, interpersonal and social-institutional, frequently are used to criticize existing patterns, with contrasts being sharply drawn. Derivative identity (Stage Three) has been supplanted by *awareness* identity.

E. Prototypical Challenges with Which Faith Must Deal

The existential challenges or crises activating Stage Four faith center around the issue of individuation. Telegraphically put, Stage Four develops in the effort to find or create identifications and affiliations with ideologically defined groups whose outlook is expressive of the self one is becoming and has become, and of the truth or truths which have come to provide one's fundamental orientation.

The transition to Stage Four involves becoming self-consciously aware of the boundaries of one's conventionally held outlook. This may arise either from confrontation with persons or groups who hold different coherent systems of belief and action, or it may come from experiencing the threatening of one's conventional synthesis under the impact of prolonged experiences of crisis that expose its limits. Or it may come from a combination of both these.

The hope and need is for affiliation with a group and its ideology that provides a style of living and seeing which both express and hold up models for further development of one's own individuating faith. Where this cannot be found or where a dominant ethos negates recognition of the need, many persons move into a potentially long-lasting transitional posture, dissatisfied with former Stage Three conventionalities, but without materials or models for construction of a Stage Four faith.

Stage Four faith provides channels and guidelines for religious or ideological orientation and for ethical and political responsibility in a world where the reality of relativism is threateningly real.

STAGE FIVE—PARADOXICAL-CONSOLIDATIVE FAITH
(Average ages: minimum ca. 30)

A. Locus of Authority

Authority has now been fully internalized. Insights are derived through a dialectical process of evaluation and criticism between one's most profound experiences and intuitions and such mature formulations of the human-ultimate relationship as are available. Multiple communities and points of view contribute to one's complex world-view, which is itself not reducible to any of these. While the normativity of tradition, scriptures, customs, ideologies and the like is taken seriously these no longer are solely determinative for the person. Personal methods and discipline have developed for maintaining a living relationship with, participation in, or deference to the transcendent of the ultimate conditions of life.

B. Criteria and Modes of Appropriation

Criteria for truth and adequacy of faith claims or insights now derive from a holding together of intentions for oneself and one's community (as in Stage Four) with intentions and hopes for a more inclusive community or humanity. There is tension between the claims of egocentric or "group-centric" loyalties and loyalties to a more comprehensive community; similarly between "objectivity" and "subjectivity" in the use of concepts and symbols. Stage Five embraces these tensions, accepting paradox when necessary, as essential characteristics of truth.

C. Symbolic and Conceptual Functioning

Stage Five affirms and incorporates existential or logical polarities, acting on a felt need to hold them in tension in the interest of truth. It maintains its vision of meaning, coherence and value while being conscious of the fact that it is partial, limited and contradicted by the visions and claims of others. It is not simply relativist, affirming that one person's faith is as good as another's if equally strongly held. It holds its vision with a kind of provisional ultimacy: remembering its inadequacy and open to new truth, but also committed to the absoluteness of the truth which it inadequately comprehends and expresses.

Symbols are understood as symbols. They are seen-through in a double sense: (1) their time-place relativity is acknowledged and (2) their character as relative representations of something more nearly absolute is affirmed.

D. Role-Taking and Extensiveness of Identification

The person has the ability not only to take the role of another person or group but also to take the role of another person's or group's world-view in its full complexity.

Stage Five must sustain political/ethical activity that has a more complex character than at Stage Four. It has a double consciousness not required of Stage Four. With opposing groups it must acknowledge a significant measure of identification—both in rights and wrongs—strengths and weaknesses. It has the burden of awareness of the degree to which "free will" or choice is always limited in fateful ways by a person's or group's history and situation. It must decide and act, but bears inevitable anguish due to a role-taking that transcends its own group's limits. Its imperatives of love and justice must be extended to *all* persons or groups.

E. Prototypical Challenges with Which Faith Must Deal

If Stage Four had to deal with the issues arising out of the in-

dividuation process, Stage Five's characteristic existential challenges
grow out of the experiences of finding the limits of one's Stage
Four ideological and communal identifications.

First there is the issue of a loneliness now experienced as cosmic. One may have relationships with other persons or groups of
great intimacy, yet there comes the recognition that one is never
fully known nor capable of fully knowing others. Though one may
work out patterns of loyalty and commitment with other person or
persons, such loyalty is always limited either by will, capacity, or
death. Great similarities and commonalities may be found or created
with others, justifying celebrations; but even with those who are
closest there may be deep-going differences which underscore the
final aloneness and uniqueness of the person. One becomes aware
of, and faith must deal with, the loneliness arising from the recognition of uncloseable gaps of experience, perspective and emotional
structure between the self and even those who are closest.

Faith must come to grips with the tensions of being ethically
responsible but finite. Whereas Stage Four faith generally offers
solutions that promise to solve the polar tensions between self-ful-
fillment and commitment to the welfare of others, Stage Five faith
has to come to terms with the tragic character of that polar pull.
Stage Five faith must sustain commitment to the worth of ethical
action and its costliness even while accepting the realities of intrac-
table ignorance, egocentricity, and limited abilities and interests—in
oneself and in human beings generally.

Stage Five maintains its faith vision without the props of authority or ideological certainty that provide guarantees for Stages
Three and Four respectively. Faith is a volitional act of paradoxical
commitment at Stage Five. Stage Five is faith that has taken its own
doubt and despair seriously.

STAGE SIX—UNIVERSALIZING FAITH
(Average age: minimum ca. 40)

A. Locus of Authority

The matter of authority is now contained within a relationship
of unmediated participation in and complementarity with the ultimate conditions of existence. There is a post-critical at-one-ness
with the ultimate conditions of one's life and of being generally.
The paradoxical quality of this in Five is overcome.

The ultimate conditions are differentiated from the mundane;
they are kept in creative tension and interpenetration.

Usually some disciplined means is employed to restore a sense of participation in or permeation by the Transcendent.

B. *Criteria and Modes of Appropriation*

Criteria for truth now require incorporating the "truths" of many different standpoints into a synthesis that reconciles without negating their particular or unique contributions. In contrast to Stage Five this reconciliation of the one and the many is no longer paradoxical, but has a quality of simplicity. For these criteria to be fulfilled the person must have an identification with being in which love of self is genuinely incorporated and fulfilled in love of Being.

C. *Symbolic and Conceptual Functioning*

One is directly and nonmediately aware of the ultimate context of life. Symbols and concepts play a secondary function, making communication possible, though inevitably distorting. Stage Six draws on insights and vision from many sources, valuing them as helpful, if partial, apprehensions of Truth.

Conflicts and paradox are embraced as essential to the integrity of Being (similarly to Stage Five) but are unified in a no-longer-paradoxical grasp of the oneness of Being.

D. *Role-Taking and Extensiveness of Identification*

Stage Six has the ability to respond to and feel commonality with the concreteness and individuality of persons while also relating to and evoking their potential.

There is the capacity for a meaningful (i.e., tested and hard-won) taking the role of a universal community. Active compassion for a commonwealth of being is expressed, including but transcending group differences and conflicts.

E. *Prototypical Challenges with Which Faith Must Deal*

Faith at Stage Six must meet the temptation to transcend and give way to complete absorption in the *All*. Ethical and historical irresponsibility can result from a genuinely universalizing perspective. Too complete a merging with the Eternal Now can result in the abdication from time and concrete responsibility.

Stage Six bears the burden and challenge of relating to persons and issues concerned at quite other stages and levels of development. It must do so with patience, compassion and helpfulness. Faith at this stage must bear the pain and potential despair of seeing ethical causes and movements of compassion exploded or subverted by less universalizing interests.

There is a crucifixion involved in seeing and having to accept the inevitability of certain tragic denouements in history. Stage Six faith must cope with seeing and understanding more than others, and with the challenge and responsibilities of universal identifications.

Faith at Six must resist the subtle temptations to pride and self-deception and the danger of corruption by adulation.

Faith must overcome the danger of ethical and political paralysis while at the same time being a source of solutional approaches that introduce genuine novelty and transcendent possibilities into situations of conflict and bitterness and deeply contested interests.

Faith must endure the misunderstandings and slanders and violent potentials (and actualities) of those who cannot comprehend, or of those who do comprehend and are threatened to the core by the person's vision and way of being.

There is the burden of being a mediator, teacher or semi-divine model for others. Faith must maintain, generate and renew the vision of a cosmic meaning that will help sustain others. This is the frightful burden of being a "Savior of God" (Kazantzakis).

SOME SIMILARITIES AND DIFFERENCES WITH
TRADITIONS OF SPIRITUALITY

Often people are initially interested in this stage theory because they believe they see or hear in it parallels with one or another of the traditions of mystical growth or spirituality. Though we can only sketchily address these issues here it is useful to clarify how our stages are like and how they are different from schemas of spiritual or mystical development. In my effort to think clearly about these matters I have been helped by William Johnston's exemplary comparison of Zen Buddhist and Christian mystical approaches (Johnston, 1971). Because the present discussion must be kept brief I will not distinguish between particular mystical traditions, but will rather treat mystical spirituality as a *genre*. I shall speak of this genre as "spiritual paths" and will contrast them with the faith stages.

Usually spiritual paths prescribe particular disciplines and contemplative exercises that have evolved in a given tradition. They are transmitted and taught because they have proven efficacious in fostering the progress of practitioners toward an ideal state of a culminating enlightenment. Typically there is a more or less developed ideological or theological perspective informing and justifying the approach and its desired end-state. In most instances phases or steps in spiritual progress have been identified. Most such ap-

proaches involve loosening the hold of discursive, controlling reason so as to allow consciousness to be deepened and expanded
through permeation by unconscious feelings and images. Most cul-
minate in an intuitive participation in and unity with being or the
ground of being in which the boundaries and restrictions of the
egoic self are transcended. Through such a process, sustained by
disciplines and guided by a master, a guru or a spiritual director, a
person grows toward an experience of union or enlightenment (satori, kensho) in which his or her self is integrated and unified with
transforming clarity (See Fingarette, 1965; Fr. Thomas et al., 1963;
Johnston, 1971). Though it is validly claimed that this transforming
integration of self and its unification with being has important
moral and social effects, the principal focus of most spiritual paths
is intra-psychic and work at spiritual progress tends to be individualistic. Stages or phases in spiritual paths are, then, blazes or stop-
ping places on particular trails leading toward the goal of ideal spirituality as epitomized by a specific tradition or by a particular
pioneer or founder of a sub-tradition within it.

    As presently described, Stage Six in our schema has some fea-
tures that closely resemble the stable and equilibrated integration
that develops in most spiritual paths after the attainment-gift of
enlightenment. This has led some readers or hearers to conjectures
that are doubly mistaken. Because of the use of language and imag-
ery characteristic of mysticism in describing Stage Six they have assumed that Stage Six is the mystical stage. Frequently connected
with this assumption is the belief that mystical spirituality is, by its
very nature, "higher" than other forms or expressions of piety.
This leads then to the second erroneous assumption that any seemingly knowledgeable use of mystical language or any serious involvement in disciplined spirituality is likely to be a portent or indication of nearness to Stage Six. While it is true that a person who is
best described by Stage Six is most likely to have strongly developed, disciplined mystical sensitivities, it is not true, conversely,
that strongly developed, disciplined mystical sensitivities necessarily indicate Stage Six.

    The faith stages, rather than describing a normative spiritual
path within a particular tradition, have as their focus a developmental sequence of systems of structurally integrated operations of
thought and feeling. The faith stages, in their formal descrip-
tiveness, take a life-span approach to understanding the person's
readiness and capacities for nurture by particular ideological or
spiritual traditions or approaches. A given faith stage, as ex-

emplified in a person or a group, is the structural consequence of their exposure to the systems of belief and practice available in their environment as these intersect with the events and circumstances of their lives. While it makes perfect sense for a Zennist to characterize the goal of his or her spiritual quest as *satori*, or for a Christian to speak with St. Teresa of "mystical marriage" with God the King as the goal of prayer, it would be awkward or peculiar for a person to claim Stage Five or Stage Six as the goal of his or her spiritual aspiration. In the practice of the spiritual disciplines of Zen or of Teresian prayer a person may well develop a faith structure best described by Stage Five or Stage Six. But that development would be the derivative of a more focused spiritual quest as informed by one or another of these traditions.

Within their character of being general, formal descriptions of patterned processes across the life-cycle, our stages are not concerned only with spiritual or religious experience. They *are*, of course, concerned with these and with the effects of such experiences on the person's pattern of knowing, valuing and acting. But the faith stages try to describe a person's mode of orienting himself or herself more generally. In this regard we are concerned with epistemological and conceptual levels, levels of social role-taking, and levels in the capacity to integrate and identify with experiences and groups other than one's own. There is concern in our stages for understanding the degree and quality of a person's self-awareness and critical self-reflection on action, belief and valuing. We try to correlate the levels or capacities just described with the life or existential issues with which a person is confronted. We are interested in the central psychodynamic and psychosocial functions of the faith system at each stage.

The foregoing should make it clear why a superficial identification of our stages with stages in one or another of the spiritual paths may be quite misleading. One is tempted to say that the spiritual paths, generally speaking, tend to be confessionally and phenomenologically *prescriptive*, while ours are empirically and structurally *descriptive*. But that would be only a half truth. For while it is true that our stages intend to be structural and descriptive in empirically verifiable ways, it is important to take note of a strong normative thrust in our stage theory that is built into it by virtue of the way we are defining faith and by virtue of the comprehensiveness and balance built into the variables included in the description of each stage. When this begins to be understood it becomes clear why, as criteria for Stage Five for example, intensity of com-

mitment and purity of heart must be placed alongside having come
to terms with genuine pluralism and the incorporation of social
perspectives different than those of one's own group.

The normative intent of our stage theory, manifest in its holding together of these diverse but interrelated criteria, is to clarify in
formal and structural terms the capacities developed by some exemplary persons in every age to live fully and responsibly in the
complexities of life, sustained by a vision or apprehension which, in
seeing life whole, brings to it transforming impulses of grace and
truth. The stages of faith constitute a necessary sequence of pat-
terned-capacities leading toward that ideal. As such the stage theory
provides a normative model against which other criteria for spiritual or personality development may be tested or clarified. But it
does not supplant particular spiritual paths or ways. This is because
in its formal generality it lacks the resonant symbolic content, the
particularity and power of methods of contemplation, and the cul-
tural-cultic richness of the particular paths or ways. The faith-stage
theory cannot make and does not want to make any claims to religious sufficiency.

On the basis of the stage theory we are able to offer some insight into the way persons at different stages may be able to appropriate or be helped by one or another spiritual path. Though our
data are by no means conclusive on this, it seems clear that the self-
conscious adoption of the methods and ideation of a particular
tradition of spirituality may occur, at the earliest, in the transition
from Stage Three to Stage Four. It is true that Helfaer (1972) and
others have documented instances of conversion and the taking on
of spiritual disciplines by children who structurally would best be
described by Stage Two. But those are not instances of what we
would call "self-conscious adoption." What becomes clear is that
typically the appropriation of a spiritual discipline and approach at
the Stages Three-Four transition will differ in decisive ways from
such an appropriation in the Stages Four-Five transition. Let's examine the reasons for this.

In the Stages Three-Four transition (or in the consolidation of
Stage Four) the person is making a bid for an individuated faith
and identity. Matters of authority and belief, of commitment and
self-definition, have become of explicit concern. Commitments and
loyalties must now be made on the basis of an identity that is self-
aware and newly concerned about authenticity and consistency.
The master-apprentice, guru-devotee, or spiritual director-directee
relationship is ready-made for these purposes. In these rela-

tionships the devotee may invest self-aware dependence in the charisma of the master and in an ideological appropriation of the ideation informing the discipline. This relationship can be the context for powerfully centering allegiances and affiliation, providing goals, models, and ideal self-images as well as a coherent and powerful world-view. In this transition the engagement in the spiritual path is made to serve the needs that go with individuation.

In the Stages Four-Five transition (or in the consolidation of Stage Five), however, a person's serious turning to a spiritual path will have to do with the need for integration into consciousness and action of that within the self, in one's past, and within one's near and far environment, which is discordant, repressed, or threatening. Whereas for Stage Four the issues have to do with boundaries and clarity of orientation, for Stage Five they concern depth, comprehensiveness, and integration. For Stage Five the need is for permeation of boundaries—self-other, subjectivity-objectivity, conscious-unconscious, *anima-animus*, and the like. Ideation and spiritual disciplines for this transition must be attuned to paradox and to the silence beyond concepts, language and other symbols.

RELATION OF FAITH STAGES TO
KOHLBERG'S MORAL STAGES

In a recent article Lawrence Kohlberg (Kohlberg, 1974) has taken a provisional step toward clarifying the relationship, as he sees it, between his stages of moral development and our faith stages. Kohlberg's principal theses on this relationship can be outlined in five points: 1) Moral development has a larger context that includes faith (p. 5). 2) For purposes of research and moral-education intervention, however, moral judgment-making and moral development can be addressed separately from any religious or faith context (p. 5). 3) Though adequate data are not yet available to determine it, one would expect to find close parallels, generally speaking, between moral-judgment stages and faith stages; and one would expect persons' developmental level in the two areas to be approximately parallel (pp. 13-14).

4) Where there are discrepancies in faith and moral levels, or where stage transition is in progress, one would expect that "the development to a given moral stage precedes development to the parallel faith stage." Two reasons support this thesis: a) A faith stage is a wider, more comprehensive system of constructs than a moral stage; it will take more time and experience to "work out a moral stage in terms of its elaboration as an organized pattern of

belief and feeling about the cosmos which Fowler calls a faith stage." b) As Kant argued, "faith is grounded on moral reason because moral reason 'requires' faith rather than that moral reason is grounded on faith." Universal moral principles cannot be dependent upon faith, "because not all men's faith is, or can be, the same" (p. 14). 5) Although Stage Six morality—universal moral principles—"can and should be formulated and justified on grounds of autonomous moral rationality, such morality . . . 'requires' an ultimate stage of faith and moves men toward it" (p. 14). (Kohlberg calls this ultimate stage of faith Stage Seven and gives an interesting account of it based on the writings of Marcus Aurelius in the article from which we are quoting, pp. 14-16).

I have substantial agreements with these theses of Kohlberg's. As the chart on page 188 indicates we expect to find significant, if not exact, parallels between his stages and ours. Our spring 1975 data, which includes Kohlberg moral-judgment interviews along with the faith interviews, support the expected correlations. Even with these new data Kohlberg is still right when he points out that adequate material is not yet available to settle the issue of precedence of development, i.e., whether moral stages develop prior to their parallel faith stages, and whether moral stages "require" and are in some sense the "cause" of a faith stage's development. It is my belief, however, that prior to examining more data in the effort to clarify these matters some central differences between us of a conceptual and theoretical nature must be worked through. I can only touch on these issues here.

First of all I am not satisfied that Kohlberg has fully grasped the reasons for differentiating between religion and faith and their theoretical implications. When he states that "moral development has a larger context including faith" (p. 5) he seems to be thinking of faith in wider than religious terms, as I find it necessary to do. But when he goes on to make his familiar point that moral development and education should be pursued in the public schools based on "universal principles of justice, not broader religious and personal values" (p. 5) it becomes less clear that Kohlberg is prepared consistently to conceptually separate the phenomenon of faith from necessary connection with institutional religion. He is still most comfortable thinking in terms of "religious faith."

The reasons for this have much to do with Kohlberg's brilliant and courageous efforts to provide a foundation and direction for approaches to moral education in the American public school. The historic doctrine of the separation of church and state and its recent evolution have made the separation of moral education and sectarian religious influences rigidly mandatory. For Kohlberg's creative contribution in this difficult juncture I have great appreciation.

It is important, however, that we not let these necessary limitations as to what can be done in moral education in one context be determinative for how we shall understand and approach moral development and moral formation, broadly speaking, in other relevant contexts. We should not let a conception of moral development which has been tailored to guide educational approaches limited by constitutional restrictions lead us to accept a truncated understanding of moral development more generally. My hope is that the focus on faith, as we are pursuing it, will provide a way for Kohlberg and those who have been influenced by him to reclaim a larger framework in which to work on moral education, but without becoming entangled in sectarian religion.[7]

The nub of my theoretical and conceptual difference with Kohlberg can be put this way: I think it is a mistake to assume that faith is or must be an *a posteriori* derivative of or justification for morality, the appeal to Kant notwithstanding. In fact, I would argue conversely, that every moral perspective, at whatever level of development, is anchored in a broader system of beliefs and loyalties. Every principle of moral action serves some center or centers of value. Even the appeals to autonomy, rationality and universality as justifications for Stage Six morality are not made *prior* to faith. Rather they are expressions of faith—expressions of trust in and loyalty to the valued attributes of autonomy and rationality, and to the valued ideal of a universal commonwealth of being (See Niebuhr, 1937; 1960; and Fowler, 1974 c).

There is, I believe, always a faith framework or matrix encompassing and supporting the motive to be moral and the exercise of moral logic. This is the case, I hold, at *each* stage of development (though a person's self-consciousness about this framework and his/her ability to articulate it in congruent ways *is* a function both of developmental level and of the availability of a "language" of faith). Let's consider the child in Kohlberg's Stage One—in the "premoral" level. Kohlberg is right when he tells us that the criteria available to the child for determining good and bad, right or wrong at this stage are largely keyed to reward and punishment, external approval and disapproval. That account is satisfactory in accounting for the source of such criteria. I find it unsatisfactorily thin and mildly cynical, however, as an account of the *motivation* to do good

7. The question of whether "faith-development education" could or should become a matter of concern for the public school is too complex for discussion here. It will receive attention in the author's forthcoming monograph.

and to avoid wrong. Our research and my observations of children lead me to the belief that one of the prime factors determining eventual development into and beyond conventional moral reasoning will be found to be the child's constructive appropriation of an ethos in which doing or being "good" is a shared, articulated and consistently embodied value. Before a child is cognitively able to give a "moral" basis for deciding good or bad, right or wrong, in specific situations, he or she can develop loyalty to the shared ethos of doing or being good. Without some such general value arch or framework legitimating punishment and reward and sustaining aspiration to goodness, it is by no means clear what motivation there could be for moving beyond Kohlberg's Stage Two. Similarly the motives for "interpersonal concord" (Stage Three) and obedience to law and constituted authority at Stage Four seem to me patently reductionistic unless it is seen that ideals of family, friendship, marriage and the state are always present eliciting our loyalties and affections. At Stage Three one does love one's wife and give her loyalty on the basis of personal, affectional ties. But a marriage based only on the subjectivity of mutual love is highly vulnerable. Marriage is a covenant when each partner's loyalty to the other is augmented by a mutually shared loyalty to the ideal or the institution of marriage. Similarly, without loyalty to the ideal of the nation-state as a center of value transcending oneself, how would persons ever be found who were prepared to give their lives for their country? In a time like ours such structures as these of trust and loyalty are revealed as much by their erosion or violation as by their presence. But if we want to be faithful phenomenologically to the dynamics of moral development we dare not leave them out of account.

My colleague, ethicist Ralph Potter (Potter, 1969, ch. 2), offers a conceptual schema that may prove helpful in showing the interpenetration of faith and moral development as I see them. In the making of any moral decision, or in the shaping of any public policy, Potter claims, four analytically separable but interpenetrating factors come into play. (For our purposes it will be most useful to examine these as factors in the deciding and acting of an individual agent.) First, there is the *empirical, factual definition of the situation* or dilemma. Such a definition includes the range of available alternative actions and assumptions about their probable consequences. When persons of good will differ on moral issues a principal point of disagreement, though frequently unrecognized, may be at the level of the factual definition of the situation. Second, there is the *mode of ethical reasoning* to be employed.[8] What sort of moral logic will the actor bring to the adjudication of differences and to the weighing of relevant moral considerations? Kohlberg's descriptions of stages in the development of moral logic are most clearly focused on the structural characteristics of the mode of ethical reasoning. Third, a person brings what Potter calls *"affirmation(s) of loyalty."* He writes, "Consciously or unconsciously, men make decisions regarding what shall be taken as their primary object of concern. They create expressive symbols that represent a center of value, locus of commitment, or source of identity. It makes a difference whether they are dedicated to a nation, an ideology, a church, 'humanity,' an ideal community, or some other object of loyalty" (Potter, pp. 23-24). We bring, consciously or unconsciously, patterns of valuing—of trust in and loyalty to centers of value—to moral decision-making and moral action. Finally, Potter holds, our decisions are shaped by what he calls *quasi-theological beliefs* or assumptions. These include beliefs "concerning God, man and human destiny. Anthropological assumptions concerning the range of human freedom and man's power to predict and control historical events have particular importance" (Potter, p. 24).

It was suggested earlier that Kohlberg's stages primarily focus on the second of these four factors, the *mode of moral decision making*. For reasons already given I find Kohlberg's account of moral motivation incomplete. While his stages clearly have and describe features that could be included under the rubrics of the third and fourth factors, I find them limited and partial in that respect, and too much subordinated to the focus on moral logic. It is the aim of our faith stages to focus explicitly on the structural characteristics of Potter's third and fourth factors, the *affirmations of loyalty* and the *quasi-theological beliefs* of persons. Complementary to and correlated with (but not subordinated to) Kohlberg's stages, they give us a much enriched structural account of moral and personal development.

Reaction to Fowler: FEARS ABOUT PROCEDURE *by* Alfred McBride, O. Praem.

William Blake, the metaphysical poet, once wrote that human development is a passage from innocence to complexity to or-

8. For my own purposes I am altering the order in which Potter presents these factors.

ganized innocence. Philosopher Paul Ricoeur speaks of this as a
journey from first to second naiveté. Present-day pioneers in developmental psychology seek to plot the inner demography of that
voyage, hoping to distill recognizable landmarks in the dense fog
that is the typical climate of the marvelously supple complexity of
the human psyche.

Piaget, Erikson, Havighurst and, more recently, Kohlberg have
provided both leadership and original insight into the field. Fowler
works in this milieu and wishes to relate developmental designs and
procedures to the question of faith knowing. His intent is daring
and presses the accolade of breakthrough. I acknowledge his daring
but regret I cannot concur he has achieved any breakthrough within the canons of his chosen field.

I wish to begin with a series of positive reactions. I will follow
these with negative observations and conclude my reaction with
some suggestions.

To begin with, Fowler's unique attempt to begin with an assumption of religious faith as a legitimate dimension of life and
worthy of honest recognition by a psychological discipline normally
committed to a reductive rationalism is both welcome and in order.
Kohlberg broke ground with his studies of moral development, but
he always studiously remained within the world of reason knowing.
Quite rightly, Fowler affirms there is such a thing as faith knowing
and it deserves the kind of scientific inquiry and trained scholar-
ship that have been exercised on other forms of knowing and perception.

The result of this kind of research holds a great appeal for educators who want to pride themselves on meeting a student where
he is and assist him to mature and develop. Today's scope and
sequence charts in every manner of curriculum reflect a respect for
and a debt to the developmentalists.

It is only natural that religious education, dealing as it does
with values, morality and faith should be especially intrigued to
find the once presumably secular psychology now making friendly
noises about morals and faith. And, in fact, Kohlberg's stages of
moral development have received a wide hearing in religious-educa-
tion circles and textbooks.

Fowler, too, is bound to receive both a respectful and influential audience among religious educators. His recovery of an old, but
long forgotten, insight that faith is a mode of knowing suits the
consciousness of the current generation of religious educators,
preoccupied with religious experience and desperately trying to

broaden the discussion beyond the overbearing ascendancy of faith as a question of truth claims.

Spiritual writers as varied as John of the Cross and Søren Kierkegaard dwelt constantly on faith as a specialized form of consciousness and perception. The Spanish mystic urged his followers and readers to cleanse the doors of perception through submission to a series of purifications. The Danish philosopher preached of the need to move beyond being a knight of infinite resignation (a world of tormented reasonings) to become the knight of faith with his higher viewpoint, i.e., mode of knowing.

Fowler, while correctly disassociating his stages from any mystical ladders and concomitant spiritual polemics, is in apostolic succession with those historical advocates of faith as a mode of perception. As I see it, this is the first and major contribution of Fowler to the question of religious faith today.

His second, but lesser achievement, is to offer a possible perspective on the stages or structures of faith knowing. He offers a persuasive chart for those about to sail in the deep waters of faith perception. They will move from the simplicity of undifferentiated beginnings through the confusions and tensions of the intermediate stages to a goal of uniting the universal and the particular in a mature faith glance. Along the way they will be buffeted by the shoals and outrageous misfortunes (the variables) of authority, shifting criteria, the mysterious tension of symbol and concept, the comforting and sometimes deceptive influence of role-taking, and lastly the recurrence of prototypical challenge.

With its six stages and five variables, the chart is neat. It possesses a seductive appeal for an educator seeking to reduce the chaotic state of faith knowing to some manageability. I like the chart. It offers me a perspective and a useful model for thinking about faith thinking. I know it is not a mystical ladder, but it gives me some sense of a beginning, middle and end to faith processes. It restores a sense of goal and motivation to my educational approach in this matter.

If existentialist philosophy challenges me to make some meaning out of life in general, Fowler's insight about faith knowing and his provisional sailor's chart comforts me that I may indeed be able to make some meaning out of faith processes in an educational context. It is a model, a grand design, a perspective that reawakens my inborn, though often atrophied, instinct for wonder about this topic.

Now having declared my positive vibrations about the Fowler

thesis, I wish to proceed with a series of negative comments. Perhaps the most devastating impression I have is that Fowler's study is not an adequate product of developmental psychology. It is rather a well-informed hunch, articulated into a broad series of unproven assumptions, a veritable library of a priori's that have not been deeply tested in any usual sense of that word. Interviews with 118 persons in a comparatively brief period of time can scarcely be called adequate research and hardly be permitted to yield the voluble conclusions of the study.

I have already said that I happen to like the conclusions because they nourish some preconceptions of my own. My objection here is that while I accept them because of some intrinsic appeal, I cannot agree that they are the mature and proven products of the sophisticated design and results of developmental psychology.

I feel the need to register this complaint loudly at least for the sake of some of my fellow religious educators who may unwittingly buy this study as a verified developmental package, when in fact it is not.

My second comment may perhaps be more debatable. Fowler seems to identify development with stages far too casually. Properly understood and with a series of cautions, this might be acceptable. But normally such an identification is fraught with pitfalls for both the researcher and the educator. The rockiest of these pitfalls is the temptation to stereotyping that is the death of both research and education.

I can see that his insistence on the variables is a way to forestall both unwarranted categorizing and to protect the astonishing uniqueness (and orneriness) of the human person. I am afraid that the very neatness of the six stages and the five variables, however, masks a logical construct imposed on people, and not a revelation of the inherent order which is the object of the research in the first place.

In a field otherwise noted for its devotion to the concrete and a modesty of judgment upon some small corner of human behavior, I find myself drowned in this study's pervasive generalities. Far from sounding like a piece of scientific research, it bears the generalizing quality of philosophizing or theologizing without owning the nuances that those disciplines would demand.

Even the reasonableness of the variables begin to possess, on second look, a univocal quality and not an intrinsic complexity in themselves. Take for example the authority variable. Developmental psychology identifies at least three kinds of major dynamics in authority-subject relationships.

For some respondents authority is simply part of nature. It's just there. They probably agree with the lady in the margarine ad, "It's not right to fool with mother nature." Other respondents view authority in the context of an adversary relationship. Their attitude is contentious. A final group approaches authority as a dialectic of restraint and free will. Admittedly, these dynamics do not appear in a pure state. Elements of all three probably reside in greater or lesser measure in everyone. One tends to dominate.

Enough hints in Fowler's five characterizations of the locus of authority persuade me to think that he has settled on the view of authority as an adversary relationship with comparatively little attention given to alternative dynamics of *just there-ness* and dialectic. I draw particular attention to this because today's erosion of authority and public trust, probably due in part to the contentious view, could well be the cause of selective perception in this study. Instead of alleviating a popular narrow view, this could tend to reinforce it.

There is another aspect of the chart that must be critiqued further. It hangs together well. It is a logical construct making a plausible appeal to reasonable people. This very virtue, however, conceals the fact that it is an external logical model imposed upon people. It proves too much and as the Latin axiom puts it, "He who proves too much, proves nothing." *(Qui probat nimis nihil probat.)*

What Fowler should be doing is revealing the inner logic of faith knowing as it discloses itself through years of patient research. The inner and inherent logic of faith knowing is not likely to be as expansive and schematic as this study indicates. Collateral developmental studies find that people generally proceed by metalogic, not through such graceful stages as outlined here.

Piaget, under whose benign patronage so much of this is written, would scarcely be this far along. In his studies he isolated topics like number, space, time and motion. He looked to mathematicians and physicists to see the types of questions they asked and the types of answers they had given. He then posed some of these questions to children and analyzed their answers. Piaget did not impose "logical" development on children. Indeed, one does not find the general term logic in his writings until after he had studied several different topics. The similarity of development in these several topic areas led to his overall formulation about logic.

The fatal flaw in Fowler's study is that he has taken the last step first, and has done so on the most general of grounds. If I may say so, he has built his approach upon the findings of Kohlberg without benefiting from the evaluations of Kohlberg from the field itself, such as by Kurtines and Greif (1974) and Simpson (1974).

In all this I know I am biting the hand that feeds me. But I think I am making my plea as an *amicus curiae*. I feel a little shy in being so direct especially since the history of the dialogue between religion and psychology has been mostly one of sniping and only recently reached the status of détente. I am hoping that the sensitivities of both sides are not still so tender that radical disagreement would reopen hostilities.

Yet I am further moved to be frank, for many religious educators have adopted an apologetic and derivative position regarding psychology. I have never been interested in the apologies and I have been annoyed by some of the derivativeness, especially from certain aspects of psychology. I am emboldened to continue in this vein since I have met enough psychologists both of the counseling and experimental strain who are as equally dismayed as I am about naive appropriations from their field by some religious educators.

I am perhaps particularly wary about the Fowler thesis because of its clearly popular appeal for religious educators. The irony is now that the psychological source itself is debatable as a good piece of research—though not as an appealing construct of religious faith. As a fascinating model I buy it. As solid research, I do not.

Let me rephrase the problem this way. Subjectively, I am in tune with Fowler's chart. I am looking, however, for at least a modest objective verification from the kind of field that earns its bread doing just that. Sadly, I do not find it. Of course I am pleased that the field even made an effort. I regret the effort faltered so badly.

I shall presume at this point to make some suggestions for the future development of this study.

1. Take more time and obtain adequate data.

2. Go back to the theologians and mystics and isolate many more of their questions and responses about the subject of faith (I detected a distinctly Tillichian perspective on faith in this study. I admire Tillich, but I think a topic of such depth deserves evidence from many other heavyweights—viz., Augustine, Aquinas, Luther, Richard Rolle and Thomas Merton).

3. Soften the equation between development and stages.

4. Find the inherent order that reveals itself rather than imposing a logical construct on the respondents.

5. Take more than a univocal view of the five variables. Furthermore, allow that other variables may be waiting in the wings.

6. Liberate the gentle reader from thinking that data from verbal responses in a test is anything less than ambiguous.

7. This may seem redundant, but find the uniqueness of the

topic. It needs to be refined. The type of ideas expressed by people on it must be distinguishable from their ideas on other topics. It is not clear what is being tested: intelligence, verbal facility, breadth of a person's literary background, amount of reflection of social issues, or—as is suggested—faith.

Despite my reservations, a good thing has been done. Developmental psychology has begun to come to grips with a most profound manner of knowing, that of faith perception. The field has boldly moved in on a major insight. Now it must treat it with the same deliberation it has given to so many other aspects of development.

What is the religious educator to do in the meantime? Years will pass before the verifications called for by this critique are found. Worse yet, they may never be found at all. Meanwhile students are present in the here and now, requiring an intelligent address to their faith needs.

The first thing that can be done is to give a favorable hearing to Fowler's recovery of the old insight about faith as a mode of knowing. Spiritual writers have always spoken of "seeing with the eyes of faith." I would urge that this faith knowing be viewed in two ways, namely, the preconceptual and the conceptual.

At the preconceptual level, the faith knowing is akin to the kind of perceptions poets talk about when they say, "You know before you know." This is the kind of faith knowing that comes through religious experience, liturgical rites, prayer and what Maslow would call oceanic events in deep human encounters. Such a faith knowing as this is a horizon making possible the ability to "faith-know" at the conceptual level.

Fowler's schema assumes the preconceptual event of faith knowing and correctly does not try to subject that to developmental apparatus. Every known attempt to dissect such forms of knowing (poetic, artistic, mystical) appears to have failed.

I think that religious educators can accept the fundamental assumption about faith knowing at the preconceptual level. Its importance for education is that students can be approached with the assumption that they inchoatively, and by divinely endowed nature, possess the capacity to faith know at this level.

As far as Fowler's schema is concerned, religious educators should be able to use it gingerly as a model, grand design and perspective with all the caveats that any good educator will retain in the use of such models. A model is like a porcupine; it should be handled with care.

Treat the six "stages" (poetic, rational, ecumenical, personalizing, tension-bearing, universalizing—my own nontechnical renaming of the stages) less as steps in a ladder and more as a mosaic of possible expressions of faith knowing at the conceptual level, surfacing in unexpected, diverse and astonishing ways in students. In this way, faith knowing retains a splendid richness. It is thus not a serpent shedding skins of "lower stages" but rather like the rings of an oak, growing sturdier with new acquisition.

Wed the insight about faith knowing, the schema of its conceptual dimensions to the many available processes of inductive learning available today. The popularity and success of valuing processes can be especially pertinent, since faith knowing is a value of supreme relevance.

Relate the assertion about faith knowing at the preconceptual level to the revival of spirituality, meditation and nonconceptual prayer. The medieval treatise *Cloud of Unknowing* and a Zen koan and the new look at the Ignatian Exercises are but three of the spirituality processes suitable not only to retreats and personal guru sessions, but also to the new styles of education practiced today in schools and learning centers.

As much as possible establish a rhythm between faith knowing at preconceptual level and its conceptual manifestation. Be wary of establishing logical links between the two. It is a matter of the preconceptual "unfolding" into the conceptual in some yet undetermined manner.

To conclude. Fowler's study is a useful and welcome model that seems to hold considerable promise for current religious educational approaches to faith knowing, as well as a future professional contribution from developmental psychology. I believe the study still needs to go through the classical paces of the canons of its own field, and I trust it will do so. While awaiting the future reports from that sector, religious educators could proceed with the chart, perhaps along the lines suggested in this paper.

I wish to conclude with the following observation from Goethe: "Epochs of faith are epochs of fruitfulness; but epochs of unbelief, however glittering, are barren of all permanent good."

Reaction to Fowler: STAGES IN FAITH OR STAGES IN COMMITMENT *by* James E. Hennessy, S.J.

This essay is not so much to be read as studied and it is well worth the effort. The research is careful, ingenious and in certain respects daring. It is the first part of an ongoing project that is not likely to be completed for many years. The prudent application of this research by educators, pastors and other religious leaders will doubtless prove its merit. Some readers, especially those familiar with the brilliant writings of Romano Guardini (1961) and Louis Monden (1965) on the crises and growth of faith at different stages of human maturing, may expect too much of this essay. For one thing Professor Fowler has an unorthodox use in his understanding of faith; he calls it a "human universal," something experienced by every man who knows himself related to ultimates in life, whatever they may be. His aim is to include all faith-commitments, a position quite sensitive to the needs of our pluralistic society.

On first glance some may expect too much from this research because the title could lead them to suppose that it is divine or Christian faith that is the subject of this investigation. Now Christian faith is essentially a mystery of grace—the believer's total response to God revealing Himself and His will in Jesus Christ. Christian faith is of course a mystery precisely because it involves God's action on the soul. It is an unmerited free gift eliciting a free response and elevating the believer to a new order of being, activity and destiny. It is a continuing gift, always fragile, constantly in need of cultivating and often facing crises of doubt and ambiguity. This grace of faith and its effects on the soul are uniquely personal; so much so that the great master of the spiritual life, St. Francis de Sales, wrote that souls differ from one another more than faces. Clearly Christian faith as such cannot be measured nor is it subject to empirical investigation.

Of course Professor Fowler does not attempt to chronicle or divide into stages the divine elements in faith. But since grace and nature are interwoven in human existence, faith does have a *human* history. It is this human history that he attempts to capture. Divine grace, of which faith is the most significant beginning in the dialogue of Christian life, comes to a person and grows within him in the concrete circumstances of his life. Parents, education, reading, environment, interpersonal relationships, joys and sorrows, successes and failures, crises and serenity—all may mediate divine grace and faith in the person. It is this *natural* history, what we may call the concomitants and effects of faith, that Professor Fowler studies empirically. For example, if a person believes (and not merely confesses) that God is Father, then he will value himself as son. Such faith in God as a loving Father will manifest itself not only in his self-image but also in his interpersonal relations and above all in his loving obedience to the Father's will. Some of these effects can be observed and studied comparatively with the faith-concomitants of others. How Professor Fowler proceeds and his preliminary findings are fascinating and challenging, even though his research up to the present is based upon insufficient sampling.

The author leans heavily on the researches of Piaget, Kohlberg and Erik Erikson. The stage theories of these investigators in cognitive, moral and psychosocial development have led him and his associates to investigate the possibility of a similar structural and developmental theory in faith-knowing. Fowler's conclusion is that faith develops in patterns or stages that can be identified empirically. The six stages he discerns are sequential, invariant, hierarchical and possibly universal (research is in progress for this last qualification). His very careful investigations over three years, and still continuing, yield results that he modestly acknowledges are as yet tentative and provisional. We hope that he and his team will continue their valuable researches, making improvements in techniques and analyses as further experience and reflection will suggest.

I mentioned that for many the word "faith" in the title may be ambiguous. In the biblical tradition this word refers to divine faith —that gift of God which is the beginning of the dialogue between a person and His Creator, Redeemer and Sanctifier. So the word "faith" has a definite meaning and connotation nuanced to be sure according to Hebrew, Catholic and Protestant traditions. Of course the word has been secularized but when this happens a modifier rescues it from its traditional meaning, as when we speak of human faith, scientific faith, political faith, etc.

"Stages in faith" for most people will probably mean stages in religious faith. But as we have noted faith in this study has a wider meaning than religious faith, for it refers to anyone's vision of and orientation to life-ultimates. Thus it may refer to the faith of a Christian, a Jew, a secular humanist, an ethical culturist and even to the faith of a communist or scientist—on the supposition that one's ultimate truth and supreme value are thereby specified.

No doubt Professor Fowler is following Paul Tillich's well-known definition of religion as the state of being grasped by an ultimate concern. Now according to this definition everyone is religious whether consciously or unconsciously. Devout believers and violent critics of religion are lumped together, with the result that some very important distinctions among human beings are obscured. In reply to this objection Tillich in his later works uses the term "quasi-religion" to stand for such phenomena as communism, nationalism or scientism when these are characterized by a kind of ultimacy of devotion and serve as a life-orienting world-vision.

It seems clear that Professor Fowler wants to include "quasi-faith" alongside faith. His desire to do so in an ecumenical age is understandable, but does it work out? Should a devout Christian and a committed communist, for example, be measured by the same rule and "averaged" together? Are they really comparable? Can they be judged by the same set of existential issues, by the same variables?

If the answer is yes, then would it not be preferable that the stages be called "stages in commitment" instead of "stages in faith"?

If the answer is no, then it seems to me that the research should be limited to the stages of faith possessed by believers in the Jewish, Catholic and Protestant religions. Were this limitation placed on the research, it would be more valuable in itself and more meaningful to religious educators. A spinoff of such a limited project could well be an investigation into the stages of quasi-faith.

Where the research project stands at the present time a separation of faith and quasi-faith would be relatively easy. Looking at the makeup of the 118 respondents used in the research (an inadequate sampling to be sure) 110 are either Protestant, Catholic or Jewish. Only 8 are listed as "other," and statistically are of minor value. So in fact, if not in theory, it is for the most part a faith stemming from a biblical tradition that is being filtered into stages. Obviously if the 8 "others" were eliminated in the final analysis and description of the stages, the study would be based upon a more homogeneous group and the results would be more worthwhile.

In addition to a more precise understanding of faith some secondary advantages would accrue. For example, Transcendent would not need to be spelled in lower case. The investigation could be more specific about such concepts as belief, religion, authority, obedience, community, etc. and about the *content* of these concepts in contemporary Christianity and Judaism.

The issues investigated in the five variables could be clarified and sharpened. Concretely here are three suggestions: 1) The respondents' concept of God might be spelled out for each stage, and not merely for the first two. 2) The horizontal aspect of faith, so well described in the introduction and so important in today's world, could profitably be explicated for each stage in order to show how faith reaches out in love and service to the neighbor. 3)

How faith expresses itself in prayer and worship, how it handles doubt, anxiety, fear and temptation in the various stages would prove enlightening. In summary, the study would then be more manageable and meaningful.

Perhaps in a subsequent publication Professor Fowler will tell us more than the age, sex and religion of the respondents. Were they randomly selected? If they were screened, on what basis? For the adults interviewed some knowledge about their education, especially religious education, would be helpful. How long and how genuinely have they been living their commitment to their faith? Some examples of how the interviewers asked their questions about the variables and existential issues, and especially examples to show how the stages were filtered out from the answers given—these are some of the questions this reader would find enlightening. It would no doubt be possible to select at random from a religiously oriented college faculty 110 members whose faith stage would fall mostly into Four and Five; while 110 freshmen picked at random in the same college would likely be in Stages Two and Three. Education, experience, and a faith lived in many crises explain the difference.

One rather practical question may occur to educators. Should students be encouraged to strive for the next faith stage? One needs prudence and caution here. A faith stage as described by Professor Fowler is a very slow and gradual achievement, resulting from many factors, not least of which is divine grace. Were anyone encouraged to advance to the next stage before he is sufficiently mature there would be surface mimicking without conviction of heart. We have to keep in mind the difference between confessing faith and believing it. What is important is that a student or anyone else be open to advance and be willing to make the effort when he is ready.

Very wisely Professor Fowler writes that each faith stage may be the best for a given individual. Each stage can be "grace-ful." Love of God and neighbor may be operating to a heroic degree in Stage Two or Three as well as Stage Six. But this love will work differently in each stage. So Professor Fowler warns us that no value judgments should be made about the intrinsic worth of each stage or implied suggestion to strive for the next stage. When one is sufficiently mature there will be a spontaneous and calm advance. It is quite different of course with the "ways" of the spiritual life, which Dr. Fowler discusses with insight and appreciation in the section "Some Similarities and Differences with Tradition of Spirituality." The purgative way, for example, is never outgrown and to some extent is always operative when one is in the illuminative or unitive way.

A final suggestion. I don't think it was the author's intention to convey the impression that faith stages are mechanical or like conditioned reflexes. Quite the contrary. They represent careful research, observation and analysis of one phase of human maturation. So it should not be too surprising that an individual, though best described by Stage Two would in fact exhibit some characteristics of Stage Four. An example that comes to mind is St. Thérèse of Lisieux who died at the age of 24. Limited in education, milieu and experience, her faith stage would probably be Three or Four. Yet her faith experience, as seen in her autobiography, *The Story of a Soul* (1975), for the last 18 months of her life can only be described as "a dark night of the soul" equal to that experienced by the greatest mystics. Similarly her charity was so universal and her identity with the divine will so complete that Stage Six would best describe these virtues in her.

I am suggesting caution in imposing categories, even theological categories. God's action on the soul defies any kind of straitjacket. Job's friends were good, orthodox theologians. They argued that Job sinned. Their proof is that he is being punished. Job rejects their "classical" proof and God confirms Job's innocence. This may have been the first but surely not the last time that theological reasoning and categorizing was punctured. Each human person is mysterious, God is *the* Mystery, and His ways with men are beyond our calculating. I feel sure Professor Fowler would agree.

Bibliography*

Almy, W., Chittender, E., & Miller, P. *Young children's thinking.* Teacher's College Press, 1966.

Archambault, R.D. Criteria for success in moral education. In B. I. Chazan and J. F. Soltis (Eds.), *Moral education and teaching.* Teachers College Press, 1973.

Ausubel, D. P. & Sullivan, E. V. *Theory and problems of child development* (2nd Ed.). Grune & Stratton, 1970.

Bakan, D. The mystery-mastery complex in contemporary psychology. *American Psychologist,* 1965, *20,* 186-191.

Bandura, A. *Principles of behavior modification.* Holt, Rinehart & Winston, 1969.

Baumrind, D. Current patterns of parent authority. *Developmental Psychology Monograph,* 4, #1, Part 2.

Beck, C. M., Crittenden, B. S. & Sullivan, E. V. (Eds.) *Moral education: Interdisciplinary approaches.* Newman Press, 1971.

Beck, C. *Ethics.* Toronto: McGraw-Hill Ryerson, 1972.

Beck, C., Sullivan, E., & Taylor, N. Stimulating transition to post-conventional morality: The Pickering High School Study. *Interchange,* 1972, *3,* 28-37.

Bettelheim, B. On moral education. In N & T. Sizer (Eds.) *Moral education.* Harvard Press, 1970.

Blatt, M. *The effects of classroom discussion program upon children's level of moral judgment.* Unpublished doctoral dissertation, University of Chicago, 1970.

Block, J. H. Teachers, teaching, and mastery teaching. *Today's Education,* 1973, *63,* 30-36.

Braginsky, B. & Braginsky, D. *Main stream psychology.* Holt, Rinehart & Winston, 1974.

Bronfenbrenner, U. *Influences on human development.* Dryden Press, 1972.

Buber, M. *I-thou.* Scribner & Sons, 1970.

Burger, H. G. Behavior modification in operant psychology: An anthropological critique. *American Educational Research Journal,* 1972, *9,* 343-360.

Campbell, D. T. On the conflicts between biological and social evolution and between psychology and moral tradition. *American Psychologist,* 1975, *30,* 1103-1126.

*In this section all the references cited by contributors have been combined to avoid repetition and to assist those who seek a pertinent bibliography.

Cauble, M. A. Formal operations, ego identity, and principles morality: Are they related? Unpublished manuscript, Arizona State University, 1974.

Chazan, B. I. & Soltis, J. F. (Eds.) *Moral education and teaching.* Teachers College Press, 1973.

Clark, K. Alternative schools. In A. C. Eurich, (Ed.) *High school, 1980.* Pitman, 1970.

Coder, R. *Moral judgment in adults.* Unpublished doctoral dissertation, University of Minnesota, 1975.

Coleman, J. *The adolescent society.* Free Press, 1961.

Coleman, J. et al., *Equality of educational opportunity.* Government Printing Office, 1966.

Coleman, J. S. The children have outgrown the schools. *Psychology Today,* 1972, *5, #9*, 72-82.

Cooney, E. & Selman, R. Social cognitive development: *Evaluation of a study in the elementary grades.* Paper presented, 1975, American Psychological Association, Chicago.

Cottle, T. Let's keep a few secrets. *Psychology Today,* 1975, *9, #5*, 22-89.

DeCecco, J. & Richards, A. Civil war in high school. *Psychology Today,* 1975, *9, #6*, 51-56; 120.

DePalma, D. & Foley, J. (Eds.) *Moral development: Current theory and research.* Wiley & Sons, 1975.

Dowell, R. C. *Adolescents as peer counselors.* Unpublished Ed. D. Thesis, Harvard Graduate School of Education, 1971.

Duska, R. & Whelan, M. *Moral development: A guide to Piaget and Kohlberg.* Paulist Press, 1975.

Elkind, D. Piaget's semi-clinical interview and the study of spontaneous religion. *Journal for the Scientific Study of Religion,* 1964, *4*, 40-46.

Elkind, D. Egocentrism in adolescence. *Child Development,* 1967, *38*, 1025-34.

Ellul, J. *The technological society.* Translated from the French, Knopf, 1964.

Erikson, E. H., *Identity and the life cycle.* International Universities Press, 1959.

Erikson, E. H., *Childhood and society* (2nd Ed.). W. W. Norton Co., 1963.

Erickson, V. L. Psychological growth for women: a cognitive developmental curriculum intervention. *Counseling and Values,* 1974, *18*, 102-115.

Eurich, A. C. (Ed.) *High school, 1980.* Pitman, 1970.

Fantini, M. & Weinstein, G. Taking advantage of disadvantage. *Teachers College Record,* 1967, *69*, 103-114.

Fingarette, H. *The self in transformation.* Harper Torchbook, 1965.

Flanagan, J. Education: How and for what. *American Psychologist,* 1973, *28*, 551-556.

Flavell, J. *Role-taking and communication skills in children.* Wiley, 1968.

Fowler, J. W., *To see the kingdom: The theological vision of H. Richard Niebuhr.* Abingdon Press, 1974 (c).

Fowler, J. W., *Faith liberation and human development: Three lectures. The Foundation,* Atlanta, Georgia; Gammon Theological Seminary, 1974, *79* (b).

Fowler, J. W., Toward a developmental perspective on faith. *Religious Education,* 1974, *69,* 207-219 (a).

Frankena, W. K. Toward a philosophy of moral education. *Harvard Educational Review,* 1958, *28,* 300-313.

Frankena, W. K. *Ethics* (2nd ed.), Prentice Hall, 1973.

Freire, P. *Pedagogy of the oppressed.* Herder & Herder, 1970.

Friedenberg, E. Z. *The vanishing adolescent.* Beacon Press, 1959.

Gardner, H. *The quest for mind.* Random House, 1974.

Goodlad, J. & Klein, M. *Looking behind the classroom door.* Jones, 1974.

Graham, R. Youth and experimental learning. In R. J. Havighurst & P. H. Dreyer (Eds.), *Seventy-Fourth Yearbook of the National Society for the Study of Education,* University of Chicago Press, 1975.

Graubard, A. The free school movement. *Harvard Educational Review,* 1972, *42,* 351-373.

Greenfield, P. & Bruner, J. Culture and cognitive growth. In A. Goslin (Ed.), *Handbook of socialization theory and research.* Rand McNally, 1969.

Guardini, R. *The life of faith.* Newman Press, 1961.

Guskin, A. & Guskin, S. *A social psychology of education.* Addison Wesley, 1970.

Gustafson, J. M. Educational for moral responsibility. In N. & T. Sizer (Eds.) *Moral education.* Harvard U. Press, 1970.

Habermas, J. *Toward a rational society.* Beacon Press, 1970.

Hapgood, M. The open classroom: Protect it from its friends. *Saturday Review,* September 11, 1971.

Haubrich, V. F. & Apple, M. W. (Eds.) *Schooling and the rights of children.* McCutchan, 1975.

Helfaer, P. M. *The psychology of religious doubt.* Beacon Press, 1972.

Hickey, J. *The effects of guided moral discussion upon offenders' level of moral judgment.* Unpublished doctoral dissertation, Boston U., 1972.

Hoetker, J. & Ahlbrand, W. P. The persistence of recitation. *American Educational Research Journal,* 1969, *6,* 145-167.

Hoffman, M. Moral development. In P. Mussen (Ed.), *Carmichael's manual of child psychology* (Vol. II). Wiley, 1970, 261-359.

Hogan, R. Moral conduct and moral character: A psychological perspective. *Psychological Bulletin,* 1973, *79,* #4, 217-232.

Hogan, R. Theoretical egocentrism and the problem of compliance. *American Psychologist,* 1975, *30,* 533-540.

Holstein, C. *Parental consensus and interaction in relation to the child's moral judgment.* Unpublished doctoral dissertation, Univ. of California at Berkeley, 1969.

Holstein, C. The relation of children's moral judgment level to that of their parents and to communication patterns in the family. In Smart, R. & Smart, M. (Eds.) *Readings in child development.* Macmillan, 1972.

Holstein, C. *Moral judgment change in early adolescence and middle age: A longitudinal study.* Paper presented at the meeting of the Society for Research in Child Development, Philadelphia, March, 1973.

Hunt, D. & Sullivan, E. V. *Between psychology and education.* Dryden, 1974.

Hurt, B. L. *Psychological development of students enrolled in an introductory education course with a psychological education component.* Unpublished doctoral dissertation, University of Minnesota, 1974.

Hurt, B. L. & Sprinthall, N. A. Psychological and moral development for teacher educators. *Journal of Moral Education* (in press).

Hymman, I. & Chreiber, K. Selected concepts and practices of child advocacy in school psychology. *Psychology in the Schools,* 1975, *12,* #1, 50-57.

Illich, I. *Tools for conviviality.* Perennial Library, 1973.

Jackson, P. *Life in classrooms.* Holt, Rinehart & Winston, 1968.

James, W. *Talks with teachers.* Norton, 1968.

Jennings, F. G. The school without walls. In A. C. Eurich (Ed.), *High School, 1980.* Pitman, 1970.

Jensen, A. R. How much can we boost IQ and scholastic achievement? *Harvard Educational Review,* 1969, *39,* 1-123.

Johnson, D. Students against the school establishment: Crisis intervention in school conflicts with organization. *Journal of Psychology,* 1971, *9,* 84-92.

Johnson, D. W. *The social psychology of education.* Holt, Rinehart & Winston, 1971.

Johnston, W. *The still point: Reflections on Zen and Christian mysticism.* Harper & Row, 1971.

Keniston, K. Psychological development and historical change, in R. J. Lifton (Ed.), *Explorations in psychohistory.* Simon & Schuster, 1974.

Kirp, D. Student classification, public policy, and the courts. *Harvard Educational Review,* 1974, *44,* 7-52.

Kirschenbaum, H. Recent research in values education. In J. Meyer, B. Burnham, & J. Cholvat (Eds.), *Values education: theory, practice, problems, prospects.* Waterloo, Ontario, Canada: Wilfrid Laurier U. Press, 1975.

Kohl, H. *Thirty-six children.* New American Library, 1967.

Kohlberg, L. *The development of modes of moral thinking and choice in the years 10 to 16.* Unpublished doctoral dissertation, University of Chicago, 1958.

Kohlberg, L. Development of moral character and moral ideology. In M. Hoffman (Ed.), *Review of Child Development Research.* Russell Sage Foundation, 1964.

Kohlberg, L. The child as moral philosopher. *Psychology Today,* 1968, *2,* #4, 24-30.

Kohlberg, L. Stage and sequence: A cognitive-developmental approach to socialization. In D. Goslin (Ed.), *Handbook of socialization theory and method.* Rand-McNally, 1968.

Kohlberg, L. Stages of moral development as a basis for moral education. In C. Beck, B. Crittenden, & E. Sullivan (Eds.), *Moral education.* Newman Press, 1971.

Kohlberg, L. A response. *The Counseling Psychologist,* 1971, 2, 80-82.

Kohlberg, L. A concept of developmental psychology as the central guide to education. In M. Reynold (Ed.), *Psychology and the process of schooling in the next decade.* University of Minnesota, Department of Audio-Visual Extension, 1972.

Kohlberg, L. *Collected papers on moral development and moral education.* Cambridge, Mass.: Center for Moral Development and Moral Education, Harvard Graduate School of Education, 1973.

Kohlberg, L. Moral development and the new social studies. *Social Education,* 1973, 5, 369-375.

Kohlberg, L. Report to N.I.H. Review Committee on a grant proposal site visit. November 22, 1974, Harvard U.

Kohlberg, L. Education, moral development, and faith, *Journal of Moral Education,* 1974, 4, 5-16.

Kohlberg, L., & Freundlich, D. *The relationship between moral judgment and delinquency.* Unpublished manuscript, Harvard U., 1973.

Kohlberg, L. & Gilligan, C. The adolescent as philosopher: The discovery of the self in a postconventional world. *Daedulus,* 1971, 100, 1050-1086.

Kohlberg, L. & Hickey, J. *Proposal to design and implement a correctional program based on moral development theory.* Unpublished manuscript, 1972.

Kohlberg, L. & Kramer, R. Continuities and discontinuities in childhood moral development. *Human Development,* 1969, 12, 93-120.

Kohlberg, L. & Mayer, R. Development as the aim of education. *Harvard Educational Review,* 1972, 42, 449-496.

Kohlberg, L. & Selman, R. L. Preparing school personnel relative to values: a look at moral education in the schools. *ERIC* Clearinghouse on Teacher Education, January, 1972 (ERIC Document Reproduction Service No. ED 058 153).

Kohlberg, L. & Turiel, E. Moral development and moral education. In G. S. Lesser (Ed.), *Psychology and educational practice.* Scott, Foresman & Co., 1971.

Konopka, G. Requirements for healthy development of adolescent youth. *Adolescence,* 1973, 31, 291-316.

Kramer, R. *Changes in moral judgment response pattern during late adolescence and young adulthood; retrogression in a developmental sequence.* Unpublished doctoral dissertation, University of Chicago, 1968.

Kuhn, D., Langer, J., Kohlberg, L., & Haan, N. *The development of formal operations in logical and moral judgment.* Unpublished manuscript, Columbia U., 1973.

Kurtines, W. & Greif, E. The development of moral thought: Review and evaluation of Kohlberg's approach. *Psychological Bulletin,* 1974, 81, 453-470.

Leacock, E. *Teaching and learning in city schools.* Basic Books, 1969.

Lickona, T. (Ed.) *Moral development and behavior: Theory, research and social issues.* Holt, Rinehart & Winston, 1976.

Linton, T. E. & Manaeker, J. The school counsellor as child advocate: Put a new trust in mental health services for children. *Canada's Mental Health,* January 1975, 3-4.

Lockwood, A. Stages of moral development and reasoning about public policy issues. In L. Kohlberg & E. Turiel (Eds.), *Moralization: the cognitive-developmental approach.* Holt, Rinehart & Winston (in press).

Loevinger, J. & Wessler, R. *Measuring ego development.* Jossey-Bass, 1970.

London, P. *Behavior control.* Perennial Library, 1971.

McColgan, E. *Social cognition in delinquents, predelinquents, and nondelinquents.* Unpublished doctoral dissertation, University of Minnesota, 1975.

MacDonald, F. The hidden curriculum: Its impact on learning. In A. T. Pearson (Ed.), *Perspectives on curriculum. Edmonton, Alberta: Faculty of Education, University of Alberta, 1973.*

McGeorge, C. The susceptibility to faking of the Defining Issues Test of moral development. *Developmental Psychology, 1975, 11,* 108.

MacIntyre, A. Against utilitarianism. In T. H. S. Hollins (Ed.), *Aims in education: The philosophical approach.* Manchester: University of Manchester Press, 1964.

McPhail, P. The Motivation of moral behaviour. *Moral Education,* 1970, *2,* 99-106.

McPhail, P. The motivation of moral behavior, and to play roles or do your thing? *The History and Social Science Teacher,* 1975, Fall.

Magnusson, P. C. Students' rights and the misuse of psychological knowledge and language. In V. F. Haubrich & M. W. Apple (Eds.), *Schooling and the rights of children.* McCutchan, 1972.

Maslow, A. *Motivation and personality* (2nd ed.). Harper & Row, 1972.

Mercer, J. A policy statement on the assessment procedure and the rights of children. *Harvard Educational Review.* 1974, *44,* 125-141.

Meyer, J., Burnham, B. & Cholvat, J. (Eds.) *Values education.* W. Laurier U. Press, Waterloo, Ont., Canada, 1975.

Miles, M. *Innovation in education.* Teachers College Press, 1964.

Milgran, S. Behavioral study of obedience, *Journal of Abnormal Social Psychology,* 1963, *67,* 371-378.

Minuchin, P. et al. *The psychological impact of school experience.* Basic Books, 1969.

Monden, L. *Sin, liberty and law.* Sheed & Ward, 1965.

Mosher, R. L. & Sprinthall, N. A. Deliberate psychological education. *The Counseling Psychologist,* 1971, *2, 4,* 3-82.

National Education Association. Parent-child communication skills, *Today's Education,* 1971, April, reprint.

Niebuhr, H. R. *Faith on earth.* An unpublished book manuscript from 1957.

Niebuhr, H. R. *Radical monotheism and western culture.* Harper & Bros., 1960.

Niebuhr, H. R. Value Theory and Theology, in *The nature of religious experience*. Harper & Bros., 1937.

Overly, N. (Ed.) *The unstudied curriculum: Its impact on children*. ASCD, NEA, 1970.

Panowitsch, H. *Change and stability in the Defining Issues Test*. Unpublished doctoral dissertation, University of Minnesota, 1975.

Peck, R. F. & Havighurst, R. J. *The psychology of character development*. Wiley, 1960.

Perkins, H. V. *Human development and learning* (2nd Ed.). Wadsworth, 1974.

Peters, R. S. *Authority, responsibility and education* (2nd Ed.). London: Allen & Unwin, 1963.

Piaget, J. *The language and thought of the child*. Harcourt & Brace, 1926.

Piaget, J. *Judgment and reasoning in the child*. Harcourt & Brace, 1928.

Piaget, J. *The child's conception of the world*. Harcourt & Brace, 1929.

Piaget, J. *The child's conception of physical causality*. London: Kegan Paul, 1930.

Piaget, J. *The moral judgment of the child*. (Gabain, M. Ed. and trans.) Collier Books, 1962. (Originally published, 1932).

Piaget, J. *Six psychological studies*. Random House, 1967.

Piaget, J. *Structuralism*. Basic Books, 1970.

Piaget, J. *The science of education and the psychology of the child*. Viking, 1970.

Piaget, J. *Main trends in inter-disciplinary research*. Harper Torchbooks, 1973.

Popham, W. J. *Providing wide ranging, diversely organized pools of instructional objectives and measures*. U.S. Office of Education, 1971.

Postman, N. & Weingartner, C. *Teaching as a subversive activity*. Delacourt Press, 1969.

Potter, R. B., Jr., *War and moral discourse*. John Knox Press, 1969.

Raths, L. E., Harmin, M. & Simon, S. B. *Values and teaching*. Merrill, 1966.

Rest, J. The hierarchical nature of stages of moral judgment. *Journal of Personality*, 1973, *41*, 86-109.

Rest, J. Developmental psychology as a guide to value education: A review of Kohlbergian programs. *Review of Education Research*, 1974, *44*, 241-259. (a)

Rest, J. R. *Manual for the Defining Issues Test*. University of Minnesota, mimeo, 1974. (b)

Rest, J. R. The cognitive-developmental approach to morality: the state of the art. *Counseling and Values*. 1974, *18*, 64-78. (c)

Rest, J. The validity of tests of moral judgment. In J. Meyer, B. Burnham, J. Cholvat (Eds.), *Value education: theory, practice, problems, prospects*. Waterloo, Ontario, Canada: Wilfrid Laurier U. Press, 1975.

Rest, J. Longitudinal study of the Defining Issues Test: A strategy for analyzing developmental change. *Developmental Psychology*, 1975, *11*, 738-748.

Rest, J. New approaches in the assessment of moral judgment. In T. Lickona (Ed.), Man and morality. Holt, Rinehart & Winston, 1976.

Rest, J., Turiel, E. & Kohlberg, L. Level of moral development as a determinant of preference and comprehension of moral judgment made by others. Journal of Personality, 1969, 37, 225-252.

Rest, J., Cooper, D., Coder, R., Masanz, J. & Anderson, D. Judging the important issues in moral dilemmas—an objective measure of development. Development Psychology, 1974, 10, 491-501.

Rogers, C. Barriers and gateways to communication, Harvard Business Review, 1952, 30, 46-52.

Rustad, K. & Rogers, C. Promoting psychological growth in a high school class, Counselor Education and Supervision, 1975, 14, 277-385.

Ryan, W. Blaming the victim. Vintage Paperback, 1971.

Sand, O. What to teach. In A. C. Eurich (Ed.), High school, 1980. Pitman, 1970.

Sanborn, S. Sins of a generation (review). Saturday Review, July 26, 1975, 25-26.

Sarason, S. B. The culture of the school and the problem of change. Allyn & Bacon, 1971.

Sarason, S. B. The psychological sense of community: prospects of a community psychology. Jossey-Bass, 1974.

Schaffer, P. Moral judgment: A cognitive developmental project in psychological education. Unpublished Ph.D. dissertation, University of Minnesota, 1974.

Schrag, P. Voices in the classroom. Beacon, 1967.

Scribner, H. Responsibilities beyond the curriculum. Conference Report to Association of Orthodox Jewish Teachers, March 12, 1972, New York.

Scriven, M. Education for survival. In D. E. Purpel & M. Belanger (Eds.), Curriculum and the cultural revolution. McCutchan, 1972.

Seeley, J. R. et al. Crestwood Heights. Basic Books, 1956.

Seeley, J. R. & Drew, C. R. Administered persons: The engineering of souls. Interchange, 1974, 5, 1-13.

Selman, R. L. The development of social-cognitive understanding: A guide to educational and clinical practice. In T. Lickona (Ed.), Moral Development: Theory, Research, Practice. Holt, Rinehart & Winston, 1976.

Selman, R. The relation of role-taking ability to the development of moral judgment in children. Child Development, 1971, 42, 79-91.

Selman, R. The relation of role-taking levels to stage of moral judgment: A theoretical analysis of empirical studies. Unpublished manuscript, Harvard U., 1973.

Selman, R. L. Social-cognitive development: application of theory to educational practice. Paper presented to 1975 American Psychological Association, Chicago.

Selman, R. L. & Byrne, D. A structural-developmental analysis of levels of role-taking in middle childhood. Child Development, 1974, 45, 803-806.

Selman, R. L. & Byrne, D. First things: Social reasoning. Guidance Associates, 1974. (Filmstrip)

Selman, R. L. & Kohlberg, L. *First things: Values.* Guidance Associates, 1972. (Filmstrip)

Selman, R. L. & Lieberman, M. Moral education in the primary grades: an evaluation of a developmental curriculum. *Journal of Educational Psychology,* 1975, *67,* 712-716.

Schaefer, R. *The school as a center of inquiry.* Harper & Row, 1967.

Shaull, R. Forward in P. Freire, *Pedagogy of the oppressed.* Herder & Herder, 1972.

Silberman, C. *Crisis in the classroom.* Random, 1970.

Skinner, B. F. *Beyond freedom and dignity.* Knopf, 1971.

Simon, S., Howe, L. & Kirchenbaum, H. *Value clarification: a handbook of practical strategies for teachers and students.* Hart, 1972.

Simpson, E. L. Moral development research, a case study of scientific cultural bias. *Human Development,* 1974, *17,* 81-106.

Sizer, N. F. & Sizer, T. R. (Eds.) *Moral education, five lectures.* Harvard U. Press, 1970.

Smart, J. J. Extreme and restricted utilitarianism. In P. Foot (Ed.), *Theories of ethics.* Oxford U. Press, 1967.

Snow, R. E. Theory construction for research on teaching. In R. M. Travers (Ed.), *Second handbook of research on teaching.* Rand McNally, 1973.

Sprinthall, N. A. A program for psychological education: Some preliminary issues, *Journal of School Psychology,* 1971, *9,* 373-382.

Sprinthall, N. A. Humanism: A new bag of virtues for guidance? *Personnel and Guidance Journal,* 1972, *50,* 349-356.

Sprinthall, N. A. A curriculum for secondary schools: Counselors as teachers for psychological growth. *School Counselor,* 1973, *20,* 361-369.

Sprinthall, N. A. A cognitive developmental curriculum: The adolescent as a psychologist. *Counseling and Values,* 1974, *18,* 94-101.

Sprinthall, N. A. & Erickson, V. L. Learning psychology by doing psychology. *Personnel and Guidance Journal,* 1974, *52,* 396-405.

Sprinthall, N. A. & Mosher, R. L. Voices from the back of the classroom, *Journal of Teacher Education,* 1971, *22,* 166-175.

Sprinthall, R. C. & Sprinthall, N. A. *Educational psychology: A developmental approach.* Addison-Wesley, 1974.

Stake, R. E. *Priorities planning: Judging the importance of alternative objectives.* Instructional Objectives Exchange, 1972.

Strommen, M. *Five cries of youth.* New York: Harper & Row, 1974.

Sullivan, E. V. *Piaget and the school curriculum.* Toronto: The Ontario Institute for Studies in Education, Bulletin No. 2, 1967.

Sullivan, E. V. *Moral learning: Some findings, issues and questions.* Paulist Press, 1975.

Thérèse of Lisieux, St. *The story of a soul: The autobiography of St. Thérèse of Lisieux* (J. Clarke, trans.). Washington, D.C.: ICS Publications, 1975.

Tomlinson-Keasey, C. & Keasey, C. B. The mediating role of cognitive development in moral judgment. *Child Development,* 1974, *45,* 291-298.

Turiel, E. An experimental test of the sequentiality of developmental stages in the child's moral judgment. *Journal of Personality & Social Psychology,* 1966, *3,* 611-618.

Turiel, E. Stage transition in moral development. In R. M. Travers (Ed.), *Second handbook of research on teaching*. Rand McNally, 1973.
Turiel, E. *The effects of cognitive conflicts on moral judgment development*. Unpublished manuscript, Harvard University, 1973.
Tyler, R. Summary of conference proceedings on YCY programs. Baltimore, Maryland, June, 1974.

Wendell, R. *Inquiry teaching: Dispelling the myths*. Clearing House, 1973.
Whitehead, A. N., *Religion in the making*. World Publishing Co. (Meridian Books), 1960.
Wilson, J. *A teacher's guide to moral education*. London: Chapman, 1973.

Zuniga, R. B. The experiencing society and radical social reform: The role of the social scientist in Chile's Unidad Popular experience. *American Psychologist*, 1975, *30*, 99-115.

THE CONTRIBUTORS

JAMES R. BARCLAY, Ph.D., Professor, Educational Psychology and Counseling, College of Education, University of Kentucky, Lexington, Kentucky
CLIVE M. BECK, Ph.D., Professor, Philosophy of Education and Coordinator of Graduate Studies, Ontario Institute for Studies in Education, Toronto, Canada
WAYNE BOHANNON, graduate student in psychology, Johns Hopkins University, Baltimore
JAMES W. FOWLER, Ph.D., Associate Professor of Applied Theology and Director Program on Research in Faith Development and Religious Education, Harvard Divinity School, Cambridge, Massachusetts
SR. BARBARA GEOGHEGAN, Ph.D., Professor, Education, College of Mount St. Joseph, Mount St. Joseph, Ohio
ROBERT J. HAVIGHURST, Ph.D., Professor of Education and Human Development, Department of Education, University of Chicago
JAMES E. HENNESSY, S.J., Ph.D., Associate Professor, Theology, St. Peter's College, Jersey City, New Jersey
THOMAS C. HENNESSY, S.J., Ph.D., Associate Professor and Coordinator of Program in Counseling and Personnel Services, School of Education, Fordham University, New York City
RONALD J. HINE, Ph.D., Assistant Professor, Graduate School of Religion and Religious Education, Fordham University, New York City
ROBERT HOGAN, Ph.D., Professor, Psychology, Johns Hopkins University, Baltimore, Maryland
MAUREEN JOY, Ph.D., Principal, Kensington Johnson School, Great Neck, New York
HARRY B. KAVANAGH, Ph.D., Assistant Professor, Education, Rider College, Trenton, New Jersey

ALFRED McBRIDE, O.Praem., Ph.D., Director, National Forum of Religious Educators, National Catholic Educational Association, Washington, D.C.

JOHN S. NELSON, Ph.D., Associate Professor, Graduate School of Religion and Religious Education, Fordham University, New York City

JAMES R. REST, Ph.D., Associate Professor, Social, Psychological and Philosophical Foundations of Education, University of Minnesota, Minneapolis

ROBERT L. SELMAN, Ph.D., Staff Clinical Supervisor, Judge Baker Child Guidance Center, Boston, and Lecturer, Graduate School of Education, Harvard University, Cambridge, Massachusetts

NORMAN A. SPRINTHALL, Ed.D., Professor, Psychoeducational Studies, University of Minnesota, Minneapolis

EDMUND V. SULLIVAN, Ph.D., Professor and Associate Chairman, Department of Applied Psychology, Ontario Institute for Studies in Education, Toronto, Canada

ANDREW C. VARGA, S.J., Ph.D., Assistant Professor, Philosophy, Fordham University, New York City